Capital utilization

Capital utilization

A theoretical and empirical analysis

ROGER R. BETANCOURT
CHRISTOPHER K. CLAGUE

Department of Economics
University of Maryland

CAMBRIDGE UNIVERSITY PRESS

Cambridge
London   New York   New Rochelle
Melbourne   Sydney

Published by the Press Syndicate of the University of Cambridge
The Pitt Building, Trumpington Street, Cambridge CB2 1RP
32 East 57th Street, New York, NY 10022, USA
296 Beaconsfield Parade, Middle Park, Melbourne 3206, Australia

First published 1981

Printed in the United States of America

Library of Congress Cataloging in Publication Data

Betancourt, Roger R

Capital utilization.

Includes index.
1. Capital productivity.   2. Capital.
3. Shift systems.   I. Clague, Christopher K.,
joint author.   II. Title.
HD57.5.B47   332'.0415   80–22410
ISBN 0 521 23583 9

to
ALICIA, MONIQUE
and to
HEATHER, HOLLY, JUAN, ROGIE

Contents

* These starred sections may be omitted without loss of continuity.

Part II. Estimation

Part III. Results

Contents

x   **Contents**

Tables and figures

Tables

Figures

Propositions

Preface

Our interest in capital utilization began to develop about ten years ago, at a time when the literature was extremely sparse and the topic seemed to be unduly neglected in light of its intellectual and practical significance. After collaborating on a number of articles on the subject, we reached the conclusion during 1975 that the time was ripe to attempt a more comprehensive treatment of the subject. Our aim was to write a book that would systematize the existing body of literature, which by then had grown much larger, while advancing the frontiers of knowledge in several important directions. The reader will be the judge of the success of our efforts.

A project as ambitious as this requires support from a number of sources. On the institutional side, sabbatical leaves to both authors during the initial phase of research for the book were extremely beneficial in two ways. They gave us time to work on the project and opportunities to interact with other researchers working on capital utilization at Boston University (C.K.C.) and at the International Labor Office (R.R.B.). In addition, the General Research Board at the University of Maryland provided summer support for one of the authors (R.R.B.) during 1977. Finally, computer time was provided by the University of Maryland Computer Science Center.

On an individual level, our thanks go to Y. Kim and G. Winston for their very useful comments. These comments led to a substantially revised manuscript that we hope will be accessible to a wide audience of economists. We would also like to thank our colleagues J. Adams, C. Harris, D. Mueller, and M. Olson for a number of suggestions, not all of which were adopted. The typing of the manuscript benefited from the resources made available for this purpose by R. Marris, then chairman of the Department of Economics at Maryland. We also want to express our appreciation for the task of deciphering our handwriting to the following individuals: P. Chiarizia, S. Gordon, S. Pressley, C. Soto, and G. Walton.

To conclude the acknowledgments, our deeply felt thanks go to our friends and especially to our families for their persistent broadening of our horizons beyond the limits of our work.

Glossary of symbols

α, α^1 The shift premium for second-shift work; α^1 refers to third-shift work.

θ The share of capital in combined capital and labor costs under single-shift operation.

$\phi(\overline{X})$ A measure of economies of scale. $\overline{X}$ is the level of output. $\phi(\overline{X}) = \frac{1}{2}$ if there are constant returns to scale and exceeds $\frac{1}{2}$ if there are increasing returns to scale.

CR, CR^1 The ratio of system 2 costs to system 1 costs; CR^1 is the ratio of system 3 costs to system 1 costs.

σ The elasticity of substitution between capital services and labor services.

β The degree of homogeneity of the production function.

e_{cx}^2 The proportionate increase in average costs generated by cutting in half the level of output under single-shift operation.

Introduction

A typical factory can be operated for eight, sixteen, or twenty-four hours per day by making use of one, two, or three shifts of workers. The decisions with respect to the number of shifts are not made, we believe, entirely by accident but depend in large part on economic considerations. Only fairly recently have economists given serious attention to explanations of what these considerations are and how they affect shift-work behavior.

The topic is of considerable intellectual interest in its own right. Moreover, the theory of production is seriously incomplete without a thorough treatment of capital utilization. But the subject should also be of interest to a rather wide audience of economists and other social scientists for at least three reasons. First, the lives of workers engaged in permanent night-work or rotating shift-work are typically adversely affected either by the disruption of biological rhythms or by the reduction in contact with family and community. Second, and on the positive side, more intensive utilization of the capital stock normally increases the output available to the society, both in the present and in the future; the additional output makes possible increased consumption by capitalists or workers or both. Third, a preliminary view of the matter suggests that the distribution of the increased output would be especially favorable to the workers, in the form of higher wages or more jobs.

The practical importance of the study of capital utilization is highlighted by two additional considerations. Not only are dramatic variations in utilization possible, but these wide variations are empirically observed across firms and countries. In addition, the degrees of utilization in various countries seem to have been increasing in recent years. A particularly dramatic example of an increase in shift-work, in this case the result of a conscious governmental decision, occurred in the Soviet Union from 1927 to 1932. A significant fraction of the increase in industrial output and employment during that period has been attributed to the increases in shift-work (Kabaj 1965).

Not surprisingly, economists and policymakers concerned with the developing countries have become intrigued by the potential employment effects of increased capital utilization. Thus studies of capital utilization in developing countries have been carried out in the last few years under the sponsorship of the World Bank (Schydlowsky 1979; Bautista et al. 1979) and the ILO (Betancourt 1977; Winston 1977b; Kabaj 1978; Phan-Thuy 1979). In addition, the study of capital utilization as an emergency employment scheme has become an ongoing part of the research program of the ILO (1976). On the other hand, in the developed countries interest in the topic has been aroused by the potential output effects of increased capital utilization. For example, the subject lies at the heart of the controversy between Denison (1972) and Jorgenson and Griliches (1972) with respect to the sources of growth in the United States. Needless to say, there are other reasons for the interest in this topic in both developing and developed countries,[1] but we shall not explore them at this point in our argument.

Despite the intrinsic importance of the subject and its practical significance, the current state of knowledge about capital utilization is severely limited in many ways. An important part of the reason for these limitations is the neglect of the subject by economists in the 1950s and 1960s. One important exception to this neglect is the contribution by Marris (1964), but the framing of his contribution in terms of discrete techniques of production no doubt led to its being ignored by many economists. In the 1970s this neglect disappeared. In his 1970 presidential address to the American Economic Association, Georgescu-Roegen discussed capital utilization and noted that it was one of the neglected areas in the economics of production. From the time of that address to the present, the literature on capital utilization has been increasing rapidly, and an excellent survey of developments up to 1974 is available (Winston 1974b). Although some theoretical progress has been made since that date, there are important aspects of the subject that have barely been treated. Moreover, the existing empirical work on the subject, which constitutes a significant portion of the literature published since 1974, is marred by serious econometric problems. In light of the situation just described, this study relates to the literature on capital utilization in two ways. First, it embeds the existing stock of knowledge on the subject in a general and consistent frame-

---

[1] For instance, in the United States, labor unions are currently showing signs of apprehension or misgivings about increased capital utilization through shift-work (Zalusky 1978); this attitude toward shift-work is prevalent in European labor unions (Maurice 1975, pp. 83–7).

work. Second, it uses the unified treatment of the subject provided by this framework to analyze many aspects of capital utilization that have not previously been investigated.

Our efforts in this book have been concentrated on two major substantive issues: explanation of the decision to utilize the capital stock of a plant, at both the theoretical level and the empirical level, and exploration of the consequences of increasing the level of capital utilization in the industrial sector. These two issues, together with our perception of the role of this study in the literature, have led us to focus on the long-run decision to utilize capital stock. In other words, this analysis will focus on the decision to utilize capital stock at the time of the investment decision, before the plant is built. Most of the theoretical literature is directed at the long-run decision, and with good reason. Because the options available are greater before the putty turns to clay, it is the more interesting decision to analyze, and in many instances the short-run analysis follows directly from imposing special assumptions on the long-run analysis. Moreover, the choices made by the firm at the investment stage condition future choices in a frequently irreversible manner. We shall show, for example, that factories that plan to utilize their capital stock in different ways are also designed and built to operate in different ways (i.e., at different levels of scale and capital intensity). Consequently, the implications that flow from the long-run emphasis are essential ingredients for proper evaluation of policy proposals to increase capital utilization.

This book is directed at two audiences: a specialized one, consisting of those who have done research or are interested in undertaking research in the economics of shift-work; a more general one, consisting of those interested in less-developed countries, economic growth, industrial organization, and labor economics who would like to be introduced to the new and relatively neglected topic of shift-work and capital utilization.[2]

Because the interests of these two audiences will differ, we have made an effort to provide guidelines for choosing where to concentrate one's efforts. The chapters all begin with material accessible to nonspecialists. Those sections that are necessarily technical or specialized are clearly indicated at the appropriate points in the discussion, and the main conclusions of each chapter are described, as far as possible, in ways that the nonspecialist can understand. In addition,

---

[2] Those interested in applied econometrics should find Chapters 4 through 7 to be worthwhile.

Chapter 0 provides a preliminary and completely nontechnical view of the subject.

In order to facilitate the reading of the subsequent chapters, we shall now describe the overall organization of the study. Chapter 0 contains a preliminary and nontechnical view of the subject. The remainder of the book consists of four parts and a concluding section. In the first of these parts, Shift-Work and the Theory of the Firm, we analyze the long-run decision to work shifts in the context of the theory of the firm. The emphasis is on understanding shift-work behavior and its determinants; nonetheless, important implications derived from the analyses of shift-work for the behavior of the firm are also identified. The focus of Part II, Estimation, is on the process of testing the propositions developed in Part I concerning shift-work behavior, on the shortcomings of previous attempts at testing these propositions, and on the procedures for avoiding these shortcomings. In Part III, Results, we present the findings from testing the theory in Part I with the procedures of Part II and data from France, India, Israel, and Japan; we also engage in international comparisons of the extent and characteristics of shift-work in a wide variety of countries. Part IV, Implications, deals with the effects of changes in capital utilization on employment and wage rates and with the relationships between capital utilization and economic growth. In the concluding section we summarize our findings, evaluate the human costs of shift-work, and suggest an approach to policy.

A preliminary view of capital utilization[1]

In most countries the vast majority of workers go to their jobs during the normal working hours. The majority of business establishments operate only one shift. A great many people, when first confronting these facts, are struck by the apparently low levels of capital utilization that are typically observed. For this reason a good way of approaching our subject is to classify the reasons for capital idleness.

We must first distinguish between intended and unintended idleness. One of the reasons that physical capital lies idle is that events do not always occur in the way that business managers expect. Demand may be less than expected, input supplies may be disrupted, or machinery may break down. These are examples of unintended capital idleness.

The reasons for intended idleness of capital depend on the type of activity involved. For example, some products and most services cannot be stored, and the timing of their production must be arranged to coincide with fluctuation in demand. In addition, many outdoor activities in agriculture, fishing, and construction are strongly affected by the weather and by the amount of daylight; obviously much idleness of capital in these sectors is explained by such factors.

The factors just mentioned do not apply to the great bulk of manufacturing activity, and yet much of the fixed capital in that sector is idle for much of the time. If the degree of capital idleness is regarded as surprisingly high, then it would be well to develop an explanation for the most difficult case, that of the manufacturing sector. The economic factors to which we shall appeal to explain capital idleness in manufacturing will also be applicable to other sectors, but the analyses for other sectors will often be complicated by the special factors mentioned in the preceding paragraph.

In the manufacturing sector, much of the intended capital idleness might be explained by cost-minimizing decisions in the presence of rhythmic variations in input prices, of which the most important is

---

[1] This chapter may be skimmed or skipped by those familiar with the general topic [e.g., those who have read Winston's survey (1974b)].

1

undoubtedly the price of labor. That is, in order to utilize fixed capital outside of normal working hours, the firm must pay, either explicitly or implicitly, higher wages to the workers for their work during abnormal hours. A second possible explanation for intended capital idleness is based on the twin assumptions of economies of scale in production and market restraint on the firm's sales. If we assume for the sake of simplicity that the factory's output level is given (e.g., by the historical level of sales), then shift-work can bring an advantage only if the decision to work shifts is made before the fixed investment is undertaken. The cost saving from double-shift operation derives from the decision to buy, for example, half as much fixed capital. But this decision may entail diseconomies of small-scale operation, and if these diseconomies are large enough, they may tip the scales against double-shift operation.

In the next section we shall develop a simple model in which we show that the profitability of shift-work depends on the shift differential in wages and the degree of economies of scale in production. We shall assume that the shift-work decision is made before the fixed capital is purchased. The reason for concentrating on this case is illustrated by the following example. Interview studies have revealed that when factory managers are asked why their factories are operating only one shift, one of the most frequently given answers is that the firm would have difficulty selling the additional output that would result from multishift operation. That answer may be a perfectly reasonable one to the question "Why don't you add another shift to your present factory?" But this lack-of-demand explanation does not answer the question "When you were building the plant or buying the machinery in the first place, why didn't you plan on multishift operation?" If the phenomenon to be explained is the intended idleness of capital, then the answer to this second question must be a more fundamental explanation than the simple lack-of-demand answer.

0.1   A simple model of capital utilization

Our purpose in this section is to describe a very simple model of capital utilization in order to lay out the issues in their clearest form. A more careful and general treatment is provided in the next chapter. Suppose a business enterprise has been operating a factory under a single-shift system. Then the time comes to scrap most of the machines and purchase new ones. The manager makes his initial plans on the assumption of continuation of single-shift operation. He determines a level of daily output, a level of capital stock (K), and a level of daily employment (L). All are assumed to be known with certainty and to be constant over the life of the plant. We designate the daily wage rate by w_1 and the daily price of capital (which includes interest and depreciation) by r. Daily costs are then $rK + w_1L$.

He then considers the possibility of double-shift operation. He must pay the second-shift workers a shift differential of α (where α might be, say, 0.15), or a total wage of $w_1(1 + \alpha)$. We assume here for simplicity that the rate of depreciation of the machinery is not affected by the fact that the machinery is worked twice as long each day; consequently the daily price of capital (r) remains unchanged. Now one of his options under the double-shift system would be to produce the same daily output, half on the first shift and half on the second shift. We shall assume that this reduction in the level of output per shift entails certain diseconomies of small-scale production. These diseconomies will be expressed in terms of a cost elasticity (e_{cx}), defined as the proportionate increase in average costs generated by cutting in half the level of output under single-shift operation. A typical value of e_{cx} might be 0.10. Under our assumptions, he would be able to produce on a double-shift operation the given level of output with $K(1 + e_{cx})/2$ units of capital and $L(1 + e_{cx})/2$ units of labor. His daily costs then would be

$$rK(1 + e_{cx})/2 + w_1L(1 + e_{cx})(2 + \alpha)/2$$

Let us define the capital share of costs $[rK/(rK + w_1L)]$ under single-shift operation as θ. Now we form the ratio of double-shift costs to single-shift costs, and after simple manipulation[2] we obtain

$$\text{CR} = [\theta + (2 + \alpha)(1 - \theta)]\frac{1 + e_{cx}}{2}$$

This expression is referred to as the cost ratio, and if it is less than unity, our particular version of the double-shift system is less costly and more profitable than the single-shift system.

It is clear from our expression for the cost ratio that the double-shift system will be less likely to be profitable for higher values of α, higher values of e_{cx}, and lower values of θ. We have now formalized the two explanations for capital idleness that were mentioned in the previous

[2] By the definition of this ratio, which will be denoted by CR, we have

$$\text{CR} = \frac{rK + w_1L(2 + \alpha)}{rK + w_1L}\frac{1 + e_{cx}}{2}$$

Use of the definition of θ (and, of course, $1 - \theta$) in this expression leads to the expression in the text.

section. The first explanation involves the trade-off between capital costs and labor costs; shift-work will be unprofitable if the shift differential is too high or if the capital share is too low. The second explanation involves the diseconomies of small-scale production; shift-work will be unprofitable if these diseconomies (measured by e_{cx}) are too large. Of course, this second explanation has been based on the assumption that the manager decides to maintain the same level of output under the two systems. The explanation will have to be modified somewhat when that assumption is relaxed. We have chosen assumptions that allow diseconomies of small-scale production to play their maximum role.

The two explanations do not provide an exhaustive list of the reasons for capital idleness. Others will be mentioned at various points in this book. At this juncture we should mention the possibility that businessmen tend to avoid the double-shift system even when it is more profitable, perhaps because they do not bother making careful calculations, or perhaps because they find multiple shifts to be personally inconvenient. For this theoretical development, however, we return to the assumption that businessmen try to minimize costs.

The model just presented has left out of account an important feature of the shift-work decision. This feature is the phenomenon of substitution, and it is the topic of the next section.·

0.2   The phenomenon of substitution

In the model in the previous section we assumed that adoption of the double-shift system would not bring about any change in the "instantaneous capital–labor ratio," that is, the amount of capital with which a given laborer is working at any point in time. Yet a proper analysis of the shift-work decision reveals that a manager would have good reason to change that ratio.

To make this point clear, we need to review the elementary theory of the choice of productive technique. The production function shows the flow of output per unit time as a function of inputs of factor services (Figure 0.1.). Let X^1 be the isoquant corresponding to the level of output that is optimal for the single-shift system. Let X_1^2 be the isoquant corresponding to half that level of output.[3] We shall assume

---

[3] If there are constant returns to scale, the isoquant X_1^2 lies halfway between the isoquant X^1 and the origin. If there are diseconomies of small-scale production, X_1^2 lies farther out than halfway. The phenomenon of substitution is basically the same in the two cases.

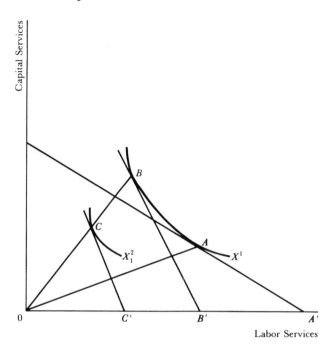

Figure 0.1. Shift-work and the choice of technique.

that the isoquant map has the property that the slopes of the isoquants are constant along any ray from the origin such as OA or OB. Because we shall continue to assume that the daily levels of output are the same for the two systems, X_1^2 is the relevant isoquant for the double-shift system.

Under single-shift operation the ratio of the price of labor services to the price of capital services is given by the line AA'. Under double-shift operation the factor service price line is steeper for two reasons: Average wages per man-hour are higher, and the price per machine-hour is lower (half as great if the rate of depreciation is unaffected). The double-shift factor price ratio is shown by the slope of BB' or CC'. Costs are minimized under single-shift operation at point A and under double-shift operation at point C. The instantaneous capital–labor ratios are given by the slopes of the rays OA and OC. It is clear that as long as the isoquants are smooth, the instantaneous capital–labor ratio will be higher under the double-shift system.

There are two important implications of this point. The first concerns the employment generated by shift-work. In the model presented in the previous section the adoption of shift-work doubled the total employment (first shift plus second shift) per unit of capital stock. In the presence of substitution possibilities, the total employ-ment per unit of capital stock will go up by less than 100% and may not even go up at all. In the example of Figure 0.1, in fact, total employment per unit of capital stock actually falls. This statement may be confirmed by comparing the slope of line *OA* with that of a line with half the slope of *OC*.

The second implication of the phenomenon of substitution is that empirical verification of the theory is rendered more difficult. The theory says that high capital intensity is a cause of shift-work. But the phenomenon of substitution shows that high utilization is itself a cause of high observed capital intensity. Empirical verification of the theory requires the development of empirical methods for separating the two influences.

0.3   Economic effects of changes in capital utilization

As mentioned in the Introduction, the topic of capital utilization is of more than academic interest because increases in utilization at the economy-wide level permit increases in total output and because at first sight the distribution of the increased output would seem to be especially favorable to workers. The reasoning behind the latter supposition may take either of two forms. If there is unemployed labor to begin with, increased utilization can provide more jobs with the same amount of fixed capital. The second form of the reasoning is based on the assumption that the total employment level is fixed, and hence an increase in utilization must bring about an increase in the ratio of capital to labor services, which in turn must increase the marginal product of labor.

Although the workers may reap economic benefits from increased utilization, it is obvious that they, rather than the capitalists, must pay the human costs of shift-work, and these costs may not be negligible. Moreover, as we shall argue in Part IV, the favorable effects of increased shift-work on workers will normally be diminished by the phenomenon of substitution. The degree of substitutability (which economists measure by the elasticity of substitution) between capital and labor services is a matter on which there is rather little firm knowledge. Consequently we do not in this study come to firm conclusions about the desirability on distributional grounds of policies to promote shift-work.

Another major economic effect of increases in capital utilization concerns the rate of economic growth. It can be shown in a wide variety of contexts that an increase in utilization has an effect rather similar (at least in the long run) to an increase in the rate of saving. This feature of capital utilization constitutes one of the strongest arguments in favor of policies to promote shift-work.

Having completed our preliminary view of the causes of capital idleness and the effects of increased capital utilization, we turn now to a more detailed exposition of the theory of the individual firm's shift-work decision.

reference, however, we shall also include an input variable that represents raw materials and intermediate products. If this variable is related to output in fixed proportions, the production process can be described by the system[3]

$$X = G(S, L); \qquad X = aM \qquad (1.1)$$

where X is the instantaneous flow of output that can be obtained from any instantaneous raw material input flow M. S and L are the instantaneous rates of services of the primary (or fund) factors utilized: capital and labor, respectively.

We shall start by assuming that the instantaneous rate of capital services available for production, UK, is a constant proportion of the size of the capital stock. U stands for the proportionality factor, which defines the period of analysis and the maintenance requirements of the machines, and K stands for the capital stock. The assumption that U is constant is tantamount to assuming that the instantaneous speed at which machines are operated is constant. The rationale for this assumption is provided in the next paragraph. Here we merely note its main implication: Variations in the instantaneous rate of capital services available for production can come about only through variations in the size of the capital stock.

The term *capital utilization* has been used indiscriminately to refer to two different dimensions of the same general phenomenon. Within a given time period of operation, the capital stock can be utilized more intensively by varying the duration of equipment operation (up to the whole period) or by varying the intensity of operation (up to the technical maximum), that is, the speed at which machines are operated. Although variations in both dimensions result in variations in the amount of capital services available or used during the given period, they have rather different (sometimes opposite) economic implications. As Winston (1974b, footnote 17) indicated, the economic explanations of capital utilization in terms of varying the speed of operation are based on capital depreciation; that is, capital is assumed to wear out faster and at an increasing rate with increasing speed of operation. He went on to note, however, that the assumption of an increasing rate of depreciation is questionable when applied to a lengthening of the duration of operations.[4] An analysis of capital utilization with two widely different implications about the nature of

---

[3] This result has been established in more general terms by Georgescu-Roegen (1935).

[4] Additional support for this statement is provided in Chapter 2, Section 2.2, footnote 9.

wear and tear would considerably complicate the exposition. Thus, in order to avoid having to choose between the simultaneous variables speed and duration, we shall assume speed to be constant. If the choice of instantaneous speed of machine operation is viewed as primarily determined by engineering considerations, which can be taken as given in determining the choice of duration, little is lost by this assumption.

It will be assumed that labor services per unit time can be freely purchased at a given wage rate within an eight-hour shift. Thus, there is neither an incentive to purchase more labor services than will actually be used in production nor a constraint to do so. This assumption ensures that it will not be optimal to plan partial shifts in the absence of indivisibilities of capital;[5] that is, only equipment that will be used throughout the whole duration of operations will be bought. Hence the instantaneous rate of capital services used in production, S, will equal the instantaneous rate of capital services available for production, UK.

For simplicity of exposition we shall define our instant to be the eight-hour shift; that is, the eight-hour shift is the basic unit of time, and the relations in (1.1) are defined in terms of rates per eight-hour shift. Because the analysis that follows is exactly the same for the double-shift and triple-shift systems, we shall deal exclusively with the former in this chapter. Relation (1.1) can now be written as

$$\overline{X} = X^1 = G(S^1, L^1); \qquad X^1 = aM^1 \tag{1.2a}$$

$$\overline{X} = X^2 = G(S_1^2, L_1^2) + G(S_2^2, L_2^2) = X_1^2 + X_2^2$$

$$X^2 = aM_1^2 + aM_2^2 = X_1^2 + X_2^2 \tag{1.2b}$$

where the superscript identifies the system of operation, the subscript identifies the shift, and $\overline{X}$ is the flow of output per calendar day that the plant must produce.

Relation (1.2a) describes the productive process if the plant is built to operate on a single-shift basis. Relation (1.2b) describes the productive process if the plant is built to operate on a double-shift system. A

---

[5] If one assumes the wage rate is a continuous function of the duration of daily operations and that it rises over the day, then partial shifts may be optimal. For instance, Winston and McCoy (1974) employed this assumption to analyze optimal capital utilization when it was less than the maximum. Because the model being developed in this section uses the same assumptions, or generalizations that contain their assumptions as special cases, in all other respects their analysis can be integrated into ours, mutatis mutandis, and used to analyze the adoption of partial shifts. Nonetheless, the planning of partial shifts under these circumstances is a somewhat special case, and it will not be explicitly pursued here.

constant instantaneous speed of operation implies that the instantaneous rate of capital services available for production is given by UK^2 for each shift of the double-shift system and by UK^1 for the single-shift system. Because under the assumptions of this chapter and the next one it will not be optimal to adopt partial shifts, the instantaneous rate of capital services employed in production is then given by

$$S_1^2 = S_2^2 = UK^2 \quad \text{and} \quad S^1 = UK^1$$

In this conceptualization of the productive process, by no means a complete description, there is before the plant is built a set of possible factory blueprints described by the function G. After the plant is built, however, we shall assume that the firm must operate with the same ratio of capital services to labor services during the day. Thus, $L_1^2 = L_2^2$. This assumption is commonly referred to as a zero ex-post elasticity of substitution. More precisely, it is a zero ex-post instantaneous elasticity of substitution of factor services in the sense of Winston (1974c). The impact on shift-work of relaxing this assumption is thoroughly discussed in the next chapter (Section 2.2). These assumptions allow the relations in (1.2) to be rewritten as

$$\overline{X} = X^1 = G(UK^1, L^1); \qquad X^1 = aM^1 \qquad \qquad (1.3a)$$
$$\overline{X} = X^2 = G(UK^2, L_1^2) + G(UK^2, L_1^2) = 2X_1^2$$
$$X^2 = a2M_1^2 = aM^2 \qquad \qquad (1.3b)$$

The choice of a system of operation can now be viewed in terms of choosing the system with the smallest cost, subject to the productive process constraints described by (1.3). That is, the double-shift system will be chosen if

$$rK^1 + w_1L^1 + P_mM^1 \geq rK^2 + w_1L_1^2 + w_2L_2^2 + P_mM^2 \qquad (1.4)$$

where inequality (1.4) is evaluated at the cost-minimizing values of the variable for each system of operation. Since $M^1 = M^2$ from (1.3), raw-material costs (and their unit price P_m) will play no role in the decision at this stage. The wage rate in the second shift of the double-shift system will be assumed to be related to the wage rate in the first shift (of both systems) as follows: $w_2 = w_1(1 + \alpha)$, where α is the shift differential.[6] The price of capital, r, equals $P_K(i + d)$, where

---

[6] When rotating shifts are used, one can think of the shift differential as being paid only for time spent on second-shift work. Parenthetically, the issue of rotating shifts versus nonrotating shifts is a trivial one in the present analytical context, but it is important in other contexts. More specifically, as we shall argue in Chapter 12, it is of great importance in evaluating the human costs of shift-work.

P_K is the price of a standard machine, i is the daily interest rate, and d is the rate of depreciation. We have assumed that depreciation is independent of utilization by allowing the daily cost of owning a unit of capital to be the same under the two systems. The impact of relaxing this assumption is also discussed in Section 2.2 in the next chapter.

Incorporating the assumptions of the previous two paragraphs into inequality (1.4) allows us to rewrite, after some manipulation, the condition for shift-work to be undertaken:

$$1 > [\theta k_1^2/k^1 + (2 + \alpha)(1 - \theta)]L_1^2/L^1 \qquad (1.5)$$

where θ is defined as the ratio of capital costs to combined capital and labor costs under single-shift operation, that is, $\theta = rK^1/(rK^1 + w_1L^1)$; k_1^2 and k^1 are the ratios of capital services to labor services utilized per shift under double- and single-shift operation, respectively, that is, $k_1^2 = UK^2/L_1^2$ and $k^1 = UK^1/L^1$; the other variables have already been defined. The right-hand side of (1.5) is the ratio of system 2 costs to system 1 costs (net of raw materials costs), which will be referred to as the cost ratio (CR).

1.2   The model and its operation: three propositions

The analysis of (1.5) requires an investigation of the optimal values of the decision variables for each system of operation. This analysis is facilitated considerably by assuming that the production function is homothetic; hence, it can be written using the output constraint as $\overline{X} = G[F(S^1, L^1)] = G(F^1)$ or $(1/2)\overline{X} = G[F(S_1^2, L_1^2)] = G(F_1^2)$, where F is linear homogeneous and $G'(F) > 0$. Using this assumption, we proceed to investigate the first-order conditions of the constrained cost minimization for each system of operations.[7]

For system 1, these conditions can be written as

$$r/w = f'(k^1)U/[f(k^1) - k^1f'(k^1)] = R(k^1)U = R^1U$$
$$\overline{X} = G(S^1, L^1) = G(F^1) = G[L^1f(k^1)] \qquad (1.6)$$

where R^1 is the rate of technical substitution of labor services for capital services in the single-shift system. Use has been made of the linear homogeneity of F, which allows it to be written as $F^1 =$

---

[7] Henderson and Quandt (1971, pp. 65-7) provided a derivation of the first- and second-order conditions for a constrained minimum in the two-variable-input case. For simplicity, we shall assume that for each factor of production the first partial of the production function with respect to a factor is positive and the second partial is negative; these assumptions ensure that the second-order conditions are satisfied.

$L^1 F(k^1,1) = L^1 f(k^1)$ (the second equality being used to simplify the notation); a prime indicates a derivative with respect to the argument.

Similarly, for system 2 the first-order conditions are

$$r/w(2 + \alpha) = f'(k_1^2)U/[f(k_1^2) - k_1^2 f'(k_1^2)] = R(k_1^2)U = R_1^2 U$$
$$\overline{X} = 2G(F_1^2) = 2G[L_1^2 f(k_1^2)] \qquad (1.7)$$

where R_1^2 is the rate of technical substitution of labor services for capital services in each shift of the double-shift system.

Turning to the production function constraint, we can solve the second equations in (1.6) and (1.7) for L^1 and L_1^2, respectively. Thus

$$L^1 = G^{-1}(X)/f(k^1); \qquad L_1^2 = G^{-1}[(1/2)\overline{X}]/f(k_1^2) \qquad (1.8)$$

where G^{-1} is the inverse function of G. Hence,

$$\frac{L_1^2}{L^1} = \left[\frac{G^{-1}[(1/2)\overline{X}]}{G^{-1}(\overline{X})} \right] \frac{f(k^1)}{f(k_1^2)} = [\phi(\overline{X})] \frac{f(k^1)}{f(k_1^2)} \qquad (1.9)$$

The bracketed term is of interest because it is directly related to the degree of economies of scale. For instance, if there are constant returns to scale, G^{-1} will be a constant multiple of $\overline{X}$, and the expression in brackets will equal $1/2$. If there are increasing (decreasing) returns to scale, more (less) of the input (F) per unit of output (X) will be necessary to produce half of the level of output, and the expression in brackets will be greater (less) than $1/2$. Finally, the homotheticity of the production function implies that economies of scale affect the cost ratio only through the bracketed term in (1.9). The three main propositions flowing from this model of shift-work will now be derived.

Proposition 1: For any prospective plant, the optimal ratio of capital to labor services in each shift of the double-shift system will be greater than the optimal ratio of capital to labor services under the single-shift system.

This proposition follows from the inverse relationship between the rate of technical substitution of labor services for capital services (R) and the ratio of capital to labor services (k) when the isoquants are convex to the origin and from the first equations in (1.6) and (1.7), which imply that $R^1 = R_1^2(2 + \alpha)$. When one views shift-work as a trade-off between capital costs and labor costs, this proposition acquires great intuitive appeal. It merely says that cost minimization implies the more intensive use of an input (capital services) that has become relatively cheaper (under system 2).

The main implication of this result is the positive association between high levels of capital utilization or shift-work and *observed* capital–labor ratios, or other measures of capital intensity. This association is the most consistently established fact in the empirical literature on capital utilization.[8] Simple and important as the result seems to be, its economic significance is somewhat limited because it obscures the existence of two entirely different influences in bringing about this association between capital intensity and utilization. That is, this association can result because the production technology available to the firm is highly capital-intensive, in which case one may think of high capital intensity as causing high utilization; or the association can result because the production technology available is one that allows easy substitution of capital for labor, in which case one may think of ease of substitution possibilities as causing high utilization and consequently high capital intensity. Clearly, the separation of these two different influences requires a more detailed characterization of the technology than has been provided here. This detailed characterization and the rigorous analysis of this issue are provided in Chapter 2 (Section 2.1) with the aid of specific functional forms for the production function.

Proposition 2: The larger (smaller) the economies (diseconomies) of scale, the higher the costs of the double-shift system.

This result follows straightforwardly from substitution of (1.9) into (1.5) and from differentiation of the cost ratio with respect to $\phi(\overline{X})$; that is, $\partial CR/\partial \phi(\overline{X}) = CR/\phi(\overline{X}) > 0$. This conclusion is easy to see intuitively. With a given level of output, shift-work entails operating each shift at half the level of output; the higher the costs of small-scale operation, the higher the costs of shift-work.

Proposition 3: The higher the shift differential, the higher the costs of the double-shift system.

It is easy to see why this proposition is true. An increase in the shift differential increases only the cost of the double-shift system. Parenthetically, it is worth taking note of an insight that can be derived directly from relation (1.7): The higher the shift differential, the higher the ratio of capital to labor services that will be observed for system 2 when it is the least-cost system. This insight will prove useful in the interpretation of empirical results.

These three propositions help emphasize and clarify several results available in the literature. One of the most important among these results is that the characteristics of the optimal factory depend on the duration of daily operations. Propositions 1 and 2 indicate the way in which the optimal factory will change with the level of utilization. That is, if a factory is designed to work shifts, it will be built to operate

---

[8] Chapter 5 provides the relevant evidence for this statement.

with a more capital-intensive technique than a single-shift factory, even if the shift differential is zero. Moreover, with a given daily output, the factory designed to work shifts will operate each shift at a lower (higher) rate of output per unit of combined capital and labor input in the presence of economies (diseconomies) of scale than will a single-shift factory.

Propositions 2 and 3 establish two of the main factors on the supply side that discourage the widespread use of shift-work in manufacturing plants. For instance, in the model developed here, if the shift differential is zero and if there are constant (or decreasing) returns to scale, shift-work will always entail lower costs than single-shift operation. This result can be demonstrated by evaluating the cost ratio at the optimal ratio of capital to labor services for the single-shift system and assuming a zero shift differential and constant returns to scale. Then (1.5) becomes

$$[\theta + 2(1 - \theta)]/2 = (2 - \theta)/2 < 1 \qquad (1.10)$$

Of course, the double-shift system will usually not be operated at the same ratio of capital to labor services as the single-shift system, but the left-hand side of (1.10) is already less than unity. Therefore, if the double-shift system were to be operated at the cost-minimizing value of the ratio of capital to labor services, the cost ratio would be even smaller than the value on the left-hand side of (1.10). Similarly, allowing for decreasing returns to scale would lead to an even lower value for the left-hand side of (1.10).

Whereas the importance of the shift differential has been consistently stressed in the literature, the treatment of economies of scale has been less systematic. For instance, Winston's survey (1974b, p. 1306) deemphasized this factor on the grounds that its effect on utilization is not clear. Proposition 2 reveals without doubt that the size of economies of scale, in the sense of the percentage increase in the rate of output flow due to a 1% increase in the rate of services from all inputs, is inversely related to the profitability of utilization. Nevertheless, ambiguity on this issue has arisen because the empirical relationship between the level of output and utilization depends on the assumed behavior of economies of scale as output increases. If one assumes economies of scale to be a decreasing function of the level of output per shift, as would be consistent with the first half of a textbook type of U-shaped average cost curve, then Proposition 2 also implies a positive association between utilization and the level of output per shift. But if one assumes, alternatively, that increasing returns proceed at a rate that is independent of the level of output, then there is no association between utilization and the level of output per shift. Nevertheless, it will still be true that the magnitude of economies of scale will be negatively related to the profitability of utilization. In terms of the cost ratio in (1.5), $\phi(\overline{X})$ will be a constant greater than $\frac{1}{2}$, and it will be greater the larger are economies of scale. Parenthetically, this assumption that economies of scale are independent of the level of output implies the following for the choice of systems: If one system is preferred at one level of output, it will also be preferred at any other level of output. The relationship between economies of scale and shift-work will be explored in more detail in Chapter 3.

*1.3   Extensions[9]

At this point we pause to indicate the main implications for the cost-minimization model of several additional factors that influence the profitability of shift-work. After being discussed here, these factors will be largely ignored in subsequent chapters.

Baily (1976) discussed several of these circumstances in her detailed study of shift-work in Kenya. Some of these factors (e.g., absenteeism on the night shift and search costs for supervisors) can be viewed, following Baily, as increasing the shift differential. Therefore, no changes are required in the theoretical framework of the previous section, which is directly applicable. In addition, two other issues stressed by Baily require only minor modifications in the cost-minimization model. If there are transport costs for workers that the firm must incur when it operates the second shift, the wage costs of the double-shift system will be $w_1(2 + \alpha)L_1^2 + tL_1^2$, where t is the average transport cost per worker. Similarly, if there is a drop in productivity during the second shift, the output constraint for the double-shift system will be $X = X_1^2 + X_2^2 = G(S_1^2, L_1^2) + \gamma G(S_1^2, L_1^2) = (1 + \gamma)G(F_1^2)$, where γ is an efficiency parameter and $0 \leq \gamma < 1$. In both cases a cost ratio that incorporates these factors will be greater than one that does not do so, because both factors can be viewed as increasing the costs of the double-shift system without affecting the costs of the single-shift system.

A consideration of overwhelming importance in some industries, ignored thus far, is the existence of large economies in prime costs due to the continuous-process nature of the technology. These economies may arise in several ways. For example, large start-up costs, particularly for fuel, may be incurred in getting the process operating at the desired specifications, or large raw-material losses may be incurred by interrupting the process. Chemicals and glass stand out among the

[9] The reader is reminded that sections carrying asterisks may be omitted without major loss of continuity.

industries where these costs are important. Yet an analysis of British industry (Marris 1964, Chapter 9) has revealed that even in these two industries the other considerations stressed earlier, apart from the continuous-process nature of the technology, are also important in the shift-work decision. In any event, from a theoretical standpoint, continuous-process technology introduces a relationship between the efficiency of the process in transforming material inputs and the duration of operations.[10]

The main consequence of incorporating this factor into the analysis is to reduce the costs of the double-shift system relative to the single-shift system. This reduction will be directly related to the magnitude of the loss in efficiency due to single-shift operation and to the importance of fuel or raw-material costs in the production process.

For simplicity of exposition, the following chapters are based on the cost ratio in (1.5), but it should be understood that the additional factors considered in this section could also be included in the subsequent analysis. This remark is well supported by the discussion of the last substantive topic in this section, to which we now turn. The analysis in this chapter has focused on a plant that uses a single productive process, but plants usually employ multiple processes or activities. Extension of the analysis to this situation is best accomplished by dealing initially with two polar cases. Let us consider first a situation in which the costs of operating each of the activities that constitute a plant are independent of one another.[11] Then the analysis of a single process can be applied to each activity exactly as before, and the factors that determine the cost ratio for each activity will determine whether or not that activity works shifts. The other polar case is a situation in which all of the activities must be operated simultaneously. In this situation the costs of all the activities must be considered in deciding whether or not to work shifts. The condition for the double-shift system to be the least-cost system becomes

$$1 > \sum_{i=1}^{n} CR_i \, TC_i \qquad\qquad (1.11)$$

[10] In other words, the coefficients of the transformation process in (1.3) differ between systems (i.e., $a^2 > a^1$).

[11] An activity or process is defined as any set of operations that can, in principle, be carried out by itself. From an economic point of view, an activity is considered to be independent of other activities if its costs are not affected by whether or not the other activities are in operation. At the very least, from an economic viewpoint, independence requires that storage costs over the twenty-four-hour day be negligible.

where CR_i is the cost ratio, defined as in (1.5), for the ith activity and TC_i is the share of total plant costs under single-shift operation that are due to the total costs of the ith activity under single-shift operation.

In these two cases, multiple processes require no conceptual changes in the analysis. The cost ratio for each activity is determined by the same factors as before. The only new element in the discussion is that where activity costs are interdependent, the cost ratios of the activities with the greatest shares in costs under single-shift operation will determine the shift-work decision. The main implication of this extreme assumption of interdependent activities is that activities that are normally labor-intensive are likely to become capital-intensive activities when shift-work is the least-cost system for the whole complex of interdependent activities.

The intermediate situation is, of course, more cumbersome to analyze. In this situation an activity can be carried out when others are not in operation, but at a higher cost. This situation requires some additional definitions because it introduces a variety of possible shift-work systems. More precisely, if there are n activities, the number (N) of possible shift-work systems is 2^n. The number of possible systems includes one system, let us say the last $(k = N)$, in which every activity is run under single-shift operation. For each of the remaining $N - 1$ systems, in which double-shift operation takes place in an activity or combination of activities, an aggregate cost ratio $CR(k)$ can be defined as follows:

$$CR(k) = \sum_{i=1}^{n} CR_i(k)TC_i \qquad \forall (k = 1, N - 1) \qquad (1.12)$$

where $CR_i(k) = CR_i + \Delta_i(k)$ if system k implies shift-work for the ith activity and $CR_i(k) = 1$ otherwise; $\Delta_i(k)$ are the increases in the costs of activity i over what they would be if every activity in system k were used under double-shift operation.[12] Among the $N - 1$ shift-work systems there is one system, let us say the first $(k = 1)$, where all activities are operated simultaneously; hence $\Delta_i(1) = 0$. If all activities are independent, in the sense that the costs of every activity are the

---

[12] Among the costs included in these interdependence functions would be, for example, storage costs or costs due to indivisibilities across activities. For instance, a two-activity plant where a single night supervisor could cover both activities would have four possible systems of operation, three of which would be shift-work systems. In two of the shift-work systems, one of the activities would not be operated at night; therefore, the $\Delta_i(k)$ functions for each of the activities operated at night in these two systems would be one-half of the daily wage for the night supervisor.

same regardless of whether or not other activities are in operation, then $\Delta_i(k) = 0$ for all i and k. TC_i and CR_i are defined as before. Thus our definitions encompass the previous two polar cases as well as the intermediate one.

A shift-work system will have lower costs than the single-shift system if and only if

$$1 > CR(k) \quad \text{for any } k \quad (k = 1, N - 1) \tag{1.13}$$

with the cost ratio for each activity, CR_i, evaluated at the optimal values of the variables for each activity. A necessary condition for the inequality in (1.13) to hold is that the cost ratio for at least one activity be less than unity. In addition, the transitivity of the aggregate cost ratio, $CR(k)$, ensures that the least-cost system among all the shift-work systems is the one for which $CR(k)$ is smallest. The aggregate cost ratio for each possible shift-work system, k, is made up of two components: some subset of single activity or process cost ratios, CR_i, and the corresponding subset of interdependence cost functions, $\Delta_i(k)$. Moreover, for every system each component enters into the aggregate as a linear combination with positive coefficients that add up to unity. Therefore any proposition that is true for a single process will also be true at the multiple-process level, other things being equal, for any shift-work system containing that process. In general, the direction of changes in the aggregate cost ratio for every shift-work system will be determined by the direction of changes in the individual process cost ratios.[13] Thus an analysis of the multiple-process case requires first an analysis of the cost ratio for each process.

To sum up, the general formulation of the multiple-process case contains the two polar cases as special cases, and it leads to the same substantive conclusions, with one possible exception. The exception arises because of the possible role of the interdependence cost functions, $\Delta_i(k)$, in affecting the outcome of the intermediate case. Undoubtedly a complete analysis of the multiple-process case necessitates further investigation of the $\Delta_i(k)$ functions and their properties; however, such an investigation would take us too far afield and would best be undertaken, in our judgment, in the context of specific plants. In light of these considerations, the remainder of the book continues the pattern of previous sections of focusing on a single process while indicating the impact of multiple-process considerations at the relevant points in the discussion.

[13] The possible exception to this statement requires that whatever produces a change in the cost ratio for one activity must also change in the opposite direction the interdependence cost functions or other individual process cost ratios in shift-work systems containing that activity.

CHAPTER 2

Specific functional forms: additional results

In this chapter we shall delve more deeply into the decision to work shifts; this will be done with the aid of specific assumptions about the productive process. The most important of these assumptions is the use of a constant elasticity of substitution (CES) production function (Arrow et al. 1961) throughout the chapter to describe the extent of ex-ante substitution possibilities between capital and labor services. Specific functional forms are also relied on to investigate more thoroughly other aspects of the productive process that are potentially important in the decision to work shifts. Finally, we also find specific functional forms to be indispensable in our subsequent empirical analysis. Thus this chapter provides the functional forms of the cost ratio that will be implemented empirically.

In the next section the CES functional form will be employed to describe ex-ante substitution possibilities in the cost-minimization model of Chapter 1. The CES assumption has already been used in the shift-work literature by Winston (1974a) and Betancourt and Clague (1975), among others. We shall follow the approach used in the latter reference because it facilitates separation of the influence of capital intensity from that of ex-ante substitution possibilities as causal factors in the shift-work decision. This separation also highlights the role of the elasticity of substitution in modifying the effect of factor prices on shift-work. This role has been particularly stressed by Winston in a number of articles, both in the context of the CES assumption (1974a) and in other settings (Winston 1974b; Winston and McCoy, 1974). In Section 2.2 specific functional forms will be used to evaluate the impact on shift-work of relaxing two assumptions made in the previous chapter: no wear-and-tear depreciation and ex-post substitution possibilities. Interestingly enough, the published literature has devoted only minor attention to the role of wear-and-tear depreciation in the shift-work decision; brief treatments are available, for example, from Marris (1964, pp. 38–41) and Baily (1976, p. 28). Yet we find this factor to be capable of having a nonnegligible impact on the cost ratio. By contrast, ex-post substitution possibilities have received a fair amount of attention in the shift-work literature (e.g., Baily 1974;

24

Millan 1975; Clague 1976), but we find their effect on the cost ratio under reasonable assumptions to be negligible when compared with the effect of wear-and-tear depreciation.

In the third section we shall discuss the decision to work three shifts in the context of specific functional forms. An explicit discussion of this decision acquires unexpected significance because it reveals a previously unknown tendency toward inferiority of the double-shift system and a similar tendency toward sequentiality in the firm's decision-making process. In the last section we shall consider two alternative formulations of the impact of working capital on the shift-work decision in the context of the cost-minimization model of Chapter 1 and the CES assumption employed throughout this chapter. A somewhat striking and novel result of our analysis is that working-capital considerations will have no effect on the shift-work decision under one of these formulations.

To put our introductory comments in a slightly different form, in this chapter we use the CES assumption with the cost-minimization model of Chapter 1 to generate the remaining two of the five most important implications of cost minimization for capital utilization that are available in the literature. We also rely on specific functional forms to explore the effect on the model of other aspects of firm behavior that are relevant to the capital-utilization decision. Although many of these aspects have been previously discussed in the published and unpublished literature, several of the results in this chapter are new. Finally, in establishing all of the results in this chapter, we rely even more heavily than in Chapter 1 on the concept of the cost ratio.

2.1   Capital intensity and ex-ante substitution possibilities

At this point we shall assume that the homogeneous production function F is of the CES variety. Hence

$$F^1 = [\delta(S^1)^{-\rho} + (1 - \delta)(L^1)^{-\rho}]^{-1/\rho} \quad \text{and}$$

$$F_1^2 = [\delta(S_1^2)^{-\rho} + (1 - \delta)(L_1^2)^{-\rho}]^{-1/\rho} \quad (2.1)$$

The first-order conditions in Chapter 1 can now be solved explicitly for the optimal ratios of capital to labor services under each system; that is,

$$k_1^2 = \{[\delta/(1 - \delta)](w_1/r)(2 + \alpha)\}^\sigma U^\sigma \quad \text{and}$$

$$k^1 = \{[\delta/(1 - \delta)](w_1/r)\}^\sigma U^\sigma \quad (2.2)$$

where σ is the elasticity of substitution and $\rho = (1 - \sigma)/\sigma$. Similarly, an explicit expression can be obtained for L_1^2/L^1:

$$L_1^2/L^1 = \phi(\overline{X})[\theta(2 + \alpha)^{\sigma-1} + (1 - \theta)]^{\sigma/(1-\sigma)} \tag{2.3}$$

The cost ratio presented in Chapter 1, relation (1.5), now becomes

$$\text{CR} = \phi(\overline{X})(2 + \alpha)[\theta(2 + \alpha)^{\sigma-1} + (1 - \theta)]^{1/(1-\sigma)} \tag{2.4}$$

For future reference, note that when $\sigma = 0$, the Leontief case, the relevant cost ratio can be obtained directly from (2.4) by setting $\sigma = 0$, which yields

$$\text{CR} = \phi(\overline{X})[\theta + (1 - \theta)(2 + \alpha)] \tag{2.5}$$

The more detailed characterization of the technology embedded in the CES assumption allows us to establish two additional propositions about the shift-work decision.

Proposition 4: The higher the capital intensity of the technology under single-shift operation (θ), the lower the relative costs of the double-shift system.

This proposition follows straightforwardly from differentiating the cost ratio, the right-hand side of (2.4), with respect to θ; that is,

$$\frac{\partial \text{CR}}{\partial \theta} = \frac{(2 + \alpha)^{\sigma} - (2 + \alpha)}{(1 - \sigma)} \phi(\overline{X})B^{\sigma/(1-\sigma)} < 0 \tag{2.6}$$

where B is the bracketed expression in equation (2.4), which is always positive. If we view the shift-work decision as a means of lowering the price of capital services while raising the price of labor services, it makes intuitive sense that the higher the share of capital costs under single-shift operation the more attractive the adoption of the high-utilization system.

It is useful to state explicitly one conceptual experiment underlying this result. Consider two plants facing the same set of factor prices and shift differential, the same level of output and economies of scale, and the same substitution possibilities, but differing with respect to the capital intensity of the technology. That is, the distribution parameter (δ) in the CES is higher for one plant than for the other, so that θ will be higher for the plant with higher δ; then the costs of shift-work will be lower for the plant with the higher θ.

Another conceptual experiment is one in which the two plants face the same situation as before, with the exception that whereas the distribution parameters are the same, the factor prices are different. It is well known that the effect of factor prices on θ depends on the elasticity of substitution. That is, if $\sigma < 1$, a fall in the wage rate leads to a rise in θ; if $\sigma > 1$, a fall in the wage rate leads to the opposite result. Therefore, Proposition 4 also allows us to predict the impact of factor prices on the cost ratio because these prices affect the cost ratio only through θ. To wit, changes in factor prices that increase θ will lower the relative costs of the double-shift system. As indicated earlier, whether or not a given change in factor prices increases θ depends on σ.[1] We shall refer to this role of the elasticity of substitution as the indirect effect of σ on shift-work.

Proposition 5: The higher the ex-ante elasticity of substitution, other things being equal, the lower the relative costs of the double-shift system.

By differentiating the logarithm of the cost ratio with respect to σ, keeping θ, α, and $\phi(\overline{X})$ constant, we obtain

$$d \log \mathrm{CR}/d\sigma = (1 - \sigma)^{-1}\theta(2 + \alpha)^{\sigma-1} \log (2 + \alpha)B^{-1}$$
$$+ \log B(1 - \sigma)^{-2} < 0 \quad (2.7)$$

The formal proof that this inequality holds is new but somewhat intricate. Therefore, in order to preserve continuity, it is relegated to Appendix 2.1. Intuitively, this result can be justified by viewing the magnitude of the elasticity of substitution as indicating the level of a constraint on the firm's decision-making process. Shift-work entails a substitution of capital for labor services in the productive process; hence, the less binding the constraint, or the easier it is to substitute capital for labor services, the lower the relative costs of shift-work.

All of our propositions, thus far, are of the other-things-being-equal variety. However, it is only with respect to Proposition 5 that we must emphasize this aspect, because when σ changes, one other thing will normally change, namely, θ. Therefore, in order to isolate the direct impact of ex-ante substitution possibilities, inequality (2.7) is derived under the assumption that θ does not change. What this assumption implies is that δ, the distribution parameter in the CES, changes when σ changes in such a way as to leave the ratio of capital to labor services under single-shift operation (and hence θ) unchanged.[2] Thus the conceptual experiment underlying this proposition is one in which two plants face the same factor prices and shift differential, the same level of output and economies of scale, and different technologies with respect to δ and σ; but these technologies are such that the two plants will use the same ratio of capital to labor services under single-shift operation. Proposition 5 says that the plant with the higher σ will face lower costs of shift-work. This effect will be dubbed the direct effect of σ on shift-work, in contrast to the indirect effect discussed earlier.

Propositions 4 and 5 clearly identify the two entirely different

---

[1] More formally, $\partial\theta/\partial(w_1/r) = \theta(1 - \theta) (r/w_1) (\sigma - 1)$.
[2] This procedure for changing the elasticity of substitution has also been used by Corden (1971, p. 48) in the analysis of effective protection.

influences that lead to the positive association between capital intensity and utilization. Hence they can be viewed as enhancing our under- standing of Proposition 1. They also suggest the necessity of character- izing the technology in greater detail, through the elasticity of substitu- tion, in order to separate the roles of capital intensity as a cause and a consequence of capital utilization.

Recognition of the role of the ex-ante elasticity of substitution in bringing about higher levels of utilization or shift-work becomes particularly important in empirical analyses, because an understand- ing of this role is a prerequisite for separating cause from effect in observed measures of capital intensity. In order to isolate the role of capital intensity as a determinant or cause of utilization, it is necessary to measure capital intensity for the single-shift system. Clearly, if plants work shifts the value of this variable cannot be observed, and therefore it must be estimated. The CES functional form allows this estimation to take place because it implies a relationship between the observed ratio of capital to labor services (k_1^2) under shift-work and the unobserved ratio (k^1); that is, $k^1 = k_1^2/(2 + \alpha)^\sigma$.[3] When the production function is that of Leontief ($\sigma = 0$), this problem is eliminated. Because there is only one possible ratio of capital to labor services in this situation, the observed ratio of capital to labor services for plants that work shifts corresponds to the unobserved ratio for the single-shift system; hence, capital intensity can operate only as a cause of utiliza- tion.

Propositions 2 through 5 summarize the most important determi- nants of the decision to work shifts, or of planned capital utilization, in the cost-minimization framework. In some particular circumstances, other factors may acquire importance, but, as illustrated earlier, the model developed here is flexible enough to accommodate other influences. In the next section we shall discuss and evaluate the impact on the shift-work decision of two factors previously ignored.

2.2   Wear-and-tear depreciation and ex-post substitution possibilities

This discussion will emphasize those aspects of these two issues that are of particular importance for the analysis of shift-work. Wear- and-tear depreciation will be discussed first.

The price of capital has been defined as $r = P_K(i + d)$ in Chapter 1

---

[3] A detailed discussion of this estimation problem is undertaken in Chapter 4, Section 4.4.

for both systems of operation. If there are capital costs that are dependent on the duration of utilization, this assumption must be changed. Because the capital equipment is operated twice as long in the double-shift system, the operating costs due to wear-and-tear depreciation should be larger for this system. The higher operating costs for the double-shift system arise, for example, because of higher frequency of repairs and/or increased maintenance activities. Differences in machine operating costs between the two systems lead to differences in the price of capital between the two systems. That is, they lead to r^2 being greater than r^1.

The impact on the cost ratio of different prices of capital for each system can easily be derived. Specifically, the cost ratio in Chapter 1, relation (1.5), becomes

$$\text{CR} = [\theta(k_1^2/k^1)(r^2/r^1) + (2 + \alpha)(1 - \theta)]L_1^2/L^1$$

where $\theta = r^1 K^1/(w_1 L^1 + r^1 K^1)$. If we impose the assumption of an ex-ante CES production function on the homogeneous function (F), a condition analogous to the one obtained by Clague (1975, Section III) follows; that is,

$$\text{CR} = \phi(\overline{X})(2 + \alpha)[\theta(2 + \alpha)^{\sigma-1}(r^2/r^1)^{1-\sigma} + (1 - \theta)]^{1/(1-\sigma)} \quad (2.8)$$

It is straightforward to prove that increases in the relative price of capital for the double-shift system increase the cost ratio. Moreover, intuitively one expects this result to be the case, as increases in r^2/r^1 can also be viewed as increases in the costs of system 2 given the cost of system 1. If wear-and-tear depreciation makes r^2/r^1 large enough, the impact on the cost ratio, and hence on shift-work, can be substantial. It is our judgment that the values of r^2/r^1 usually lie between 1.0 and 1.35.

In order to support this judgment, we must take a closer look at the determinants of r^2/r^1. Wear-and-tear depreciation takes place as a result of both the passage of time after a machine is built and the extent to which the machine is used. In both cases the maintenance costs incurred will be assumed to restore the machine to its original state; that is, the machine yields the same rate of services per unit of time (eight-hour shift) throughout its life if properly maintained. Given the life of the machine, the daily maintenance costs due to the passage of time (c) will be the same for both systems; however, the daily maintenance costs due to usage, $M(s)$, given the same machine life as before, will differ between systems because the accumulated usage will be twice as much in the double-shift system (i.e., $s^2 = 2s^1$) and because maintenance costs are an increasing function of usage [i.e., $M(s^2) =$

$M(2s^1) > M(s^1)$]. Wear and tear due to usage is the sole source of differences in the prices of capital between systems.[4]

Let us now assume that machine life is fixed under both systems at the optimal replacement life of the machine under single-shift operation. Then the ratio of the prices of capital in the two systems can be written as $r^2/r^1 = [i + d^1 + c^1 + M(2s^1)]/[i + d^1 + c^1 + M(s^1)]$.[5] The assumption of nonoptimal replacement for the double-shift system ensures that we have an upper bound to r^2/r^1, given the values of i, d^1, c^1, and $M(s^1)$; that is, $d^{2*} + c^{2*} + M(s^{2*}) \leq d^1 + c^1 + M(2s^1)$, where the asterisk indicates the optimal values of the variables in the double-shift system.[6] Rewriting, we have

$$r^2/r^1 \leq \{1 + [M(2s^1)/M(s^1)] Q^1\}/(1 + Q^1) \qquad (2.9)$$

where $Q^1 = M(s^1)/(i + d^1 + c^1)$, or the optimal ratio of user costs to other capital costs under single-shift operation. It can be seen from the inequality in (2.9) that the range of values of r^2/r^1 depends critically on the functional form of the user cost function $M(s)$ and increases with Q^1.

The literature does not shed much light on either the values of Q^1 or the functional form of the user cost function, but a frequent assumption is that user costs are proportional to use. This assumption will be used here because it is likely to overstate the importance of wear-and-tear depreciation due to a lengthening of the duration of operations[7] (e.g., Marris 1964, pp. 9, 38–41). Then $M(2s^1)/M(s^1) = 2$, and

[4] This formulation accentuates the main aspects of wear-and-tear depreciation relevant to the present context; for a more general treatment of wear and tear, see Feldstein and Rothschild (1974) or Clague (1975, Section III).

[5] This formulation of the price of capital in each system requires that maintenance costs be proportional to the value of the machine.

[6] In general, the inequality will hold. For instance, Clague (1975, Section III) found that under a variety of assumptions the optimal life of machines in the double-shift system was greater than 66% but less than 100% of the optimal life under single-shift operation. He also found a range of 1 to 1.25 for r^2/r^1 when buildings are included as part of capital. Incidentally, the inequality in the text will hold even though it will generally be the case that the optimal depreciation rate will be larger for the double-shift system than for the single-shift system (i.e., $d^{2*} > d^1$).

[7] Maintenance activities are subject to economies of scale with respect to a lengthening of the duration of operations, which provides one of the main reasons for the overstatement discussed in the text. This factor also provides one of the reasons for objecting to the assumption that depreciation increases at an increasing rate when utilization increases. Economies of scale in maintenance activities render this assumption implausible.

Table 2.1. *Wear-and-tear depreciation and ex-post substitution*

Wear-and-tear depreciation[a]						
	r^2/r^1 ($\sigma_1 = 0.4$)			r^2/r ($\sigma_1 = 1.4$)		
	1.0	1.2	1.3	1.0	1.2	1.3
$\theta = 0.3$	0.997	1.035	1.054	0.915	0.980	1.009
$\theta = 0.4$	0.918	0.967	0.991	0.832	0.909	0.943
Ex-post substitution[b]						
	σ_2 ($\sigma_1 = 0.4$)			σ_2 ($\sigma_1 = 1.4$)		
	0		0.2	0	0.2	0.6
$\theta = 0.3$	0.997		0.979	0.915	0.909	0.897
$\theta = 0.4$	0.918		0.910	0.832	0.828	0.821

The entries in the body of the table are values of the cost ratio calculated using the alternative table values. For this purpose it is assumed that α, the shift differential, is 0.5 and that there are no economies of scale; σ_1 is the elasticity of substitution in the ex-ante CES production function, and σ_2 is the elasticity of substitution in the ex-post CES production function.
[a]No ex-post substitution was allowed in the calculations presented in this part of the table (i.e., $\sigma_2 = 0$).
[b]No wear-and-tear depreciation was allowed in the calculations of this part of the table (i.e., $r^2/r^1 = 1$).

(2.9) collapses to $r^2/r^1 \leq (1 + 2Q^1)/(1 + Q^1)$. Even if user costs are as high as one-half of the other capital costs under single-shift operation, our upper bound for r^2/r^1 will equal 1.33. Two additional considerations neglected in the previous discussion should be mentioned. A substantial portion of the capital equipment is in the form of buildings rather than machines (about 40% of the value of capital in our samples). For buildings, the ratio $M(2s^1)/M(s^1)$ will be considerably less than 2. Finally, obsolescence has been ignored in the discussion, but high rates of obsolescence lead to shorter optimal lives for equipment. Insofar as shorter equipment life raises the depreciation unrelated to use (d^1) more than it lowers the daily maintenance costs unrelated to use (c^1), it tends to decrease Q^1 and thus r^2/r^1.

To conclude the discussion of wear-and-tear depreciation, we present in the top half of Table 2.1 a brief sensitivity analysis of the impact of r^2/r^1 on the cost ratio in (2.8). For example, this table shows that a 20% increase in the price of capital for system 2 leads to increases in the cost ratio that are less than 10% in all four cases in the table. Because the theoretical impact of wear-and-tear depreciation on shift-work is straightforward, as demonstrated here, and because our data provide us with no information on this variable, the next few chapters will make only passing reference to this issue. On the other hand, this section also demonstrates that the effects of wear and tear on shift-work are of somewhat uncertain magnitude and are expected to be small but not negligible; therefore the role of wear and tear will be taken up again in some detail when we assess the policy implications of our results in Chapter 9.

Ex-post substitution possibilities present a different and less diffi-cult set of problems. Intuitively, relaxing the assumption of zero ex-post substitution should decrease the costs of shift-work. For if one views the value of the ex-post elasticity of substitution as indicating the level of a constraint on the firm's decision making, it is a constraint that is not binding on single-shift operation but is binding on the double-shift system. Hence, other things being equal, relaxing the constraint should decrease the costs of the double-shift system without affecting the costs of single-shift operation by allowing for the possibility of using a smaller amount of the higher-priced services of night workers in the double-shift system. The new cost ratio corresponding to (1.5) in Chapter 1 is

$$\mathrm{CR} = [\theta(k_1^2/k^1) + (2 + \alpha)(L_2^2/L_1^2)(1 - \theta)](L_1^2/L^1) \tag{2.10}$$

Further progress at the analytical level becomes difficult and cumber-some, particularly when allowing for nonconstant returns to scale. Moreover, it is of dubious value, as the assumption of zero ex-post substitution may be an accurate reflection of the actual situation that prevails at the process level during the twenty-four-hour day. Thus, we limit our discussion to a brief summary of the main results available in the literature.

Baily (1974, Chapter 2) has shown that shift-work will always be optimal with a constant-returns-to-scale production function, which is the same ex-ante and ex-post, as long as the marginal product of labor is not bounded above (e.g., the CES with $\sigma \geq 1$). A more realistic case is one in which ex-post substitution possibilities exist but are less than ex-ante substitution possibilities. This case is difficult to analyze, however, as shown by Clague (1976). Even under the assumption of constant returns to scale, with an ex-ante CES and either a variable elasticity of substitution (VES) or ex-post CES, an analytical solution is not possible. Nevertheless, Clague's numerical analysis clearly shows that the higher the ex-post elasticity of substitution, the lower the costs of shift-work. The second part of Table 2.1, which reproduces some of his results, serves to illustrate this point. It is also worth stressing the main implication of this numerical analysis; namely, the quantitative impact of ex-post substitution possibilities on the cost ratio is of very limited importance. For instance, whereas changes in r^2/r^1 usually lead to changes in the second decimal of the cost ratio, equal or even larger changes in the value of the ex-post elasticity of substitution frequently lead to changes in the third decimal of the cost ratio. Therefore, in the remainder of this book, ex-post substitution possibilities are usually ignored.

*2.3   The decision to work three shifts

Not surprisingly, the previous theoretical results are not altered by introducing the possibility of a third shift. The easiest way of dealing with the three-shift possibility is to define an additional cost ratio: the ratio of the costs of the triple-shift system to the costs of the single-shift system, CR^1.

The cost ratio CR^1 must, of course, be evaluated at the optimal values of the decision variables for each system of operations, subject to the technological constraints embedded in the production function. The results for the CES and Leontief cases, comparable to equations (2.4) and (2.5) in Section 2.1, are presented in equations (2.11) and (2.12), respectively.[8]

$$CR^1 = [3 + (1 + b)\alpha]\{\theta[3 + (1 + b)\alpha]^{\sigma-1}$$
$$+ (1 - \theta)\}^{1/(1-\sigma)}\phi^1(\overline{X}) \quad (2.11)$$

and

$$CR^1 = \{\theta + [3 + (1 + b)\alpha](1 - \theta)\}\phi^1(\overline{X}) \quad (2.12)$$

where b is the ratio of the shift differential for the third shift (α^1) to the shift differential for the second shift (α), $b \geq 1$;[9] $\phi^1(\overline{X}) = G^{-1}[(\frac{1}{3})\overline{X}]/G^{-1}(\overline{X})$. The term $[3 + (1 + b)\alpha]$ plays exactly the same role in this cost ratio as the term $(2 + \alpha)$ did in the earlier one. The same five propositions established with respect to the previous cost ratio will also hold, mutatis mutandis, with respect to this one. In addition, it will be true that the higher the ratio of shift differentials b, the higher the new cost ratio CR^1; that is,

8   The derivation is exactly analogous to that for the two-shift case.
9   We speak of the third shift as the night or graveyard shift and of the second shift as the evening shift. There is widespread evidence that the night shift receives slightly higher compensation than the evening shift (Maurice 1975, pp. 79–81).

$$\partial \log \mathrm{CR}^1/\partial b = (1 - \theta)\alpha/[3 + (1 + b)\alpha]B^1 > 0 \qquad (2.13)$$

where $B^1 = \{\theta[3 + (1 + b)\alpha]^{\sigma-1} + (1 - \theta)\}$.

Instead of belaboring the same considerations as before, it will be more profitable to consider an interesting feature of the relationship between the two cost ratios, CR and CR^1, that provides another view of the impact of the (ex-ante) elasticity of substitution on shift-work. The essence of the argument is that under certain circumstances the double-shift system has a tendency not to be the best system among the three systems, a tendency that becomes stronger as the elasticity of substitution increases. We speak of this phenomenon as a tendency toward inferiority. An inferior system is, of course, a system that is never optimal among the three systems.

It is convenient to assume constant returns to scale in the remainder of this section. This assumption implies that $\phi^1(\overline{X}) = \frac{1}{3}$ in (2.11) and (2.12) and $\phi(\overline{X}) = \frac{1}{2}$ in (2.4) and (2.5). The tendency toward inferiority of the double-shift system can now be seen most easily in terms of Table 2.2. In the body of this table we present the range of values of the capital share under single-shift operation for which the double-shift system will be optimal, given different values of the elasticity of substitution. The lower bound is the minimum value that the capital share can take on (in terms of the shift differential) while the double-shift system is preferred or indifferent to the single-shift system (i.e., while $\mathrm{CR} \le 1$). The upper bound is the maximum value that the capital share can take on while the double-shift system is preferred or indifferent to the triple-shift system (i.e., while $\mathrm{CR}/\mathrm{CR}^1 \le 1$).[10]

If the lower bound of the capital share is greater than the upper bound, the double-shift system can never be optimal. Hence it is an inferior system. Numerical analysis of the bounds in Table 2.2 reveals that, for given values of the day–evening differential (α), the range of values of the evening–night differential (b) for which the double-shift system is an inferior system increases as the elasticity of substitution increases. Thus the tendency toward inferiority of the double-shift system is least pronounced in the Leontief case ($\sigma = 0$). In this situation the double-shift system will be an inferior system or at best an indifferent system if b equals unity. If b is greater than unity, there will always be some value of the capital share for which the double-

---

[10] Incidentally, except for the Cobb-Douglas case, the upper bound depends on the capital share itself. More precisely, as the capital intensity of the production process increases, measured by θ, the value of the upper bound decreases (recall that $\alpha \ge 0$ and $b \ge 1$).

Table 2.2. *Optimality of the double-shift system*

σ	Lower bound	Optimal	Upper bound
0	$\alpha/(1 + \alpha)$	$< \theta$	$< [\alpha/(1 + \alpha)][(2b - 1) + 2\theta\alpha(1 - b)]$
1	$\log(2 + \alpha)/\log 2$	$< 1/(1 - \theta)$	$< \log\{[3 + \alpha(1 + b)]/(2 + \alpha)\}/\log(3/2)$
2	$(1/2)[\alpha/(1 + \alpha)]$	$< \theta$	$< [\alpha/(1 + \alpha)][(2b - 1)(1 - \theta)]\{(1 + \alpha)/(2 + \alpha)[3 + \alpha(1 + b)]\}$

shift system is optimal. On the other hand, if σ is greater than zero, even with positive values of b, the double-shift system can still be an inferior system. In fact, it can be shown that under a Cobb-Douglas function with constant returns to scale, if b is less than 1.377 and α is positive, the double-shift system will always be inferior. Finally, it can also be shown from Table 2.2 that regardless of σ, if α is equal to zero, the double-shift system must be an inferior system provided that θ is positive.

A phenomenon related to inferiority is that of sequentiality. The decision-making process of the firm can be defined as sequential if the firm can decide whether or not shift-work is optimal from a single binary comparison. Note, however, that if shift-work is optimal, a further comparison will be needed in order to ascertain whether the double-shift system or the triple-shift system is the better alternative. In more precise terms, the decision-making process can be defined as sequential if $CR > 1$ implies $CR^1 > 1$, or vice versa. It is worth noting that with constant returns to scale, the structure of the shift-work decision-making process will tend to be sequential. More important, the order of the sequence depends on the elasticity of substitution. That is, if the production function is Leontief, it can be shown that $CR > 1$ implies $CR^1 > 1$. If the production function is Cobb-Douglas, however, it can be shown for values of b less than 1.377 that $CR^1 > 1$ implies $CR > 1$. The demonstration of these results is undertaken in Appendix 2.2.

The phenomena of inferiority and sequentiality illustrate another aspect of the role of the (ex-ante) elasticity of substitution in affecting the shift-work decision. That is, the higher σ is, the lower the costs of both the double-shift system and the triple-shift system will be, the impact of an increase in σ being greater on the triple-shift system. This is an intuitively plausible result, since shift-work involves in both cases a substitution of capital for labor services, and the extent of this substitution is greater for the triple-shift system.

These findings should be viewed as merely suggestive, because if other factors are introduced into the analysis (e.g., economies of scale or wear-and-tear depreciation) the tendency toward inferiority of the double-shift system and the tendency toward sequentiality of the decision-making process are reduced. To conclude this section, we offer the following interpretation of these results: In general, the double-shift system and the triple-shift system are to be viewed as fairly close substitutes relative to the single-shift system; however, as the elasticity of substitution increases, there is a definite tendency for the triple-shift system to become the dominant alternative among the shift-work systems.

*2.4   Working capital and shift-work[11]

Our interest in this topic stems from three somewhat different concerns. First, it provides an opportunity to add realism to the cost-minimization model by incorporating another characteristic of the productive process into the analysis. Second, our data provide some information on the subject; hence this section provides the basis for the development of alternative hypotheses that will be tested empirically in Chapter 7. Finally, working-capital costs in the presence of imperfect capital markets have been suggested as one of the main obstacles to increased utilization in the short run (Schydlowsky 1974), but these costs can be shown to be far less important in the long-run decision. The nature of working-capital requirements and working-capital costs will be discussed first; subsequently the implications of working-capital costs for the cost ratios will be derived.

Working capital is needed to bridge the gap between the payment of productive factors and the receipt of revenue from the sale of the product. Part of the working-capital requirements stem from the need to finance the holding of inventories. Inventories can be divided into materials (T_1), work-in-process (T_2), and finished products (T_3). We can let P_i $(i = 1, 2, 3)$ be the period of turnover for the ith category of inventories, expressed as a fraction of a year. Then if $P_3 = 0.085$, for example, finished goods remain on the shelf for an average of one month before they are sold. The other part of working-capital requirements depends on the net credit position of the enterprise vis-à-vis its customers and suppliers. We can let P_4 be the period for which credit is extended to purchasers of the product, with P_5 being the period for which credit can be obtained from suppliers on material purchases.

---

[11] This section is a specialized one that also relies heavily on our earlier work on the subject (Betancourt and Clague 1976a).

Total working-capital requirements can now be stated in terms of various categories of costs and the periods of turnover previously defined. Two possibilities will be considered:

$$\text{WK} = P_m M P^* + wLP + rKP \tag{2.14}$$

or

$$\text{WK} = P_m M P^* + wLP \tag{2.15}$$

where WK are the working-capital requirements, $P_m M$ and wL are material and labor costs, respectively, P^* is the average period of financing required for materials (i.e., $P^* = P_1 + P_2 + P_3 + P_4 - P_5$) or the average time between payment for materials and receipt of payment for the product, P is the average period of financing required for labor and capital costs (i.e., $P = P_2 + P_3 + P_4$) or the average time between payment for labor and capital and receipt of payment for the product.[12]

It will be assumed that the periods of turnover P and P^* are given from the point of view of the firm. For the inventory ratios, P_1, P_2, and P_3, the assumption is that the technical characteristics of the production process determine these ratios in an inflexible manner. For the other two ratios, P_4 and P_5, the assumption is that the institutional setting in which the firm operates determines these periods in an inflexible manner. Clearly, given a choice, the firm has an incentive to seek to reduce P and P^*, and the higher the rate of interest on working capital, the greater this incentive. The advantage of the assumption is that it avoids the need for an incursion into inventory theory or into the determinants of interfirm credit. In any event, the assumption provides an upper bound to the impact of the rate of interest on working-capital requirements. Thus this assumption is relatively innocuous because its impact on the analysis is straightforward.

In the first formulation of working-capital requirements, equation (2.14), fixed capital costs are assumed to give rise to working-capital requirements in the same manner as the variable labor costs. It immediately follows from our production-function assumptions that in this situation working-capital costs will have no effect on the shift-work decision. In this case working-capital costs can be viewed as leading to redefinition of the prices of capital and labor as $r^* = r(1 + IP)$ and $w^* = w(1 + IP)$, where I is the interest rate on working capital. Because the homotheticity of the production function ensures that optimal factor proportions depend only on factor prices, working capital will not affect optimal factor proportions for either system,

---

[12] We assume that labor and capital are paid at the beginning of period P_2.

because $r^*/w^* = r/w$. At the given level of output, total costs for both systems will be higher than when working-capital costs are ignored, but these higher costs will not affect the choice of system. Thus, if (2.14) holds, working capital will have no effect on shift-work, and the analysis in this book up to this point holds without modification. This hypothesis will be referred to as the zero-effect hypothesis in subsequent chapters, but it will not be considered further here.

The second formulation of working-capital requirements, equation (2.15), assumes that fixed capital costs do not give rise to any working-capital requirements. One way of justifying this assumption is to suppose that the interest payments or the interest income foregone on the fixed capital are scheduled to coincide with the receipt of payments from sales. Alternatively, one can justify this second formulation by assumimg that any working-capital costs associated with the fixed capital are already incorporated into the price of capital, and the interest rate on working capital for the financing of labor (I) is higher than the interest rate on fixed capital (i). Then (2.15) can be used together with the difference in interest rates ($I - i$) to analyze the impact of this type of working-capital market on shift-work. We shall rely on the first justification because it facilitates the exposition while leading to the same analytical conclusions as the second justification.

The interest costs of working capital (I) will depend on the nature of the working-capital market. One important dimension has already been mentioned; that is, the interest cost on working capital (I) will be assumed to be higher than the interest cost on fixed capital (i). It will also be assumed that the firm does not perceive its actions as influencing the interest rate that prevails in the working-capital market.[13] Whereas this assumption is consistent with a perfectly competitive working-capital market, it is also consistent with other market settings. For example, the rationing of working capital may be accomplished through the use of criteria other than interest rates (e.g., creditworthiness, type of collateral, customer goodwill). This situation is implicit in the arguments behind the availability thesis put forth in the context of developed countries.[14] In less-developed countries, capital

[13] A situation in which there is a rising supply curve for working capital has been analyzed in our earlier work (Betancourt and Clague 1976a, Section IV). Nevertheless, our attempts at empirically implementing the rising-supply-curve models yielded very poor results. These two considerations, together with Mme Simplicity and Mlle Brevity, lead us to drop these models from consideration.

[14] The discussion of the availability thesis in Wonnacott (1974, pp. 168–74), for example, illustrates this point.

markets are frequently segmented.[15] This segmentation provides a setting wherein different firms may face different interest rates, depending on the segment of the capital market available to them; yet in each segment of the capital market, criteria other than interest rates may be used to allocate loans, and any one firm correctly perceives its working-capital needs as having no influence on the interest rate it faces.

The implications of the formulation in (2.15) for the impact of working-capital costs on the shift-work decision can now be established. Working-capital costs for the two systems of operation will be given by

$$IWK^1 = (w_1 L^1 P + P_m M^1 P^*)I \quad \text{and}$$

$$IWK^2 = [w_1 L_1^2 (2 + \alpha)P + P_m M^2 P^*]I \tag{2.16}$$

where we have already made use of the assumption that the ex-post elasticity of substitution is zero. The double-shift system will be chosen over the single-shift system if

$$TC^1(\overline{X}) = rK^1 + w_1 L^1 (1 + IP) + P_m M^1 (1 + IP^*) >$$

$$TC^2(\overline{X}) = rK^2 + w_1 L_1^2 (2 + \alpha)(1 + IP) + P_m M^2 (1 + IP^*) \tag{2.17}$$

As before, the production assumptions embedded in relation (1.3) of Chapter 1, together with the given-level-of-output assumption, result in eliminating from the decision the terms involving material costs. Hence the condition for the double-shift system to be undertaken, analogous to (1.5) in Chapter 1, is given by

$$1 \geq [\theta^* k_1^2 / k^1 + (2 + \alpha)(1 - \theta^*)] L_1^2 / L^1 \tag{2.18}$$

where $\theta^* = rK^1 / [rK^1 + w_1 L^1 (1 + IP)]$, and the right-hand side of (2.18) is the ratio of costs of the double-shift system to those of the single-shift system. Both sets of costs are net of all material costs but include working-capital costs due to labor.

Once more the cost ratio (2.18) must be evaluated at the optimal values of the variables k_1^2, k^1, and L_1^2 / L^1. The first-order conditions can be used to show that a higher ratio of capital to labor services will be chosen for both systems in the presence of working-capital costs. Assuming the homogeneous function of our homothetic production function to be CES will lead to the following expression for the cost ratio:

---

[15] An interesting discussion of capital market segmentation in the present context is available from Thoumi (1975, Annex 5).

$$\text{CR}(I, P) = \phi(\overline{X})(2 + \alpha)[\theta*(2 + \alpha)^{\sigma-1} + (1 + \theta*)]^{1/(1-\sigma)} \qquad (2.19)$$

Thus the difference between the cost ratio in Section 2.1, equation (2.4), and the cost ratio here lies only in the difference between the old and the new capital share (i.e., between θ and $\theta*$). Similarly, the CES cost ratio for three shifts versus one shift can be obtained through replacement of θ by $\theta*$ in equation (2.11).

It is useful to derive an explicit relationship between the capital shares with and without working-capital costs. By use of the optimal capital–labor ratio for the single-shift system in both cases, the following explicit relation can be obtained:

$$\theta*/(1 - \theta*) = [\theta/(1 - \theta)](1 + IP)^{\sigma-1} \qquad (2.20)$$

This relation demonstrates that $\theta* \gtreqqless \theta$ as $\sigma \gtreqqless 1$. Therefore, if the elasticity of substitution is less than unity, working-capital costs will make shift-work less attractive because they decrease the capital share and thereby increase the cost ratio.[16] If the elasticity of substitution is greater than unity, the opposite will be the case. It is also clear from (2.20) that the negative impact of working capital on shift-work will be greatest when $\sigma = 0$.

How important are working-capital costs as an obstacle to shift-work in the long run? A sensitivity analysis (Betancourt and Clague 1976a, Table 1) has shown that these costs change the cost ratio by less than 2% in a setting where working-capital costs are allowed to have a potentially substantial impact; namely, when $\sigma = 0$, the interest rate on working capital (I) is set at 40%, P is set at 0.40, and θ is also set at 0.4. Recall that by not allowing the value of P to adjust to the interest rate I, we are providing an upper bound to this role of working capital. Thus, even if the interest rate paid to finance working-capital requirements due to labor costs is substantially higher than the interest rate on fixed capital costs, the negative impact on shift-work tends to be small in magnitude, and if σ is greater than unity, it may even increase the desirability of shift-work in a cost-minimization framework.

A by-product of the analysis of working capital in this section is another illustration of the robustness of the cost ratio as a tool for analysis of the shift-work decision. As a matter of fact, the CES cost ratios in equations (2.4) and (2.11) in this chapter provide the basic functional form that will be used in the empirical analysis of shift-work. Because the results in this chapter, as well as those in the previous chapter, are based on the assumption of the same level of output per day for each system, the question of the robustness of the

---

[16] This result follows from Proposition 4.

cost ratio to changes in this assumption must be explored. It will be shown in the next chapter that the cost ratio continues to play a critical role in the decision to work shifts under alternative assumptions about the determination of the level of output for each system.

Appendix 2.1 Proof of Proposition 5

Repeating inequality (2.7)

$$\frac{d \ln \mathrm{CR}}{d\sigma} = \frac{1}{1 - \sigma} \frac{\theta(2 + \alpha)^{\sigma-1} \ln (2 + \alpha)}{B} + \ln B \frac{1}{(1 - \sigma)^2} \le 0 \qquad (2.\mathrm{A}1)$$

where $B = \theta(2 + \sigma)^{\sigma-1} + 1 - \theta > 0$. B can be rewritten as $B = 1 - \theta[1 - (2 + \alpha)^{\sigma-1}] = 1 - A$, where $A = \theta[1 - (2 + \alpha)^{\sigma-1}]$. Then (2.A1) can be written as

$$\frac{-(\sigma - 1)\theta(2 + \alpha)^{\sigma-1} \ln (2 + \alpha) + (1 - A) \ln (1 - A)}{(1 - A)(1 - \sigma)^2} < 0 \qquad (2.\mathrm{A}2)$$

The sign of expression (2.A2) will be determined by the numerator, N, which can be expressed as

$$N = -\theta(2 + \alpha)^{\sigma-1} \ln (2 + \alpha)^{\sigma-1} + (1 - A) \ln (1 - A) \le 0 \qquad (2.\mathrm{A}3)$$

Since $\theta(2 + \alpha)^{\sigma-1} = \theta - A$ and $(2 + \alpha)^{\sigma-1} = 1 - A/\theta$, (2.A3) becomes

$$N = -(\theta - A) \ln (1 - A/\theta) + (1 - A) \ln (1 - A) \le 0 \qquad (2.\mathrm{A}4)$$

or

$$(1 - A)^{1-A} \le \left(\frac{\theta - A}{\theta}\right)^{\theta-A} \qquad (2.\mathrm{A}5)$$

We want to show that (2.A5) holds.

I. If $\sigma > 1$, then $A < 0$, and for $\theta = 1$, the equality holds; that is, $(1 - A)^{1-A} = (1 - A)^{1-A}$. But as θ decreases, the right-hand side (RHS) increases; that is,

$$\partial\{(\theta - A) \ln [(\theta - A)/\theta]\}/\partial\theta < 0$$

or let $x = (\theta - A)/\theta$; then $1 < x$, and

$$\partial(\mathrm{RHS})/\partial\theta = 1 + \ln x - x < 0$$

Proof: At $x = 1$, the expression equals zero. For any value of x greater than 1, the rate of change of the negative term is larger in absolute value than that of the positive term (i.e., $|-1| > 1/x$). Therefore $\partial(\mathrm{RHS})/\partial\theta < 0$; hence, for any value of θ less than 1, the inequality in (2.A5) holds.

II.   If $\sigma < 1$, then $0 < A < 1$, $\theta > A$, and $0 < (\theta - A) < 1$. Once more, for $\theta = 1$, the equality in (2.A5) holds. And as θ decreases, the right-hand side increases, but this is somewhat harder to prove. As before, let $x = (\theta - A)/\theta$; then $0 < x < 1$, and

$$\partial\,(\text{RHS})/\partial\theta = 1 + \ln x - x < 0$$

Proof:[1] For the range $x < 1/e$, where e is the base of the natural logarithms, $1 + \ln x < 0$. Thus we are left with the range $1/e \le x \le 1$. Let $x = f(x)$, $1 + \ln x = g(x)$, and the difference function $d(x) = g(x) - f(x)$. At $x = 1/e$, $d(x) = -f(x) < 0$. At $x = 1$, $d(x) = 0$. Over the interval $1/e \le x \le 1$, the difference function is continuously increasing; that is, $\partial d(x)/\partial x = 1/x - 1 > 0$. Thus it attains its maximum at the upper boundary of the interval $1/e \le x \le 1$, and therefore $d(x) \le 0$ over this interval. Consequently, for $0 < x < 1$, $\partial(\ln \text{RHS})/\partial\theta < 0$; hence, for any value of θ less than 1, the inequality in (2.A5) holds.

Appendix 2.2 Sequentiality

If the production function is Leontief ($\sigma = 0$) and there are constant returns to scale, a necessary and sufficient condition for shift-work not to be optimal is that the single-shift system be preferred to the double-shift system. To establish this result, note that the single-shift system is preferred to the double-shift system if and only if $CR > 1$, which implies, using (2.5), that $\theta/(1 - \theta) < \alpha$. Now the necessary and sufficient condition for the single-shift system to be preferred to the triple-shift system is that $CR^1 > 1$, which implies, using (2.12), that $\theta/(1 - \theta) < \alpha(1 + b)/2$. Since the minimum value of b is unity, then $CR > 1$ implies that $CR^1 > 1$, which is what we wanted to demonstrate in order to establish sequentiality.

The cost ratios for the Cobb-Douglas case ($\sigma = 1$) under constant returns to scale are

$$CR = (2 + \alpha)^{1-\theta}/2 \qquad \text{(two-shift case)} \tag{2.A6}$$

and

$$CR^1 = [3 + (1 + b)\,\alpha]^{1-\theta}/3 \qquad \text{(three-shift case)} \tag{2.A7}$$

In this case the necessary and sufficient condition for shift-work not to be optimal (given low values of b) is that the single-shift system be preferred to the triple-shift system.

The need for the qualification arises because for a sufficiently high

---

[1] We would like to thank, without incriminating, D. Madan for his help in this part of the proof.

value of b (the evening–night differential) the triple-shift system will never be preferred to the double-shift system. After all, b affects the costs of the triple-shift system but not those of the double-shift system. The results that follow indicate that this qualification is not very restrictive in practice.

To establish sequentiality, note that the single-shift system is preferred to the triple-shift system if and only if $CR^1 > 1$. This condition implies, using (2.A7), that $1/(1 - \theta) < \log[3 + \alpha(1 + b)]/\log 3$. Similarly, the necessary and sufficient condition for the single-shift system to be preferred to the double-shift system is that $CR > 1$. This condition implies, using (2.A6), that $1/(1 - \theta) < \log(2 + \alpha)/\log 2$. Therefore, if $CR^1 > 1$ is to imply $CR > 1$, it must be shown that

$$\log[3 + \alpha(1 + b)]/\log 3 < \log(2 + \alpha)/\log 2 \qquad (2.A8)$$

First note that if $\alpha = 0$, the inequality becomes an equality. Second, both sides of (2.A8) increase with α, but the left-hand side (LHS) increases more slowly than the right-hand side (RHS), given low values of b; that is,

$$\frac{\partial(\text{LHS})}{\partial \alpha} = \frac{(1 + b)}{[3 + \alpha(1 + b)] \log 3} < \frac{1}{(2 + \alpha) \log 2} = \frac{\partial(\text{RHS})}{\partial \alpha} \qquad (2.A9)$$

Rewriting (2.A9), we have $\alpha > [(1 + b)(2 \log 2) - 3 \log 3]/[(1 + b) \log 3 - \log 2]$. Now, if $b < 1.377$, a sufficient condition for (2.A9) to hold, and hence for (2.A8) to hold, is $\alpha > 0$. Normally the shift differential will be greater than zero.

Just as in the case of the Leontief production function, the preceding result may be viewed as establishing the sequentiality of the decision-making process of the firm. The first step in the sequence for the Cobb-Douglas case, however, is a single comparison between the triple-shift system and the single-shift system. To conclude, in the Cobb-Douglas case we note, without proving, that if sequentiality holds, the double-shift system will be an inferior system.

CHAPTER 3

Profit maximization

In the previous chapters the analysis has relied on the assumption that the level of output that the firm plans to produce during the day will be the same for all systems of operation. With this assumption, profit-maximizing behavior leads to the same results as cost-minimizing behavior. In this chapter we shall investigate the consequences of relaxing this assumption for the previously established results, and we shall establish several additional results.

In the next section we discuss the issues that arise for the analysis of the shift-work decision when each system operates at its optimal level of output under the criterion of profit maximization. The discussion of these issues suggests the need to analyze the decision to work shifts under two different types of technologies. This analysis is undertaken in Section 3.2 under the assumption of a constant-β technology, which is a technology such that the degree of economies of scale is independent of the level of output. The results presented in this section are by and large available in the literature, primarily in the work of Clague (1975, Section II) and Millan (1975, Chapter 3). As a matter of fact, one of the main conclusions of this section is that the cost ratio discussed in earlier chapters always provides an accurate guide to the choice of system under profit maximization (Proposition 6A), and this conclusion is available in our earlier work (Betancourt and Clague 1975, footnote 13). Thus our treatment of this case will be brief, and it will emphasize those aspects relevant to the subsequent discussion.

In Section 3.3 we undertake an analysis similar to the one in Section 3.2 under the assumption of a semi-U technology, which is a technology such that the degree of economies of scale depends on the level of output in a manner consistent with the behavior of the first half of the usual textbook type of average cost curve. Analytical results are difficult to obtain with this assumption, and in our earlier work (Betancourt and Clague 1975, Section III) we resorted to simulation. Nevertheless, in this section we are able to obtain several analytical results not previously available. For instance, we show that any change in the determinants of the cost ratio that makes shift-work more attractive under cost minimization will also have the following similar effects under profit maximization: It increases the range of outputs in

44

which shift-work may be profitable; it increases the profitability of shift-work if, prior to the change in the cost ratio, the firm is operating in the range of outputs where shift-work may be profitable; it increases the profitability of shift-work at all levels of output if the change in the cost ratio does not affect the marginal cost curve for the single-shift system. We also show that outward shifts in the position of the demand curve, or increases in the elasticity of demand, will always increase the profitability of shift-work if, prior to the change in the demand condition, the firm is operating in the range of outputs where shift-work may be profitable. Finally, one of the main results established under this assumption is the following: Demand conditions and their interactions with the degree of economies of scale influence the choice of system through their effect on the cost ratio in such a way as to make shift-work more likely to be profitable when the optimal level of output under single-shift operation is large (Proposition 6B). There-fore, even with a semi-U technology the cost ratio plays a dominant role in the capital-utilization decision under profit maximization.

An important implication of the analysis in Sections 3.2 and 3.3 is that decreases in the cost ratio tend to increase the profitability of shift-work and the optimal level of output under shift-work relative to the optimal level of output under single-shift operation. This implica-tion is of crucial importance for empirical analysis of capital utiliza-tion. Our interpretation of the empirical literature, which is reviewed in Chapter 5, makes extensive use of this result.

The results in Sections 3.2 and 3.3 are important because the main propositions presented there (Propositions 6A and 6B), together with the other five propositions presented in Chapters 1 and 2, can be said to contain the principal insights about the shift-work decision that are offered by the neoclassical theory of firm behavior. Hence, in Section 3.4 we rely on these insights to analyze the impact on shift-work of dynamic considerations known to be relevant to the firm's behavior. Specifically, we discuss intertemporal decision making, output fluctua-tions, and uncertainty. The second of these considerations is the only one discussed at any length in the previous literature on shift-work (e.g., Marris 1964, pp. 94–7), and the propositions developed earlier allow us to obtain new results even with respect to this consideration.

We conclude the chapter by discussing briefly the effect on our results of postulating alternative objective functions for the firm.

3.1 The issues

Under profit maximization the entrepreneur will choose the system that yields the highest profits at the optimal level of output for each system of operation. That is, shift-work will be an inferior, indifferent, or superior alternative as $\pi^1 - \pi^2 \gtrless 0$, or

$$\pi^1 = TR(X^1) - TC^1(X^1) \gtrless TR(X^2) - TC^2(X^2) = \pi^2 \qquad (3.1)$$

where π indicates profits, TR is total revenues, TC is total costs, and X is the level of output. Expression (3.1) is more conveniently rewritten as

$$CR(X^1)[TC^2(X^2)/TC^2(X^1)] \gtrless$$
$$\{[TR(X^2)/TR(X^1)] - 1\}(1 + m^*) + 1 \qquad (3.2)$$

where $CR(X^1)$ is the cost ratio evaluated at the optimal level of output for system 1, $1 + m^* = [TR(X^1)/TC(X^1)]$, and m^* is the profit margin for system 1 in terms of that system's costs. From expression (3.2) it appears that the cost ratio developed in earlier sections will play a similar role under profit maximization.[1] That is, other things being equal, the higher the cost ratio at X^1, the lower the profitability of shift-work. Of course, in general, other things need not be equal, and how they can differ is the main subject for discussion.

Just as in the cost ratio discussed in earlier chapters, the terms in (3.2) must be evaluated at the optimal values of all the variables for each system of operation. The homotheticity of the production function ensures that the choice of the optimal level of output for system 1 can affect the cost ratio at X^1 only through its effect on the degree of economies of scale prevailing at X^1. And for both systems of operation, the choice of the optimal level of output will not affect the choice of the optimal ratio of capital to labor services. Changes in factor prices, however, can affect both the choice of the optimal ratio of capital to labor services and the choice of the optimal level of output for each system of operation. This result can be seen from the first-order conditions for each system of operation developed in Chapter 1, equations (1.6) and (1.7), which allow the marginal costs (the Lagrange multiplier) to be expressed in terms of the (no longer constant) level of output for each system, as follows:

$$MC^1(X^1) = \frac{r}{G'(F^1)f'(k^1)U} = \frac{w}{G'(F^1)[f(k^1) - k^1 f'(k^1)]}$$

$$MC^2(X^2) = \frac{r}{2G'(F_1^2)f'(k_1^2)U} = \frac{w(2 + \alpha)}{2G'(F_1^2)[f(k_1^2) - k_1^2 f'(k_1^2)]} \qquad (3.3)$$

The discussion, thus far, suggests that we want answers to the

[1] Incidentally, if the levels of output are the same for both systems of operation, then (3.2) collapses to the previous condition; that is, $CR(X) \gtrless 1$.

following questions: What determines the choice of system under profit maximization? What is the effect of demand conditions on the choice of system? What is the effect of supply conditions on the choice of system?

In order to answer these questions we must specify the nature of demand conditions in greater detail. Throughout, demand conditions will be characterized by a function of the form $p = AX^{-1/n}$, where n is the absolute value of the elasticity of the demand curve and p is the value added price; that is, the product price minus the costs of raw materials used per unit of output. It is well known that the marginal revenue curve, MR, can in general be expressed as $MR = AR(1 - 1/n) = p(1 - 1/n)$, where n is not necessarily constant.[2] Thus, with our specification, changes in demand conditions that shift the marginal revenue curve throughout the output range can be formulated in terms of either changes in the position of the demand curve ($\partial MR/\partial A > 0$) or changes in n ($\partial MR/\partial n > 0$).[3]

Next we come to the specification of those factors that determine the nature of economies of scale. As mentioned in Chapter 1, there are (at least) two alternative formulations that have very different implications for the relationship between output and the cost ratio. In one of these formulations, henceforth referred to as the constant-β technology, the degree of economies of scale is independent of the level of output.[4] In the other formulation, henceforth referred to as the semi-U technology, the degree of economies of scale decreases as the level of output increases up to a point at which it is assumed that (marginal) costs become constant. It should be stressed that we are focusing exclusively on economies of scale at the process level. Therefore, we view both of these formulations as reasonable potential descriptions of reality. They are supposed to describe the percentage increase in the potential flow rate of output due to a 1% increase in the amount of capital and labor services available per eight-hour shift (e.g., Georgescu-Roegen 1972, p. 288).

The constant-β technology is frequently criticized by economists because it implies decreasing (marginal) costs throughout the output range for $\beta > 1$. Whereas we are somewhat sympathetic to this

---

[2] Henderson and Quandt (1971, p. 168).

[3] We are assuming that n is greater than unity, a condition that will always be satisfied for a monopolist.

[4] With this assumption the homothetic production function becomes a homogeneous production function of degree β, where β is the degree of economies of scale.

criticism in general, many of the reasons advanced for the lack of realism in this model are not applicable to our formulation. For instance, there may be economies and diseconomies associated with a given plant site; distribution costs can be and usually are an increasing function of output; economies and diseconomies may arise in marketing. But none of these sources of economies or diseconomies provides valid criticism of the constant-β-technology assumption at the process level, because they are not associated with the size of output per eight-hour shift. Instead, they depend on the existence of fixed costs, or they depend on the (total) level of output produced but are invariant to the system of operation under which the output is produced. On the empirical side, the engineering estimates usually favor the constant-β technology, and the interview estimates the semi-U technology.[5] But recent interview data from a six-nation sample can be interpreted as suggesting that the constant-β technology is most appropriate for several industries precisely because of the implication of decreasing costs throughout the output range.[6] Without trying to resolve this issue, we merely conclude that both formulations are worth exploring, given the state of knowledge on the subject.

Because the answers to some of the questions raised turn out to be substantially affected by which of the two hypotheses about the degree of the economies of scale is postulated, the two cases are considered separately.

*3.2   The constant-β technology

The factors that determine the cost ratio can be categorized into those that may be affected by the level of output and those that are not. That is, $CR(X^1) = CR^*\phi(X^1)$, where CR^* refers to those elements of the cost ratio that are independent of X^1, and $\phi(X^1)$ is, as before, an expression incorporating economies of scale. Now, by the hypothesis of the constant-β technology, we have $\phi(X^1) = 2^{-1/\beta}$.

The implications of the constant-β technology for the expression in (3.2) are as follows:

$$CR(X^2/X^1)^{1/\beta} \gtreqless [(X^2/X^1)^{1-1/n} - 1](1 + m^*) + 1 \qquad (3.4)$$

1. The cost ratio is independent of the level of output; that is, $CR = CR^*/2^{1/\beta}$. Therefore, if one system has lower costs at one level of output, it will have lower costs at every level of output.

[5] In Chapter 6, Section 6.4, we provide the relevant references.
[6] Scherer et al. (1975, p. 79).

2. The term $(X^2/X^1)^{1/\beta}$ follows from the constant degree of homogeneity of the production function; that is, $X = [\mu TC(X)]^\beta$, where μ is a constant that depends on factor prices. Therefore, $TC^2(X^2)/TC^2(X^1) = (X^2/X^1)^{1/\beta}$.

3. The term $(X^2/X^1)^{1-1/n}$ follows from the assumption of a constant elasticity of demand. That is, $TR(X) = (1/A)^{-1/n}X^{1-1/n}$. Hence $TR(X^2)/TR(X^1) = (X^2/X^1)^{1-1/n}$.

The profit margin for system 1 in terms of that system's revenues, m, can be written as[7]

$$m = 1 - \frac{TC(X^1)}{TR(X^1)} = 1 - \frac{MC^1(X^1)\beta}{MR(X^1)n/(n-1)} = 1 - \beta\frac{n-1}{n} \qquad (3.5)$$

and the ratio of the optimal outputs for each system can be written as follows [using equation (2.5) from the work of Clague (1975, Section II)]:

$$X^2/X^1 = (CR^{-1})^{\beta/m} \qquad (3.6)$$

Rewriting (3.4) and using (3.5) and (3.6), we obtain

$$(\pi^1 - \pi^2)/TC^1(X^1) = m*(1 - CR^{1-1/m}) \gtreqless 0 \qquad (3.7)$$

The second-order conditions for a maximum (the marginal revenue curve must intersect the marginal cost curve from above) require the profit margin, m, to be positive. Since in the monopolist's case n must be greater than unity, $0 < m < 1$ and $1 - 1/m < 0$. Therefore, in this case the answer to the question of what determines the choice of system under profit maximization can be formulated in terms of the following proposition derived from (3.7).

Proposition 6A: With a constant-β technology, the necessary and sufficient condition for shift-work to be chosen under profit maximization is that the cost ratio be less than unity.

Since $0 < m < 1$, $m* > 0$. Furthermore, the sign of the left-hand side of (3.7) will be negative if and only if the cost ratio (CR) is less than unity, which makes $CR^{1-1/m}$ greater than unity. Thus, with the constant-β technology, other things are indeed equal, and the results presented in previous chapters hold without qualification.

In terms of the questions raised in the previous section, neither the position of the demand curve nor its elasticity will determine the choice of system. The degree of economies of scale, which determines the rate of change of the marginal cost curve as output changes, will help determine the choice of system, but only through its effect on the cost ratio. Similarly, the factors that determine the position of the marginal

---

[7] Note that $m* = m/(1 - m)$.

cost curve will help determine the choice of system only through their effect on the cost ratio. Finally, the optimal levels of output for either system of operation will not affect the choice of system. Hence, demand conditions or the interaction between demand and supply conditions cannot be used to explain the choice of system. These results stem from the fact that when the degree of economies of scale is constant, the marginal cost curves for the two systems never intersect.

For future reference, we note an implication of (3.7) and (3.6) that is important in the evaluation of empirical work:

$$\partial[(\pi^1 - \pi^2)/\mathrm{TC}^1(X^1)]/\partial \mathrm{CR} = -m^*(1 - 1/m)\mathrm{CR}^{-1/m} > 0 \quad (3.8)$$

and

$$\partial(X^2/X^1)/\partial \mathrm{CR} = -(\beta/m)\mathrm{CR}^{-\beta/(m-1)} < 0 \quad (3.9)$$

That is, increases in the cost ratio decrease the profitability of shift-work and the optimal level of output for system 2 relative to the optimal level of output for system 1.

Incidentally, one of the main results presented in this section, equation (3.7), is useful in the analysis of perfect competition in the product market. This analysis is carried out in a brief appendix to this chapter.

*3.3   The semi-U technology

With a semi-U technology, the analysis must start again from relation (3.2), which yields the condition for shift-work to be an inferior, indifferent, or superior alternative. Whereas in principle there seem to be four different terms in this relation, one answer to the question of what determines the choice of system can be expressed in terms of the cost ratio.

If the marginal cost curves for the two systems of operation do not intersect each other, and if the marginal revenue curve is downward-sloping, the profit-maximizing system will always be the one with the lower marginal cost curve. Hence the choice of system can be determined in terms of the cost ratio. That is, the system with the lower (marginal and total) costs at any level of output will also be the profit-maximizing system. Undoubtedly, the more interesting case arises when the marginal cost curves of the two systems intersect each other. Thus the discussion that follows will focus solely on this situation.

Our assumption of a semi-U technology implies that $\mathrm{CR}_x(X) = d\mathrm{CR}(X)/dX = \mathrm{CR}^*\phi_x(X) \leq 0$, with the equality holding only at large levels of output, where constant returns to scale set in and $\phi_x(X)$

= 0. We shall also assume that the two marginal cost curves decline smoothly up to their respective constant-returns-to-scale points; hence there is only one intersection point. In these circumstances the marginal cost curve of system 2 must cut the marginal cost curve of system 1 from above. We shall establish this proposition as follows: First, we show that at the point of intersection of the marginal cost curves, $\overline{X}$, the cost ratio must be greater than unity; second, we show that at the point (X^*) where the cost ratio equals unity, $X^* > \overline{X}$, and the marginal cost curve for system 2 lies below the marginal cost curve for system 1.

From the definition of the cost ratio we know that for every level of output, $TC^2(X) = CR(X)TC^1(X)$. Differentiating both sides with respect to X yields

$$MC^2(X) = CR_x(X)TC^1(X) + MC^1(X)CR(X) \qquad (3.10)$$

Recall that $\overline{X}$ is the output at which the marginal cost curves intersect [i.e., $MC^2(\overline{X}) = MC^1(\overline{X})$]; hence, from (3.10) we have

$$\frac{MC^1(\overline{X})}{TC^1(\overline{X})} = \frac{CR_x(\overline{X})}{1 - CR(\overline{X})}$$

Because the left-hand side is positive and $CR_x(\overline{X})$ is negative, $CR(\overline{X})$ must be greater than unity.

Now X^* is the point where the cost ratio equals unity. We have just shown that $CR(\overline{X})$ exceeds unity, and we know that $CR_x(X)$ declines with X. Thus it is obvious that $X^* > \overline{X}$. Moreover, from (3.10) we see that at X^*, $MC^2(X^*) \leq MC^1(X^*)$, and because $MC^2(X) = MC^1(X)$ implies that $CR(X) > 1$, we must conclude that at X^*, $MC^2(X) < MC^1(X)$. At this juncture, a diagram becomes useful. Figure 3.1 depicts the two marginal cost curves (the two unbroken lines) and the points $\overline{X}$ and X^*.

With a downward-sloping marginal revenue curve, which must intersect the marginal cost curves from above for a maximum, Figure 3.1 reveals a partitioning of the range of feasible outputs into three distinct regions with respect to the choice of system. If the optimal levels of output lie to the left of $\overline{X}$ (region I), shift-work will always be unprofitable, and the optimal level of output under system 1 (X^1) must exceed the optimal level for system 2 (X^2). $X^1 > X^2$ holds because the MR curve is downward-sloping and $MC^2(X) > MC^1(X)$ to the left of $\overline{X}$. At $\overline{X}$, $CR(\overline{X}) > 1$. To the left of $\overline{X}$, $CR(X^1)$ increases as X^1 decreases; therefore the single-shift system will be the more profitable system in this area even if it is forced to operate at the optimal level of output for the double-shift system. If the optimal level of output under single-shift operation lies to the right of X^* (region III), then

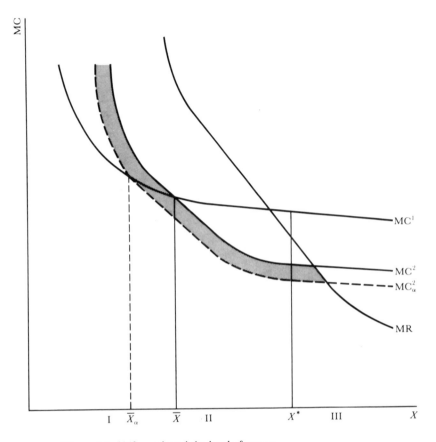

Figure 3.1. Shift-work and the level of output.

shift-work will always be profitable, and $X^2 > X^1$. At X^*, $CR(X^*) = 1$. To the right of X^*, $CR(X)$ decreases as X increases; therefore shift-work will be more profitable than single-shift operation in this region. Between $\overline{X}$ and X^*, however, lies a region of uncertainty in which $X^2 > X^1$, but shift-work may or may not be profitable.

The foregoing discussion leads us to advance the following proposition as the main new dimension in the answer to the question of what determines the choice of system with a semi-U technology.

Proposition 6B: With a semi-U technology, the larger the optimal level of output under single-shift operation (X^1), the more likely is shift-work to be the profit-maximizing system of operation.

Because a large value of X^1 is required for $X^1 > X^*$, and hence for shift-work to be always profitable, the proposition is obviously true in this limited sense. What is not so obvious is the range of phenomena encompassed by the proposition. Namely, it provides the framework in which to answer the questions raised about the impact of demand and supply conditions on the choice of system.

With respect to demand conditions, let us consider first a change in the position of the demand curve (i.e., a change in the value of A). In terms of Figure 3.1, an increase in A, for example, will be depicted by a shift to the right in the marginal revenue curve; therefore it will lead to an increase in X^1, which in turn will increase the likelihood that the firm will end up operating in the region where shift-work is profitable. As a matter of fact, it can be shown rigorously that if the firm is operating in either region II or region III before the increase in A, the profits of system 2 will always increase by more than the profits of system 1 as a result of the increase in A. Let

$$Z = \pi^2 - \pi^1 = [\text{TR}(X^2, A) - \text{TC}^2(X^2)]$$
$$- [\text{TR}(X^1, A) - \text{TC}^1(X^1)] \quad (3.11)$$

Then, differentiating both sides of (3.11) and collecting terms yields

$$\frac{dZ}{dA} = \frac{\partial \text{TR}(X^2, A)}{\partial A} - \frac{\partial \text{TR}(X^1, A)}{\partial A}$$
$$+ [\text{MR}(X^2) - \text{MC}^2(X^2)]\frac{dX^2}{dA} - [\text{MR}(X^1) - \text{MC}^1(X^1)]\frac{dX^1}{dA}$$

which, using our specification for the demand function and the first-order condition for both systems, collapses to

$$dZ/dA = [\text{TR}(X^2) - \text{TR}(X^1)]/A \quad (3.12)$$

If the firm is operating in region II or III, $X^2 > X^1$, and therefore $dZ/dA > 0$.

A similar argument applies to increases in the elasticity of demand, n. That is, increases in n increase the optimal level of output for system 1 and thus make it more likely that shift-work will be profitable. Moreover, it can be shown rigorously by an argument exactly analogous to the previous one that if the firm is operating in region II or III, an increase in n will always increase the profitability of shift-work; that is,

$$\frac{dZ}{dn} = \frac{d(\pi^2 - \pi^1)}{dn} = \left[\text{TR}(X^2)\log\frac{X^2}{A} - \text{TR}(X^1)\log\frac{X^1}{A}\right] \quad (3.13)$$

Turning to the impact of supply conditions on the choice of system, we consider first the impact of changes in the shift differential, because such changes will affect only the marginal cost curve for system 2. Hence, they are easier to analyze than other changes that affect the marginal cost curves for both systems. A decrease in α decreases the cost ratio at X^1 and shifts the marginal cost curve for system 2 downward. This second change is depicted by the broken-line curve (MC_α^2) in Figure 3.1. Thus a decrease in α will shift the point $\overline{X}$ to the left and increase the size of the region where shift-work may be profitable. The profitability of shift-work increases at every level of output, including the previously optimal level of output for system 2; hence, a decrease in α increases the profitability of shift-work, and the increase in profits is represented by the shaded area between the two marginal cost curves in Figure 3.1. Therefore, with respect to this change in the cost ratio, other things are also equal, even with the semi-U technology, because changes in α do not affect the optimal level of output for system 1.

At this stage in the discussion it is convenient to pause briefly and note an implication of the results in this chapter for the literature on optimal plant size.[8] Under both the constant-β technology and the semi-U technology the following result holds: An other-things-being-equal decrease in the shift differential always increases the optimal level of total output for the double-shift system (X^2). This result follows from equation (3.9) in the constant-β technology and from the analysis of Figure 3.1 in the previous paragraph for the semi-U technology. Other things will, in general, not be equal in comparisons of firm sizes across industries or across countries with widely different shift differentials, but if they were, these comparisons should reveal larger observed levels of total output for those firms that work shifts in the low-shift-differential industries or countries than for firms that also work shifts in the high-shift-differential industries or countries.

Returning to our main theme, we note that changes in the other determinants of supply conditions [namely, the other determinants of the cost ratio $\mathrm{CR}(X)$] entail changes in both marginal cost curves and hence in the optimal levels of output for both systems. In order to analyze these changes, one must return to the relationship between the costs of the two systems; that is, $\mathrm{TC}^2(X) = \mathrm{CR}(X)\mathrm{TC}^1(X)$. The percentage change in the costs of system 2 as a result of a change in any

---

[8] Scherer et al. (1975) provide an excellent survey of the theoretical literature on optimal plant size (Chapter 2) as well as substantial empirical research on this topic (Chapters 3 and 4); nevertheless, the influence of shift-work in determining optimal plant size is ignored in their brief discussion of multiple-shift operation (p. 133).

one of the determinants of the cost ratio d will be given by

$$\frac{\partial TC^2(X)/\partial d}{TC^2(X)} = \frac{\partial CR(X)/\partial d}{CR(X)} + \frac{\partial TC^1(X)/\partial d}{TC^1(X)}$$

or, equivalently,

$$\frac{\partial TC^2(X)/\partial d}{TC^2(X)} - \frac{\partial TC^1(X)/\partial d}{TC^1(X)} = \frac{\partial CR(X)/\partial d}{CR(X)} \qquad (3.14)$$

Any change that decreases the cost ratio will decrease the costs of system 2 at every level of output by more than the costs of system 1. The previously analyzed change in α is simply a special case of (3.14) in which $\partial TC^1(X)/\partial d = 0$. The relation in (3.14) can be used to describe changes in the cost ratio due to a change in the production function that changes the degree of economies of scale or to changes in the other determinants of the cost ratio that are independent of the level of output (i.e., changes in CR*). The main difference between the two types of changes is that the changes in the cost ratio due to changes in the degree of economies of scale need not be the same at every level of output, whereas the percentage change in the cost ratio due to changes in CR* will be the same at every level of output.[9]

The diagrams in Figure 3.2 are helpful in analyzing the impact of changes in any of the determinants (d) of the cost ratio $CR(X)$ on the choice of system. The main difference between the diagrams in Figure 3.2 is that the curves in Figure 3.2A have been drawn to ensure that the marginal revenue curve will intersect the marginal cost curves to the right of $\overline{X}$, the intersection point of the marginal cost curves prior to the change in d. However, in Figure 3.2B the MR curve will intersect the marginal cost curves to the left of $\overline{X}$.[10] Both parts of Figure 3.2 depict changes in d that shift the marginal cost curves downward, but it is possible for changes in d to decrease the cost ratio while shifting both marginal cost curves upward. In either circumstance, it follows from (3.14) that $\overline{X}$ will move to the left because at

[9] Incidentally, a simulation analysis of the impact of changes in demand elasticity and the degree of economies of scale on the profitability of shift-work is available (Betancourt and Clague 1975, Section III). In the present terminology, the simulation analysis is confined to changes that take place in region III.

[10] To put it another way, in Figure 3.2A the firm will be operating in region II or III before and after the change in d; on the other hand, in Figure 3.2B the firm will be operating in region I before and after the change in d.

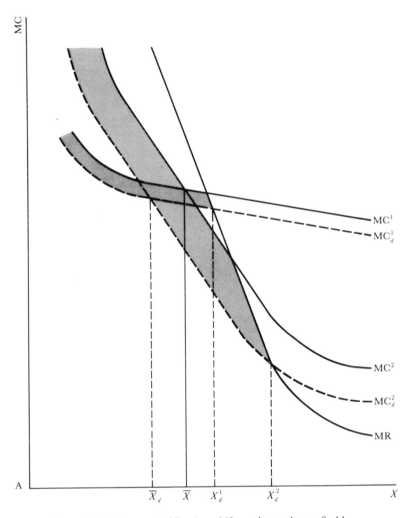

Figure 3.2A. Change in CR when shift-work may be profitable.

every level of output the costs of system 2 are reduced by more (or increased by less) than the costs of system 1. Therefore any changes that lower the cost ratio increase the likelihood of shift-work by increasing the range of outputs in which shift-work can be profitable. Moreover, if the firm is operating in region II or III prior to the decrease in the cost ratio (Figure 3.2A), the profitability of shift-work will always increase as a result of a decrease in the cost ratio. Even if system 2 is forced to operate at the new optimal level of output for system 1, X_d^1, its profits will increase by more (or decrease by less

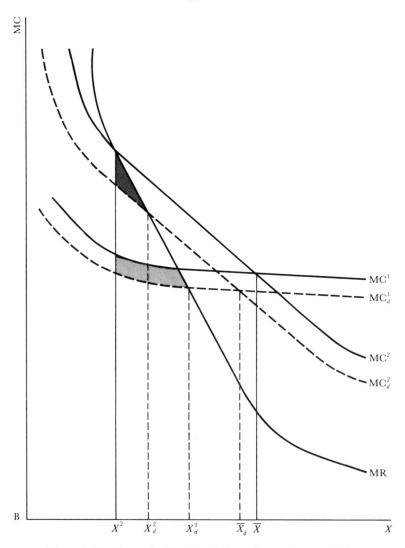

Figure 3.2B. Change in CR when shift-work must be unprofitable.

when the marginal cost curves shift up) than those of system 1; and if system 2 is allowed to operate at its new optimal level of output, X_d^2, the profits of system 2 will be even larger than at X_d^1, as can be seen by comparing the two shaded areas in Figure 3.2A. In Figure 3.2B, however, this conclusion does not hold. It is true that at the initial optimal level for system 2, X^2, its profits will have increased by more than those of system 1. But it is possible that the increase in profits for system 1 in going from output level X^2 to output level X_d^1, the light-shaded area in Figure 3.2B, is greater than the increase in profits for system 2 in going from X^2 to X_d^2, the dark-shaded area in Figure 3.2B, plus the increase in profits of system 2 over system 1 up to output level X^2.

To summarize, the determinants of the choice of system are quite similar under both profit maximization and cost minimization. This similarity is so strong that with a constant-β technology the cost ratio always predicts correctly the choice of system under profit maximization. Even with a semi-U technology, any change in the determinants of the cost ratio that makes shift-work more attractive under cost minimization will also have the following similar effects under profit maximization: It will increase the range of feasible outputs in which shift-work can be profitable (i.e., it will decrease the size of region I relative to regions II and III); it will increase the profitability of shift-work if the firm is operating in region II or III prior to the change; it will increase the profitability of shift-work at all levels of output if the change in the cost ratio does not affect the marginal cost curve for the single-shift system (e.g., changes in the shift differential). Nevertheless, a semi-U technology introduces a new dimension to the choice of system under profit maximization. This new dimension is embodied in Proposition 6B, and it is worth reiterating its main implication: Demand conditions and their interactions with the degree of economies of scale affect the choice of system in such a way as to make shift-work more likely to be profitable when the optimal level of output under single-shift operation is large.

3.4   Dynamic considerations

To broaden the scope of our inquiry into shift-work and the theory of the firm, we shall briefly sketch the relationship between the results of our analysis and other important topics in the analysis of firm behavior. These topics can be lumped together under the rubric of dynamic considerations. In particular we shall consider intertemporal aspects of decision making, output fluctuations with their consequent adjustment costs, and uncertainty. The analysis in this section is meant to be suggestive rather than exhaustive. Our primary objective is to indicate the impact of these dynamic considerations on the choice of system.

In an intertemporal setting the firm is assumed to maximize the present value of profits or cash flow subject to the production-function constraint in every period.[11] The results presented in this book are consistent with an intertemporal objective function for the firm. More specifically, the intertemporal model of investment behavior underlying the analysis of each system of operation is a special case of the one developed by Sandmo (1971). This special case is obtained by assuming that the price of capital goods, P_K, is not expected to change between the time the investment decision is made, $t = 0$, and the time the investment comes on line, $t = 1$, in Sandmo's model. The decision maker in Sandmo's model carries out his decisions only with respect to the first period beyond the initial one; he makes plans for the remaining periods, and whether or not these plans are realized depends on whether or not expectations are realized. The first-order conditions for the first period beyond the initial one (period 1) are exactly the same as those developed here in a seemingly static framework. Thus a comparison of profits for each system leads to the same behavior as a comparison of the present value of profits or cash flow. This result arises because our definition of the price of capital, $r = P_K(i + d)$, incorporates the main intertemporal aspects of the decision that can be derived from Sandmo's model.

Output fluctuations, with their consequent adjustment costs and uncertainty, are also important aspects of the investment decision. Although these topics are intimately related, the analysis is facilitated by considering them separately. Thus we shall consider first output fluctuations in a simple setting where the decision maker knows with certainty that he must produce different levels of output in different periods. Such fluctuations can arise, for example, from seasonal variations in demand or input supplies. An extreme instance, useful for analysis, is one in which the entrepreneur knows with certainty that he will have to produce an output X_H for a certain proportion of the year (λ) and an output of zero for the rest of the year $(1 - \lambda)$, for example, sugar refining in some developing countries. A way of proceeding is to compare this firm with another one that is expected to produce under single-shift operation an output X every day of the year, where $X = \lambda X_H + (1 - \lambda)0$ (hence $X = \lambda X_H$). The question we wish to answer is the following: Which of the two firms is more likely to design the factory to work shifts?

The yearly profits of the two firms under single-shift operation will

---

[11] If properly defined, the two objectives are equivalent, and both of them can be derived from the criterion of utility maximization over time by the owners of the firm (e.g., Sandmo 1974, pp. 288–91).

be given by $D(pX - rK^1 - w_1L^1)$ for the nonseasonal firm and $\lambda D(pX_H - w_1L^1) - DrK^1$ for the seasonal firm, where D is the number of days in the year. Using the first-order conditions for profit maximization, we can show that the seasonal firm will choose a ratio of capital to labor services that will satisfy $1/R^1 = w_1/(r/\lambda)$, where R^1 is the rate of technical substitution of labor for capital services under single-shift operation. In other words, the effective daily price of capital r/λ is higher for the seasonal firm. Hence, it will use a lower ratio of capital to labor services under single-shift operation. Thus, one way this type of seasonality affects shift-work is through its impact on the capital share under single-shift operation, θ. An increase in the price of capital will increase the capital share if the elasticity of substitution (σ) is less than unity (Chapter 2, footnote 1). Hence, by Proposition 4, the seasonal firm will be more likely to work shifts than the nonseasonal firm if σ is less than unity. With the constant-β technology, this effect of seasonality will be the only effect of seasonality on shift-work; however, with the semi-U technology there will be another effect on shift-work. Because of its higher level of daily output under single-shift operation ($X_H > X$), the seasonal firm will be more likely to work shifts than the nonseasonal firm (by Proposition 6B of the previous section).

It is relatively straightforward to generalize the previous analysis. Once more we shall proceed by comparing two firms: one that is expected to produce under single-shift operation an output X every day of the year and another that is expected to produce (also under single-shift operation) an output X_H a certain proportion of the year (λ) and an output X_L the remaining proportion of the year. Of course, peak output corresponds to the nonzero output in the previous example, and off-peak output (X_L) corresponds to zero in the previous example. As in that situation, we shall assume that $X = \lambda X_H + (1 - \lambda)X_L$. We are still assuming that the producer knows X_H, X_L, and λ. We shall also assume that the firm always wants to meet demand as it arises. The firm does so either because X_H is not "too large" and the price of the product is "sufficiently greater" than marginal cost or because the firm desires to maintain customer goodwill or brand loyalty.

The average daily profits of the two firms under single-shift operation will be given by $pX - rK^1 - w_1L^1$ for the stable-output firm and by $\lambda(pX_H - w_1L_H) + (1 - \lambda)(pX_L - w_1L_L) - rK^1$ for the fluctuating-output firm. With a zero ex-post elasticity of substitution between high-output and low-output days, the firm will adjust by adopting a partial shift and operating part of the capital equipment (q)

during the low-output days, but using the same instantaneous ratio of capital to labor services; that is, $qK^1/L_L = K^1/L_H$. The first-order conditions can again be used to show that the effective daily price of capital is higher for the fluctuating-output firm than for the stable-output firm; that is, $1/R^1 = w_1/\{r/[\lambda + (1 - \lambda)q]\}$. As in the previous case, one consequence of fluctuations in output will be to make shift-work more likely if the elasticity of substitution is less than unity, through its effect on the capital share (Proposition 4).[12]

With a constant-β technology, the previously described effect of output fluctuations will be the sole effect on the choice of system. With a semi-U technology, on the other hand, the incentive to work shifts provided by the high level of peak output, X_H, will be counterbalanced by the disincentive provided by the low level of off-peak output, X_L (Proposition 6B). Incidentally, the disincentive effect will tend to be greater than the incentive effect because of the convexity of the semi-U type of technology. For example, given that $\lambda = 0.5$ and hence that X_H and X_L are the same distance from X, the increase in costs due to the diseconomies of small-scale operation $(X_L - X)$ will be larger than the cost savings from the economies of large-scale operation $(X_H - X)$. We have not explicitly discussed how the double-shift system is affected by these output fluctuations, although the analysis is similar to the preceding one. We simply note here that the effect of output fluctuations on the price of capital is the same for both systems, and partial shifts will always be planned first for the second shift of the double-shift system because the variable labor cost is higher in the evening. That is all we need to say on the subject, for the impact of known fluctuations in output on the choice of system has been ascertained by analyzing their effect on the behavior of a single-shift firm, which, together with our earlier results, has allowed us to determine their impact on the choice of system.

The nature of the adjustment costs introduced by output fluctuations should now be clear. There are two types of adjustment costs introduced by the fact that output fluctuations force the firm to plan to operate at different levels of output. One cost is that capital must be left

---

[12] Parenthetically, our analysis brings out an error of Marris (1964, p. 97), who wrote: "If firms were following this principle we should expect to observe that, other things being equal, in industries where demand was known to be variable, the average occurrence of shift-work, taking one year with another, would be relatively frequent." Interpreting reductions in λ or q as increases in the variability of output, we note that Marris's statement is correct only if the elasticity of substitution is less than unity.

idle for part of the time. This cost is incorporated in what we have called the effective daily price of capital. The other cost arises from the need to operate at different positive levels of output; low levels of output will be accompanied by the diseconomies of small-scale operation. If we view output fluctuations as occurring because of the stochastic nature of the demand curve rather than because of known seasonal patterns, the essence of these adjustment costs remains unaltered. Moreover, under the assumption that the decision maker maximizes expected profits, the impact of this type of uncertainty on the choice of system has implicitly been analyzed in the previous paragraphs. That is, if one lets λ stand for the probability that on any given day output X_H must be produced and $1 - \lambda$ stand for the probability that on any given day output X_L must be produced, then the maximization of expected profits entails maximizing the same objective functions as discussed in the previous paragraphs. Therefore, the impact of uncertainty on the choice of system will be the same as the impact of known output fluctuations already discussed.

If the behavior of the entrepreneur depends on his risk preferences, however, uncertainty introduces additional considerations into the analysis. In particular, if there is risk aversion on the part of the entrepreneur, he will be willing to pay a premium in order to hedge against the consequences of uncertainty. The capital stock is the source of the undesirable consequences stemming from uncertainty, because it must be paid whether or not it is used; consequently, risk-averse behavior will induce a preference for a smaller capital stock, under either single or multiple shifts, in the presence of uncertainty.[13] In the absence of uncertainty, a plant designed to work shifts tends to use a smaller capital stock than a plant designed for a single shift if the elasticity of substitution is less than unity (Betancourt and Clague 1975, p. 74). Therefore, the introduction of uncertainty in this situation will tend to favor the adoption of shift-work. Because the amount of capital used by the shift-work firm is smaller than that used by the single-shift firm, the adoption of shift-work reduces the amount of risk that the decision maker must bear as a result of the output fluctuations generated by the introduction of stochastic demand.

The discussion undertaken in this section is sufficient to reveal the main impact of these dynamic considerations on the choice of system. More important, it illustrates the usefulness of the main propositions

---

[13] This result has been rigorously established in the analysis of firm behavior under uncertainty (e.g., Batra and Ullah 1974; Holthausen 1976). These analyses of firm behavior under uncertainty assume (implicitly) that the system of operation is given.

developed in this chapter and in earlier ones for the analysis of the firm's behavior with respect to the choice of system in a variety of contexts.

3.5   Concluding remarks

By way of concluding our discussion of shift-work and the theory of the firm, we consider briefly the impact on the choice of system of alternatives to profit maximization, or its variants, as objective functions for the enterprise. Two alternatives will be discussed: sales maximization (which is very similar to profit maximization) and maximization of income per worker (which is very different from profit maximization).

Under a sales-maximization objective (e.g., Baumol 1959) the cost ratio still plays a crucial role in the analysis. Insofar as profits are used as a fund for sales-increasing activities, the firm will be concerned with profits, and much of the preceding analysis will still be relevant. To the extent that the firm sacrifices profits for additional current output, a new element is introduced. As an extreme case, let us suppose that the firm increases output to the point that profits are zero. This assumption means that the firm selects, for each system of operation, a level of output such that the average revenue curve intersects the average cost curve for that system. With a constant-β technology, of course, the average cost curves cannot intersect, and the choice of system depends exclusively on the cost ratio. With the semi-U technology, assuming the average cost curves do intersect,[14] system 1 will be chosen if the average revenue curve cuts the average cost curves to the left of X^*, and system 2 will be chosen if it cuts them to the right of X^*.

With an objective function for the firm as different as the maximization of income per worker, it is not surprising that some major changes are required in the analysis. Nonetheless, a tool of analysis analogous to the cost ratio, the income ratio, has been used to establish three propositions exactly comparable to Propositions 3 through 5 of the first two chapters (Betancourt and Clague 1977, p. 466). Other similarities in the capital-utilization decisions of the two types of firms can also be established.[15]

In summary, these remarks suggest that the basic propositions

[14] If the average cost curves intersect, they must do so at X^*, where the cost ratio equals unity.

[15] We shall demonstrate this proposition in a monograph (currently in preparation) on shift-work in a labor-managed system.

developed in these chapters, particularly in the first two chapters, are quite robust with respect to the use of alternative objective functions for the firm. Instead of pursuing further variations in the theory, we find it more productive at this point to turn our efforts toward the process of testing the main propositions presented in the first part of this book.

Appendix 3.1 Perfect competition in the product market

Under long-run competitive equilibrium, the profit margin will be zero, at least for the marginal firm in the industry, because the price elasticity of demand is infinite ($n = \infty$) and because the (marginal) firm operates at the constant-returns-to-scale point ($\beta = 1$) with a U-shaped long-run average-cost curve. Therefore the expressions in (3.2) collapse to the old cost ratio of Chapters 1 and 2 (i.e., CR $\gtreqless$ 1) where $\phi(X) = \frac{1}{2}$ in the cost ratio because of constant returns to scale.

With a constant-β technology, constant returns to scale ($\beta = 1$) imply that the preceding result holds for every firm and that the level of output is indeterminate. We do not need to consider increasing returns to scale throughout the output range ($\beta > 1$) because it is well known that they are inconsistent with perfect competition. Finally, the constant-β technology with decreasing returns to scale ($\beta < 1$) implies that the profit margin of the competitive firm is positive (i.e., $m = 1 - \beta$), and the shift-work profitability condition is the same as (3.7).

The last result in the previous paragraph is also of interest because it can be used to describe the inframarginal, perfectly competitive firm at its equilibrium point, when the technology is U-shaped. Because $\phi(X) = \frac{1}{2}$ for the marginal firm and $\phi(X) < \frac{1}{2}$ for the inframarginal firm, it is possible for the two firms to make different decisions with respect to the choice of system. Hence, perfect competition does not necessarily imply that all firms must make the same shift-work decision.

PART II

Estimation

CHAPTER 4

The estimation framework

Bridging the gap between the theory and the data is frequently a difficult task in economic research. Successful accomplishment of this task is the aim of the estimation process. This process, which is the focus of the second part of this book, will be critically influenced by the nature and implications of the theory, the characteristics of the data, and the purpose of the estimation.

The principal purpose of the estimation in our context is, of course, the testing of the theory of capital utilization presented in the previous part of this book. We lay the foundation for such testing in this chapter through an analysis of the implications of certain characteristics of the theory (and to a lesser extent of the data) for the estimation process. Without going into details at this point, it is worth noting that the analysis in this chapter yields insights of interest and significance for the empirical analysis of other qualitative variables as well as shift-work. By contrast, in the next chapter the discussion focuses exclusively on capital utilization or shift-work; there we use the theoretical results from Part I and the results from this chapter to provide a novel interpretation of previous attempts at testing the theory. In so doing we furnish a review of the existing econometric literature on capital utilization. In Chapter 6 we describe in detail the procedures employed to implement the models empirically. An important aim of these procedures is avoidance of some of the shortcomings exhibited by previous tests of the theory. The results of testing the theory with our data are presented in Part III.

Because the discussion in this chapter is rather technical and specialized, we begin with a nontechnical presentation of the main issues that arise in the estimation process (Section 4.1). The general reader may prefer to read this section and move on to the next chapter. Nevertheless, the reader with an interest in methodology will want to go on to the subsequent sections in this chapter, where we develop our estimation procedure in the course of a more detailed discussion of the following topics: issues that arise in the specification of the dependent variable (Section 4.2), issues that arise in the specification of the independent variables (Section 4.3), and estimation problems stemming from the existence of unobservable variables (Section 4.4). In Section 4.5 we discuss the estimation techniques appropriate for the analysis of shift-work in the light of the previous discussion. Finally, in Section 4.6 we introduce measures of predictive performance that have been developed specifically for the evaluation of models in which the predicted values can be interpreted as probabilities (the relevant case for our purposes).

4.1   A nontechnical overview of the estimation process

The characteristics of the theory developed in Part I have several important implications for the estimation process. For instance, the theory suggests the number of shifts that a plant is designed to operate as a dependent variable, although other measures of capital utilization can also be appropriate. In addition, the theory provides us with information on the main causal influences on the utilization decision (Propositions 2 through 5, for example) as well as on the functional form in which these influences interact to affect this decision (the functional forms of the cost ratio). Moreover, one of these causal influences (capital intensity under single-shift operation) is not directly observable for some of the observations in a sample, and the theory suggests that utilization influences the variable actually observed for these observations (Proposition 1). All of these character- istics affect the selection of estimation procedures, because taking account of these characteristics either introduces desirable properties into estimation procedures or eliminates undesirable properties from these procedures.

If the dependent variable is regarded as a categorical variable rather than an interval-scale variable, the usual statistical technique employed for the analysis of causal relationships (i.e., regression analysis) is in general not suitable. In recent years statistical tech- niques designed to deal with categorical variables have been developed under various assumptions. Their applicability to a problem, however, is dependent on whether or not these assumptions are satisfied. The most popular among these techniques requires the assumption that the choice alternatives be truly distinct. On the other hand, our theoretical analysis suggests that the double-shift system and the triple-shift system are, under reasonable circumstances, similar or like alterna- tives, particularly when compared with the single-shift system. This conclusion is implied by our analysis of sequentiality and inferiority in Chapter 2. For example, the double-shift system was found to be an inferior system under some assumptions, because whenever it was preferred to the single-shift system it was not preferred to the triple-shift system. This characteristic suggests that from the point of view of choosing between the three alternatives, it makes better sense to view the double-shift system as being the same as the triple-shift system than to treat it as a truly distinct alternative. Thus our dependent variable is a categorical variable, but the relevant categories are shift-work and no shift-work. The property of sequentiality leads to a similar conclusion, except that it leads one to view the shift-work/no-shift-work dichotomy as the first step in a sequence. The second step is the choice between the triple- and double-shift systems when shift-work is the chosen system of operation. In both steps of the sequence, however, we have a dichotomous dependent variable.

Statistical techniques for dealing with dichotomous choices are more readily available than are those for dealing with choices among many alternatives. Among the possible techniques are probit analysis, logit analysis, and even ordinary regression analysis with the dependent variable defined as a binary (0–1) variable. Each of these techniques has attractive properties for linking the theory and the data under different assumptions about the stochastic process generating the observations. Because logit analysis and probit analysis give very similar results and because logit analysis is computationally simpler, we shall use it rather than probit analysis. On the other hand, both logit analysis and ordinary regression analysis will be applied to our data, because empirical results that hold under these two fairly different methods are more robust than those that arise under only one of these two methods. We also present a measure of predictive performance for statistical techniques that yield predicted values that can be interpreted as probabilities. The need for this measure stems from the shortcomings of the traditional measure (R^2) when the dependent variable is a categorical one (e.g., when the categorical dependent variable has more than two alternatives, it is not even feasible to compute the R^2). This measure indicates the amount of accurate information provided by the sample predictions obtained from any particular combination of statistical techniques and economic models; it ranges from minus unity (maximum misinformation) to plus unity (maximum information).

In testing a causal relationship, it is customary to employ statistical techniques, such as multiple regression, that control for the effects of various independent variables. In this causal context, two issues arise for our analysis: How much information from the theory should be brought to bear on the data in the specification of the independent variables? Are the assumptions underlying the statistical model valid for the specific problem at hand?

With respect to the specification of the independent variables, we pursue two different approaches. In one, which we label the restricted-form specification, we utilize as much information from the theory as possible. For instance, we view any one of the CES cost ratios in Chapter 2 as the main explanatory variable under this approach. In the other approach, which we label the free-form specification, we merely try to identify individual explanatory variables (and their expected signs) that correspond to the main causal elements suggested by the theory. These explanatory variables are put forth as independent causal influences in the utilization decision. In our view, the two approaches should be thought of as complementary rather than competitive; in any event, we find that the use of both approaches strengthens our results.

With respect to the second issue, the main source of problems lies in the requirement imposed by most statistical techniques that the explanatory variables be statistically independent of (or at least have a zero covariance with) the stochastic component generating the dependent variable. In the case of shift-work, capital intensity under single-shift operation is one of the appropriate independent variables (Proposition 4), but it is not observable for firms that work shifts. Typically one uses instead the observed capital intensity for those firms that work shifts, and thus observed capital intensity becomes an explanatory variable. Unfortunately, it is not logical to assume that observed capital intensity is statistically independent of the random variable generating levels of utilization, because Proposition 1 suggests a positive relationship between levels of utilization and observed capital intensity. Violation of this important assumption (of no reverse causation) in the statistical model makes tests of the theory suspect. If one can estimate the elasticity of substitution, however, the problem can be eliminated, because with this information it is possible to estimate the capital share under single-shift operation for those firms that work shifts. We show that it is possible to estimate the elasticity of substitution by traditional methods if one pays careful attention to the proper definition of the variables. Hence, we are able to avoid this problem in our estimation process. In the next chapter we interpret the prior econometric literature on capital utilization in light of the problem just described and a similar one that arises with respect to the level of output under the semi-U technology.

*4.2   Specification of the dependent variable

At the theoretical level we have been primarily interested in the long-run decision to work shifts. This interest has led us to focus on the choice of a system of operation before the factory is built. We shall pursue the implications of this emphasis in this section and in the next two. Conceptually, we are viewing the decision maker as choosing an optimal system of operation by comparing the value of the objective function for each system of operation when this objective function is evaluated at the optimal values of all the other decision variables for each system.[1] Such a conceptualization of the decision-making process clearly suggests the number of shifts as the (qualitative) dependent variable. Nevertheless, it would not be unreasonable to put forth a continuous index of utilization as the dependent variable (e.g., one defined in terms of the number of hours during the year that a plant or a process is in operation). When the focus is on the intended level of utilization from a long-run point of view, however, the number of shifts is preferable as a dependent variable. The main reason, as noted elsewhere (Betancourt 1977, pp. 56-7), is that one would expect the continuous measure to be more sensitive to variations in the firms' short-run intended levels of utilization or actual levels of utilization than would the number of shifts.

*4.2.1 Literature on estimation of choice probabilities

A consequence of specifying a qualitative dependent variable is that the estimation problem becomes one of estimating choice probabilities. The estimation techniques appropriate for such problems are dependent on the underlying structure of the choice-probability model that is assumed to generate the probabilities. There are two general forms of these models in the theoretical literature (e.g., Sattah and Tversky 1976): the random-utility model and the constant-utility model. A critical distinction between the two models is that the former attributes uncertainty to the determination of the value of the objective function, whereas the latter attributes uncertainty to the application of the decision rule that follows from the objective function. Because the theoretical development of the objective function in the previous chapters has been undertaken in a deterministic framework, a constant-utility model is a natural specification of the choice probabilities for this study.[2] It must be noted, however, that one of the most widely used choice-probability models in the economic literature is the

---

[1] Of course, this conceptualization is also applicable to other economic problems (e.g., choice of travel mode).

[2] In the case of continuous dependent variables, the usual specification of the disturbances for econometric work corresponds conceptually to the constant-utility model.

conditional logit model[3] (McFadden 1974), which is an example of the subclass of random-utility models known as independent random-utility models.

Conditional logit is quite popular in applied work because it is extremely difficult to develop estimation techniques with known and desirable properties from the specification of either random-utility models or constant-utility models for the choice probabilities, and conditional logit accomplishes these tasks superbly. These accomplishments, however, require an assumption that is very objectionable in the analysis of shift-work. A discussion of the reasons for our objection is necessary because these reasons suggest an alternative assumption leading to the estimation technique employed in this study, which is based on the constant-utility model. Hence, the subsequent discussion will provide a rationale for our departure from what may be viewed as the standard procedure in the analysis of qualitative dependent variables.

The source of our objection to the conditional logit model is that it is based on the axiom of independence of irrelevant alternatives. This axiom requires that the odds of choosing one alternative over another be independent of whether or not other alternatives are excluded from the choice set. As McFadden (1974, p. 7) pointed out, this axiom makes the model inapplicable when there are substantially different patterns of substitutability and complementarity among the alternatives.[4] The theory developed in the previous chapters provides a strong argument for the existence of substantially different patterns of substitutability between the three systems of operation in a variety of circumstances. For instance, in the Leontief case it was established that the decision maker can ascertain whether or not single-shift operation is desirable from a single binary comparison using the cost ratio for two shifts versus one even when three shifts is the optimal alternative. Under somewhat more restrictive assumptions it was also shown that the two-shift system will be an inferior system. Similar results were established in Chapter 2 for other functional forms.[5] Finally, we interpreted these results as suggesting that two- and three-shift opera-

---

[3] The special case of this model relevant to our discussion is also known in the literature as multinomial logit (Maddala and Nelson 1974).

[4] This axiom has also been used in other models in the theoretical literature on choice probabilities (Luce 1959), and it has been criticized in this literature on similar grounds (Debreu 1960).

[5] As a matter of fact, similar results can be established under the postulate that the firm maximizes income per worker. These results will be presented in the monograph mentioned in Chapter 3 (footnote 15).

tions are to be viewed as fairly close substitutes relative to the single-shift system and that the pattern of substitutability between two shifts and three shifts depends, among other things, on the elasticity of substitution.[6]

An example will bring out these points most clearly. If the odds for choosing between the double-shift system and the single-shift system are equal to unity when the triple-shift system is excluded from the choice set, then the axiom of independence of irrelevant alternatives implies that, when three shifts are included in the choice set, the odds for choosing between two shifts and one shift and the odds for choosing between three shifts and one shift are also equal to unity. Thus the probabilities are given as follows: $P_1 = P_2 = \frac{1}{2}$ for the restricted choice set; $P_1 = P_2 = P_3 = \frac{1}{3}$ for the complete choice set. The first theoretical result mentioned in the previous paragraph suggests, however, that a more reasonable assignment of probabilities in the expanded choice set would be $P_1 = \frac{1}{2}$ and $P_2 + P_3 = \frac{1}{2}$, and the only restriction on P_2 and P_3 is that they must vary between 0 and $\frac{1}{2}$. The same initial assignment of probabilities also follows if either two shifts or three shifts are inferior alternatives, but then we would expect either P_2 or P_3 to equal zero. Finally, this initial assignment is also consistent with the existence of unobserved aspects of choice that are similar for two-shift and three-shift systems but different for the single-shift system (see footnote 6).

Mention should also be made at this point of a very recent development in the literature on random-utility models. Hausman and Wise (1978) have been able to relax the assumption of independence of irrelevant alternatives in a random-utility model that they term the covariance probit model. The solution they offer to the independence problem is based on the assumption that variations in the unobserved characteristics of choice behavior are small relative to variations in tastes across decision makers. For example, in the limiting case that they discuss (p. 415), this assumption implies that the unobserved characteristics of choice behavior are the same across alternatives and

---

[6] On a more heuristic level, it can also be argued that the single-shift system is the "normal" system of operation both from the point of view of how individuals conduct their affairs and from the point of view of market interactions between economic agents. Since both two- and three-shift systems can be viewed in this sense as abnormal, this unobservable aspect of choice behavior induces a pattern of substitutability between two shifts and three shifts in relation to the single-shift system that is substantially different from the pattern that exists between two shifts and three shifts in relation to each other.

individuals; the randomness in the utility function results exclusively from variations in tastes among decision makers over the measured attributes. Their assumption does not seem plausible when applied to the analysis of shift-work. For instance, it implies that variations in the tastes of entrepreneurs over the measured profitability of shift-work must be large relative to variations in unobserved characteristics such as managerial attitudes toward shift-work systems, productivity differentials, and implicit shift differentials. Moreover, their model is derived on the assumption that the unobserved characteristics of choice behavior are independent across alternatives. Further exploration of the applicability of this random-utility model to the analysis of shift-work may be a worthwhile subject for future research, because such research could very well overcome the difficulties mentioned here. Nevertheless, in light of our preceding discussion, we shall not pursue this line of inquiry any further in this study.

We conclude this brief incursion into the literature on random-utility models by noting a procedure suggested by Domencich and McFadden (1975, pp. 77-9) for situations in which the independence axiom is violated. They offer as an approximation a sequential process in which the decision maker chooses first between the like alternatives and subsequently is viewed as choosing between the "unlike" alternative and the best of the like alternatives. This procedure provides an interesting contrast to the one we shall follow.

4.2.2 Our estimation procedure

The essence of our approach to the estimation problem is our treatment of the double- and triple-shift systems as the same in relation to the single-shift system for the assignment of choice probabilities in the first step of a sequence. In order to arrive at an estimation technique it is necessary to impose this assumption on the assignment of choice probabilities, and this task is easily accomplished by defining a binary dependent variable that takes on the value 1 if the firm works shifts (either two or three shifts) and the value 0 otherwise. Then estimation techniques applicable to binary models can be selected, and the restriction will be automatically satisfied by every observation. Thus, our estimation procedure can also be viewed as a sequential process, but the order of the sequence will be reversed. That is, the first step in the sequence is determined by the process just described, wherein the decision maker chooses between working shifts and not working shifts. The second step is, of course, the choice between two shifts and three shifts for those firms that choose shift-work. Although this assumption also places restrictions on choice behavior, we find it preferable to the existing alternatives for analysis of shift-work. If the conditions for sequentiality discussed in Chapter 2 were to hold for every observation in our samples, then this approach could be justified as the most appropriate estimation procedure in light of our theory and the use of a constant-utility model for the assignment of choice probabilities.[7] Nevertheless, we think those conditions are too stringent to be met by every observation in practice. Therefore we see our approach to the estimation problem as an approximation to a more general approach that is yet to be developed. Consequently, some sensitivity analysis of the results to alternative estimation procedures has been undertaken and will be discussed briefly in Chapter 7.

At this point it is worthwhile to note some implications for reductions of the sample. Because there are three alternatives, it is always possible to drop the observations that chose one of the alternatives (e.g., the single-shift firms) and apply an estimation technique for binary dependent variables to the remaining observations. The estimated probabilities, however, cannot be interpreted in general as estimates of the conditional probabilities of choosing, for example, three shifts or two shifts, given that the single-shift system is excluded from the choice set. The choice set for any one firm or observation remains the same after the sample is reduced. Instead, these estimates from the restricted samples are simply estimates conditional on the set of observations that is dropped. Considering the basis for the estimation procedure, one can argue that the estimates of the coefficients and the probabilities in the restricted samples should not be very different from the unrestricted-sample estimates if the observations that chose system two or those that chose system three are dropped from the sample, and the performance of these experiments will provide an informal test of our approach. On the other hand, no restriction follows from our approach to the estimation problem with regard to what happens when the sample is restricted by dropping the observations that chose the single-shift system. This restricted sample merely provides the information for estimating the choice probabilities for the double- and triple-shift systems (i.e., for the second step in our sequence).

*4.3 Specification of the independent variables

One can characterize the specifications of the independent variables in applied econometric work by two broad categories: free form (where at best the theory is used as a guide to select variables available in the

[7] In these circumstances, the statistical properties of sequential estimation procedures are the ones presented by Amemiya (1975).

data that are supposed to capture the influence of a particular theoretical factor) and restricted form (where the theory is also used to derive information on the functional form in which variables should enter into the statistical analysis). Most empirical work lies somewhere in between, and judgments on the particular problem play an important role in determining where on the spectrum the analyst wants to be (Goldberger 1968, Chapter 9, provides a discussion of these issues). As we mentioned in Section 4.1, we shall pursue two alternative types of specifications of the independent variables:[8] one corresponding to the restricted-form specification and the other corresponding to the free-form specification. In the restricted-form specification we shall be calculating the various conditions on the desirability of shift-work developed in earlier chapters (i.e., the cost ratios of Chapter 2) for every observation in a sample. Clearly, this is a rather formidable task that will require going beyond the straightforward use of our sample data. Thus, most of Chapter 6 is devoted to a systematic presentation of our efforts in this direction. In the free-form approach we shall be looking at the theory of the previous chapters and extracting information regarding the variables in the data that capture these theoretical factors and regarding their expected signs. These variables will be introduced, usually in linear form, as independent variables. The actual variables used, and the rationale behind the specific definition, will also be discussed in Chapter 6.

The two approaches previously mentioned need not be viewed as substitutes. On the contrary, we found in our earlier work (Betancourt and Clague 1978) that they tend to complement each other. In order to bring out this complementarity and to set the stage for the discussion in subsequent chapters, we shall describe briefly the nature of the difference between the two approaches. In the restricted-form approach one must specify how each variable enters into the decision to work shifts and how in interacts with other variables. In our case this process is heavily influenced by the assumptions made about the production function; for instance, our empirical analysis will be based on the use of a CES production function to describe substitution possibilities, which under the maintained hypothesis of cost minimization leads to the cost ratios of Chapter 2. Thus our models under the restricited-form specification will contain a single independent variable that will be a nonlinear function of other (elementary) variables [e.g., see equation (2.4)]. In the free-form approach there is no need to

---

[8] We speak of types of specifications because within each broad category several additional choices or judgments are usually made in arriving at an equation that is capable of being tested with actual data.

assume any particular functional form to describe substitution possibilities or to assume any specific type of interaction between the variables. In the most extreme version of this approach, each elementary variable entering the shift-work decision can be viewed as an independent variable in a regression equation.

In principle, the restricted-form specification has a substantial advantage over the free-form specification on the following grounds: In general, the more a priori knowledge that is brought to bear on a body of data, the more information that can be extracted from the data if the prior knowledge is correct (e.g., Rothenberg 1973). In practice, this advantage of the restricted form need not be realized, because the prior knowledge may not be correct. It is this possibility that provides the basis for the complementarity between the two approaches. This complementarity manifests itself in the different implications of the two approaches for the testing of alternative hypotheses and for the analysis of the sensitivity of the results to the econometric problems that normally occur in applied work. A thorough examination of these different implications, however, is best undertaken in the contexts in which they arise; hence, it will be undertaken at the relevant points in the subsequent sections, particularly throughout the next three chapters.

To conclude the discussion, we note an advantage of the restricted-form specification in the treatment of the policy implications that follow from the analysis. With the free-form specification, the investigator frequently does not (although in principle it is possible to) attempt to relate the implications of the results for policymaking to the actual way in which the policy variables operate. The restricted-form specification forces on the analyst a degree of precision in deriving the implications of the theory that, besides being unusual in most applied work, leaves him little choice in this matter, because the problem is already formulated in terms of the precise form in which the variables affect the decision. This feature of the restricted form will be relied on extensively in Chapter 9.

*4.4   Unobservable variables in the analysis of shift-work

In recent years econometricians have become interested in the overlap between the estimation problems raised by unobservable variables and simultaneous-equation models (e.g., Goldberger 1974). The analysis of shift-work provides an interesting example of this overlap, because the estimation problems that arise can be analyzed in either framework.

From the point of view of shift-work, a critical aspect of the estimation problem is the unobservable nature of the variables at the time of the investment decision. When the observed values of these variables are also affected by the firm's decision to work shifts, an estimation problem will arise that can be interpreted either as an error-in-the-variables problem or as a simultaneous-equation problem. This situation is potentially present in most economic contexts that can be modeled in terms of qualitative dependent variables.

In the analysis of shift-work there are two different contributors to the unobservable-variable problem: capital intensity and the level of output. An important difference between the problems raised by these two variables is in the extent of the problems. The estimation problem with respect to the level of output arises only when the degree of economies of scale is made a function of the level of output for the profit-maximizing enterprise. The estimation problem with respect to capital intensity, however, is far more pervasive, for it affects all the models of firm behavior mentioned in the last three chapters. The former problem will be discussed in Chapter 6, where we discuss the specification of the degree of economies of scale; in this section we shall focus on the problems that arise because of the dual role of capital intensity as a cause and consequence of high utilization.

*4.4.1 Estimation of a model of shift-work

Because the theoretical considerations leading to the problem have been adequately discussed in Chapters 1 and 2, they will not be repeated here. Instead, we shall illustrate the problem and its solution in terms of a concrete example.[9] For simplicity of exposition the discussion in this section will be set in the familiar context of linear regression. The illustration will be carried out in terms of one of the models implemented empirically in Chapter 7 that is defined by the hypothesis of zero effect of working capital (Chapter 2, Section 2.4) and a constant-β technology (Chapter 3, Section 3.2). The regression equation to be estimated for this model will be

$$S_i = \beta_0 + \beta_1 X_{1i} + u_i \qquad (4.1)$$

where S_i takes on the value of zero if the firm works one shift and the value of unity otherwise.[10] X_{1i} is the cost ratio that follows from

---

[9] This illustration also brings out some of the differences between the restricted-form specification and the free-form specification alluded to in the previous section.

[10] To keep the notation from becoming cumbersome, we shall assume throughout this section that all shift-working firms work just two shifts.

putting together equation (2.4) with the assumption of a constant-β technology [i.e., from replacing $\phi(X)$ in (2.4) by $2^{-1/\beta}$]. Thus

$$X_{1i} = 2^{-1/\beta}(2 + \alpha_i)[\theta_i(2 + \alpha_i)^{\sigma-1} + (1 - \theta_i)]^{1/(1-\sigma_i)} \tag{4.2}$$

Under the free-form specification the same model can be implemented by introducing the elementary variables in (4.2), or suitable proxies, into a regression equation. For instance

$$S_i = \gamma_0 + \gamma_1 Z_{1i} + \gamma_2 Z_{2i} + \gamma_3 Z_{3i} + u_i \tag{4.3}$$

where S_i is defined as before, Z_{1i} is a measure of capital intensity under single-shift operation (e.g., the capital–labor ratio[11]) Z_{2i} is the shift differential, and Z_{3i} is the elasticity of substitution.

The first point to be made is that the estimation problem under consideration arises regardless of whether one specifies equation (4.1) or equation (4.3). Under (4.1) the appropriate measure of capital intensity, θ_i, is the capital share *under single-shift operation* for the ith firm. But if the ith firm works shifts, this share is not directly observable. If the elasticity of substitution and the shift differential are known, however, the single-shift capital share for these firms can be estimated from the following equation, which is derived from (2.2) and the definition of the capital share:

$$\frac{\theta_i}{1 - \theta_i} = \frac{r}{w_1}k_i^1 = \frac{r}{w_1}\frac{k_i^2}{(2 + \alpha_i)^{\sigma_i}} \tag{4.4}$$

Exactly the same problem arises under the free-form specification. That is, the relevant measure of capital intensity, Z_{1i}, will be, in our example, the capital–labor ratio per shift *under single-shift operation*.[12] If the elasticity of substitution and the shift differential are

---

[11] Strictly speaking, the appropriate elementary variable in the free-form approach would be θ_i, but it is rarely used in practice because of measurement problems. We choose to specify (4.3) in terms of the capital–labor ratio for two reasons: It is a common specification in empirical work (see Chapter 5), and it facilitates establishing the connection between this estimation problem and a closely related one, the estimation of the elasticity of substitution.

[12] Henceforth we are using k_i to denote capital–labor ratios $(K/L)_i$ per shift as well as ratios of capital to labor services $(UK/L)_i$ per shift in order to simplify the notation. This notational convention implies that we are setting the proportionality constant U equal to unity. As the reader may recall from Chapter 1, this proportionality constant defines the period of analysis (eight-hour shifts in our case). Because the relationship in (4.4) also holds in terms of capital–labor ratios per shift, nothing is lost by adopting this convention at the present stage in our argument.

known, then k_i^1 can also be estimated from (4.4) for those firms that work shifts.

By use of the free-form specification the estimation problem can be set up in terms of the errors-in-the-variables framework, as follows: The observed capital–labor ratio per shift, k^0, equals the true one, k^*, times a disturbance term, v. Incidentally, the assumption of normality is not appropriate for v. If we assume the elasticity of substitution and the shift differential to be constant across the sample observations, the estimation problem can be described in terms of the following relations:

$$S_i = \gamma_0 + \gamma_1 k_i^* + u_i \tag{4.5}$$

$$k_i^0 = k_i^* v_i = k_i^* (2 + \alpha)^{\sigma S_i} \tag{4.6}$$

$$S_i = \gamma_0 + \gamma_1 k_i^0 + u_i^* \tag{4.7}$$

where $u_i^* = \gamma_1(k_i^* - k_i^0) + u_i$. Relation (4.5) is the true relation; (4.6) describes the error in the variable; and (4.7) is the relation to be estimated when the observed capital–labor ratio per shift is used instead of the true one. Undoubtedly, the assumption of uncorrelated-ness between the regressor and the disturbance is not tenable for (4.7) even in large samples. If (4.7) is estimated by ordinary least squares (OLS), it follows under the usual stability assumptions that

$$\text{Plim } \hat{\gamma}_1 = \frac{\gamma_1 \text{ COV } (k^0, k^*) + \text{COV } (k^0, u)}{\text{VAR } (k^0)} \tag{4.8}$$

The asymptotic bias, η, will be given by

$$\eta = \gamma_1 \left[\frac{\text{COV } (k^0, k^*)}{\text{VAR } (k^0)} - 1 \right] + \frac{\text{COV } (k^0, u)}{\text{VAR } (k^0)} \gtrless 0 \tag{4.9}$$

In general, the sign of the bias is ambiguous, but it is still instructive to discuss the signs of the components of (4.9). COV (k^0, k^*) will be positive because high values of capital intensity under single-shift operation lead to shift-work, which in turn leads to high values of observed capital intensity k^0. Similarly, COV (k^0, u) will be positive because high values of u also lead to shift-work, which once more leads to high values of k^0. γ_1 is also positive according to our theory. For future reference, we also note that

$$\text{Plim} \left(\frac{R_{k^0}^2}{R_{k^*}^2} \right) = \frac{(\gamma_1 + \eta)^2}{\gamma_1^2} \frac{\text{VAR } (k^0)}{\text{VAR } (k^*)} \tag{4.10}$$

Thus if the bias is positive ($\eta > 0$), R^2 will be higher in a regression that uses the observed measure of capital intensity (k^0) than in a regression that uses the true measure of capital intensity. Note that

VAR (k^0) can be expected to be larger than VAR (k^*) because $k^0 = k^*v$, and the covariance of k^* and v will be positive for the same reasons that COV (k^0, k^*) is positive.[13] If the bias is negative, we can then have Plim $(R_k^{20}/R_k^{2*}) \gtreqless 1$.

Although the preceding discussion has been carried out exclusively in terms of the free-form specification, similar results hold for the restricted-form specification. In order to see this point, it is convenient to put the two specifications on comparable footing by redefining X_{1i} as the inverse of the cost ratio (CR_i^{-1}), which implies that $\beta_1 > 0$. With this reformulation we can replace k^0 by X^0, k^* by X^*, γ_1 by β_1, and v by w in equations (4.5) through (4.7); the same results as in the free-form specification can now be obtained by a parallel argument. The essence of this argument is that the true variable is θ_i^*, the observed variable is θ_i^0, and $\theta_i^0 > \theta_i^*$ for the same reasons as before, which can be seen from (4.4). Since $\partial(CR_i^{-1})/\partial\theta_i$ is greater than zero, $X_i^0 = X_i^* w_i$ and $w_i \geq 1$ as $S_i \geq 0$.[14] To conclude, we reiterate that if the production function is Leontief $(\sigma = 0)$, the unobservable-variable problem disappears in both specifications. Namely, $k^0 = k^*$ for the firms that work shifts, as can be seen from (4.4), which implies that $v_i = w_i = 1$ for $S_i = 1$.

The preceding results have been obtained in terms of simple linear regressions; nevertheless, it is not difficult to show that the unobservable-variable problem leads to similar conclusions in a multiple-regression framework, or with other estimation methods (e.g., with maximum-likelihood estimation). Moreover, although the unobservable-variable problem with respect to capital intensity has been illustrated using one specific model of shift-work, this problem is present in every model of shift-work (and/or capital utilization) that does not assume the capital stock to be fixed or the production function to be Leontief. Fortunately the previous discussion also provides us with the solution to the unobservable-variable problem. Frequently

---

[13] The asymptotic approximation to the variance of this product is VAR $(k^0) \simeq (Ek^*)^2 \sigma_v^2 + 2E(k^*)E(v)$ COV $(k^*, v) + (Ev)^2$ VAR (k^*). By definition, $v \geq 1$; therefore $Ev > 1$. Hence $(Ev)^2$ VAR $(k^*) -$ VAR $(k^*) > 0$, and VAR $(k^0) -$ VAR $(k^*) > 0$, because the other two terms in the approximation for VAR (k^0) are positive. We tried to prove the same result using the formula for the exact variance of a product (Goodman 1960), but we were unable to do so.

[14] Note that $X_i^0 = CR^{-1}(\theta_i^0)$, $X_i^* = CR^{-1}(\theta_i^*)$, and $w_i = X_i^0/X_i^*$. It is the nonlinearity of the cost ratio in the elementary variables that makes the results for the restricted form similar to, rather than identical with, the free-form results.

the shift differential for those firms that work shifts is an observable variable. Thus, if one knows or is able to estimate the elasticity of substitution, the "true" capital share and/or capital–labor ratio can also be calculated or estimated for those firms that work shifts. Because the elasticity of substitution is not known, it must be estimated. As we shall demonstrate immediately below, our analysis of the shift-work decision has important implications for the estimation of the elasticity of substitution.

*4.4.2 Estimation of the elasticity of substitution

Because we rely exclusively on the CES functional form in our empirical work, we concentrate our discussion on this functional form.[15] One of the methods of estimating the parameters of the CES is derived from the first-order conditions for cost minimization in Chapter 2. That is, taking logarithms of both sides of the equation for the single-shift system in (2.2), we have[16]

$$\ln k_i^1 = \sigma\{\ln[\delta/(1-\delta)]\} + \sigma \ln (w_1/r)_i + \ln \tilde{u} \qquad (4.11)$$

If firms use only the single-shift system, or if the values of k_i^1 and w_1/r are observable for those firms that work shifts, then no problem arises in estimating σ from (4.11). Nonetheless, for those firms that work shifts, k_i^1 and w_1/r are not directly observable, and therefore problems can arise in the estimation of (4.11) with actual data. The nature of the problems will depend on what is actually done in the course of estimation.

To keep the discussion brief, we shall consider in greater detail the possibility that is of greatest interest for our purposes. For those firms that work shifts, a natural measure to use for the dependent variable in (4.11) is the capital–labor ratio in the first shift of the double-shift system (i.e., k_1^2). Moreover, a natural measure to use as the independent variable for these firms is the average wage–rental ratio over the two shifts. That is, in our notation,

$$\frac{\bar{w}}{\bar{r}} = \frac{w_1(1+\alpha/2)}{r/2} = \left(\frac{w_1}{r}\right)(2+\alpha) = \left(\frac{w}{r}\right)^*(2+\alpha) \qquad (4.12)$$

---

[15] Nonetheless, problems similar to the one discussed next will arise with other functional forms.

[16] Because we are setting U equal to unity, it follows that $\ln U$ equals zero. In any event, in general U affects the intercept in (4.11), not the slope. Hence it does not affect our argument. Also, we are letting σ be the same for every firm to facilitate the exposition, but this assumption is not necessary, and we do not rely on it for our empirical analysis.

It turns out that with these measures no problems arise in the estimation of the elasticity of substitution.

The estimation problem in this situation can be described by the following relations:

$$\ln k_i^* = \delta_0 + \sigma \ln (w/r)_i^* + \ln \tilde{u}_i \tag{4.13}$$

$$\ln k_i^0 = \ln k_i^* v_i \tag{4.14}$$

$$\ln (w/r)_i^0 = \ln (w/r)_i^* \epsilon_i \tag{4.15}$$

$$\ln k_i^0 = \delta_0 + \sigma \ln (w/r)_i^0 + \ln \tilde{u}_i \tag{4.16}$$

Equation (4.13) is simply a reparameterization of (4.11); equation (4.14) is just a repetition of (4.6); equation (4.15) describes the new error in the variable arising in this problem. Note that $\epsilon_i = (2 + \alpha_i)^{S_i}$; that is, $\epsilon_i \geq 1$ as $S_i \geq 0$. Equation (4.16) describes a relation in terms of the observable measures defined in the previous paragraph. This relation can be estimated by OLS, and no problems of dependence between the regressor and the disturbance term need arise. Relation (4.16) can be easily derived from the previous three. To wit, from (4.14) and (4.15) we can write $k_i^* = k_i^0/v_i$ and $(w/r)_i^* = (w/r)_i^0/\epsilon_i$. If we plug these two results into (4.13), we obtain

$$\ln \frac{k_i^0}{v_i} = \delta_0 + \sigma \ln \frac{(w/r)_i^0}{\epsilon_i} + \ln \tilde{u}_i \tag{4.17}$$

which becomes (4.16) because $\ln v_i = \sigma \ln \epsilon_i$. Thus we have a feasible method of estimating the elasticity of substitution when we apply OLS to (4.16); furthermore, the OLS estimators will have the usual desirable properties as estimators of the corresponding population parameters.

At this point it is worth noting that the conclusion of the previous paragraph holds only if the variables are measured exactly as described here, which is not the way it is done in the empirical literature discussed in Chapter 6, Section 6.3. For instance, the independent variable may be measured as the ratio of the average wage rate to the price of capital; that is, instead of (4.12) we may have in our notation

$$\frac{\overline{w}}{r} = \frac{w_1(1 + \alpha/2)}{r} = \left(\frac{w}{r}\right)^* \frac{2 + \alpha}{2} \tag{4.18}$$

In this situation (4.16) becomes

$$\ln k_i^0 = \delta_0 + \sigma \ln (w/r)_i^0 + \tilde{u}_i^* \tag{4.19}$$

where $\tilde{u}_i^* = \ln \tilde{u}_i + \sigma S_i \ln 2$. Thus the assumption that the disturbance in (4.19) is independent of the regressor is untenable because both depend on S_i.

4.4.3   A simultaneous-equation interpretation

To conclude, we present a simultaneous-equation formulation of the issues discussed in this section. The estimation problem in terms of unobservables is described by a recursive system if u_i and $\ln \tilde{u}_i$ have a zero covariance; that is,

$$S_i = \gamma_0 + \gamma_1 k_i^* + u_i \qquad (4.5)$$

$$\ln k_i^* = \delta_0 + \sigma \ln(w/r)_i^* + \ln \tilde{u}_i \qquad (4.13)$$

On the other hand, the estimation problem in terms of observables cannot be viewed as a recursive system. It is true that the following relations hold:

$$S_i = \gamma_0 + \gamma_1 k_i^0 + u_i^* \qquad (4.7)$$

$$\ln k_i^0 = \delta_0 + \sigma \ln(w/r)_i^0 + \ln \tilde{u}_i \qquad (4.16)$$

But $u_i^* = u_i + \gamma_1(k_i^* - k_i^0)$. Thus u_i^* and $\ln \tilde{u}_i$ will not have a zero covariance. Note that (4.16) can be estimated independently of (4.7), although the reverse is not true.

Because we have shown that (4.16) is equivalent to (4.13) and that in order to estimate (4.5) what one needs is a reliable estimate of σ, which can be obtained from fitting (4.13), we shall be working with the recursive specification.[17] Parenthetically, a similar approach will be adopted for the restricted-form specification of the independent variables, in which case the system will be (4.1) and (4.13). Whereas the estimation of (4.13) is straightforward, the estimation of equations such as (4.1), (4.3), and (4.5) is somewhat more complicated because of the presence of a qualitative dependent variable; therefore the next section is devoted to this subject.

*4.5   The estimation technique

In light of the discussion in Section 4.1, the estimation problem may be conceptualized as follows (Goldberger 1964, p. 250):

$$S_i = 1 \quad \text{if} \quad Y_i > Y_i^*$$

$$S_i = 0 \quad \text{if} \quad Y_i < Y_i^*$$

where S_i takes on the value 1 if the firm works shifts (either two or

---

[17] Our estimates will be consistent but not fully efficient. The reason is that in estimating (4.5) we do not use k_i^* but $\hat{k}_i^* = k_i^0/(2 + \alpha_i)^{\hat{\sigma} S_i}$; thus a gain in efficiency will be available from incorporating into the estimation method the knowledge that σ appears in both equations.

three shifts) and the value 0 otherwise, Y_i is an index that is a function of the independent variables, and Y_i^* is an unobservable critical value that plays the same role as a disturbance term in the classical model. Thus Y_i^* incorporates errors of measurement in the dependent variable, other influences, and the firm's preferences. This conceptualization allows us to formulate the probability that the ith firm works shifts as a function of the factors that determine the desirability of working shifts for the ith firm:[18]

$$P(S_i = 1 \mid Y_i) = \text{Prob } (Y_i^* \leq Y_i \mid Y_i) = f(Y_i) = f(X_i\beta) \qquad (4.20)$$

where X_i is a row vector of independent variables, β is a column vector of parameters that measure the impact of the independent variables on the probability of working shifts, and the expected signs of these parameters can be ascertained from the theory under either specification of the independent variables.

Several methods have been suggested to deal with this type of estimation problem (e.g., Warner 1962). The simplest method is to assume that the probability is linearly related to the conditioning variables (i.e., f is the identity function), and then it becomes possible to run a simple regression on the binary dependent variable.[19] The two main difficulties with this method are that the assumption of homoscedasticity cannot be satisfied and that the estimated probabilities will not in general be in the interval of 0 to 1 (thereby impairing their interpretation as probabilities). Goldberger (1964) and, more recently, Pindyck and Rubinfeld (1976) have suggested the use of weighted least squares to correct for the former problem. This suggestion does not seem to have much practical value, however, for it also transforms the estimation problem from one involving a qualitative dependent variable into one involving a limited dependent variable; that is, the zeros will remain zeros after the transformation to correct for heteroscedasticity has been applied to the dependent variable. Furthermore, there is no satisfactory solution to the second difficulty in the context of the simple regression model.

Because for our purposes the interpretation of the predicted values as probabilities is important, it is necessary to use another approach that restricts the probabilities to lie in the 0–1 interval. From the many

---

[18] Similarly, binary dependent variables can be defined for the three types of restricted samples mentioned at the end of Section 4.2, and the resulting probabilities will be conditional on the excluded observations. More important for our present purpose, the same estimation techniques to be discussed next can be applied in each case.

[19] This method is the one underlying the analysis of the previous section.

possible functions (f) that impose this restriction, the following one was selected:[20]

$$P(S_i = 1 \mid Y_i) = e^{X_i\beta}/(1 + e^{X_i\beta}) \qquad (4.21)$$

Because the probability that the ith firm does not work shifts is given by the logistic function, this approach is referred to in the literature as logit analysis (Theil 1971, p. 632). Equation (4.21) is nonlinear in its parameters, but the maximum-likelihood estimators of these parameters can be obtained by iterative methods, and either the likelihood ratio test or the t ratio test based on the estimates of the standard errors obtained from the estimated inverse of the information matrix can be employed to test hypotheses on the β coefficients.[21]

Our presentation of the results in this text will rely heavily (at times exclusively) on the estimates derived from the maximum-likelihood method. Nevertheless, all our models were also estimated by OLS. In our earlier work (Betancourt and Clague 1978) we found the two methods to yield similar results. This similarity was quite pronounced with respect to the signs and the statistical signficance of coefficients; however, sometimes these estimation methods differed appreciably with respect to predictive power. The wisdom of using both methods is illustrated by the conflicting evidence from the few Monte Carlo studies available. Those studies reported by McFadden (1974) and Domencich and McFadden (1975) tended to favor the maximum-likelihood method even for sample sizes as small as fifty, a typical size in our analysis; but the Goldfeld and Quandt (1972) experiments comparing OLS and probit analysis (which is quite similar to logit analysis) tended to favor OLS for sample sizes as large as 200.

*4.6   Measures of predictive performance for qualitative dependent variables

In the restricted-form specification, alternative hypotheses about the relevant theoretical factors lead to alternative regressions using a single independent variable. Therefore, the usual tests of significance on the coefficients of this independent variable are quite likely to fail to discriminate between alternative hypotheses because several of them may turn out to be significantly different from zero. Thus it is highly

---

[20] The main alternative available in the literature is probit analysis, but logit analysis was selected because of its simplicity and lower computational cost.

[21] A recent thorough discussion of the statistical properties of maximum-likelihood estimation of the binomial logit model is available (Domencich and McFadden 1975, pp. 110–12).

desirable to have a measure of predictive performance that indicates which of these hypotheses best explains the data. Traditionally, of course, the R^2 statistic is employed for these purposes. However, when the estimation method is nonlinear, the R^2 statistic, although it can be calculated, loses some of its desirable properties; for example, the usual decomposition of total variation is not applicable. Furthermore, there has been controversy regarding the appropriate upper bound of this statistic in the case of binary-choice models (e.g., Morrison 1972, Goldberger 1973).

Qualitative dependent-variable models, where the predicted values are probabilities, provide an opportunity to use alternative measures of predictive performance based on the concept of entropy [see the work of Theil (1971) for a discussion of entropy]. The actual measures used in this study are simple extensions of an earlier one developed by the authors (Betancourt and Clague 1978), and we now turn to a discussion of these measures.

The concept of entropy can be defined for any observation in a sample in terms of the predicted probabilities as

$$E_i = -\left(\sum_{j=1}^{k} \hat{P}_{ij} \log \hat{P}_{ij}\right) \tag{4.22}$$

where k is the number of alternatives. In the dichotomous case, equation (4.22) collapses to

$$E_i = -[\hat{P}_i \log \hat{P}_i + (1 - \hat{P}_i) \log(1 - \hat{P}_i)] \tag{4.23}$$

where, for example, $\hat{P}_i$ is the estimated probability that the ith firm will work shifts. Entropy, which may be interpreted as a measure of the amount of uncertainty associated with a distribution, takes on its maximum value at $\hat{P}_{ij} = 1/k$ for all j and its minimum value at $\hat{P}_{ij} = 1$ for any j. We seek a measure of the amount of information contained in the predicted probabilities $\hat{P}_{ij}$; this measure will be defined by

$$I_i = 1 - E_i/E_{max} \tag{4.24}$$

where E_{max} is the maximum amount of entropy associated with the distribution.[22] For instance, E_{max} occurs at $\hat{P}_{ij} = \frac{1}{2}$ in the dichotomous case and at $\hat{P}_{ij} = \frac{1}{3}$ for three possible outcomes. I_i thus takes on its maximum value at $\hat{P}_{ij} = 1$ for any j and its minimum value at $\hat{P}_{ij} = 1/k$ for all j. In the dichotomous case, for example, the minimum occurs at $\hat{P}_i = \frac{1}{2}$.

Entropy has the attractive property that the joint entropy of two

---

[22] Although entropy is unique up to a factor of proportionality [set at unity in (4.22)], the measure of information in (4.24) will not be affected by the proportionality factor.

independent random variables is the sum of their individual entropies. The amount of information I_i has the same property. Therefore, defining a correct prediction as $\hat{P}_{ij} > 1/k$ when alternative j is chosen and $\hat{P}_{ij} < 1/k$ when it is not chosen,[23] we can define the amount of information contained in a set of predictions as

$$\bar{I} = (I_1 - I_2)/N \tag{4.25}$$

where I_1 is the sum of information for all the correct predictions, I_2 is the sum of misinformation for all the incorrect predictions, and N is the number of observations. $\bar{I}$ ranges from -1 (all probabilities incorrectly predicted as 1 or 0) to $+1$ (all probabilities correctly predicted as 1 or 0).

Intuitively, this summary measure scores each prediction in a given set by giving it points not only in accordance with whether the prediction is right (positive points) or wrong (negative points) but also in a way that reflects the degree of certainty of the prediction. In other words, more credit (discredit) should be and is given to a correct (incorrect) prediction if a high probability underlies the prediction than if a low probability underlies the prediction. For example, in the dichotomous case, more credit (discredit) is given to a correct (incorrect) prediction that is close to 1 or 0 than to a prediction that is close to 0.5.

The measure of information in (4.25) was applied to the dichotomous case in our earlier work (Betancourt and Clague 1978), and it has also been applied to the trichotomous case by Abusada (1975). Nevertheless, this measure has a shortcoming[24] that becomes particularly acute when the distribution of the observations over the choices is very uneven. $\bar{I}$ can be calculated for the predictions that result from bringing no information from the theory to bear on the data. That is, the proportions of observations in a sample that choose an alternative can be used as an estimate of $\hat{P}_i$ for every observation in the sample. If the observations are fairly evenly divided, the amount of information from this set of predictions for the whole sample will be relatively low; however, if the observations are very unevenly divided, the amount of information contained in these "naive" predictions can be relatively high. Because the focus of interest by most investigators is on how the introduction of the theory enhances the ability to explain and predict a

---

[23] When there are several alternatives, this definition of a correct prediction may be too strict. In these cases, a more suitable definition is simply $\hat{P}_{ij} > 1/k$ when alternative j is chosen (Lago 1979).

[24] The need for some normalization was brought to our attention by Tom Louis of Boston University.

particular phenomenon, we define a new measure of predictive performance, I_A, that captures the absolute amount of additional information provided by the introduction of the theory into the statistical analysis (i.e., in addition to the information already contained in the sample proportions). Thus

$$I_A = \bar{I} - \bar{I}_M \tag{4.26}$$

where $\bar{I}_M$ is the amount of information provided by the sample proportions. Because this measure will now have a different range for different samples, it is also desirable to calculate a measure of the amount of information provided by the introduction of the theory relative to the maximum amount of information that the theory can capture in a given sample.[25] Hence,

$$I_R = I_A / I_{A\max} \tag{4.27}$$

where $I_{A\max}$ is simply $1 - \bar{I}_M$. Finally, because the range of I_R is the same as the range of R^2, a degrees-of-freedom correction can be defined as follows:

$$\bar{I}_R = I_R - [K/(N - K - 1)](1 - I_R) \tag{4.28}$$

where K is the number of independent variables.[26]

The three measures defined by (4.26) through (4.28) provide a basis for evaluating predictive performance in models with qualitative dependent variables, and they will be used throughout this text. It is worth noting that in our initial application of $\bar{I}$ to the dichotomous case, as mentioned earlier, we found the behavior of $\bar{I}$ to be very similar to that of R^2, defined for the nonlinear case as $1 - \Sigma(S_i - \hat{S}_i)^2 / \Sigma(S_i - \bar{S})^2$. A major advantage of all our four measures of information over R^2, however, is that they are equally applicable to situations with more than two alternatives; in contrast, R^2 cannot be defined for these cases. Moreover, we can use the relative measures of information, I_R and $\bar{I}_R$, to compare sets of predictions with different numbers of alternatives. This point will be illustrated in the next chapter.

---

[25] In principle, one can also define a measure relative to the minimum, but in practice a theory that predicts worse than the sample proportions is of little value.

[26] For the case involving multiple choices the definition will be

$$\bar{I}_R = I_R - [JK/(N - JK - J)](1 - I_R) \tag{4.29}$$

where J is the number of alternatives minus one.

CHAPTER 5

Econometric literature on capital utilization: an interpretation

At this point it is useful to review the current state of empirical knowledge about the long-run determinants of capital utilization in light of both the theory developed in Part I and the analysis in the preceding chapter. Given the long-run emphasis of our analysis, cross-sectional studies rather than time-series studies constitute the appropriate focus of our review.[1] Because a major aim of this survey is to provide a perspective from which to view the empirical measurements and the results presented in the next two chapters, we shall discuss these cross-sectional studies from the point of view of testing propositions about the long-run determinants of capital utilization. Therefore, comments on descriptive material in these studies and comments on solely descriptive studies will be postponed until Chapter 8.

All but two of the studies under consideration are based on data for individual plants. The two exceptions are the early empirical studies

---

[1] Normally one expects short-run factors to be far more prominent in determining the behavior of a given variable in a time series than in a cross section. In our analysis this possibility acquires added importance because in the long run the decision to utilize capital can be viewed as synonymous with the decision to work shifts. In the short run, however, the decision to utilize capital encompasses a broader range of decisions (e.g., overtime) than the decision to work shifts (e.g., Betancourt 1977, Sections I and III). As a matter of fact, Ramos (1975, pp. 17–20) presented direct evidence that many firms do not view shift-work as a desirable instrument for adjusting capital utilization in the short run; but the evidence is not completely one-sided, for Millan's results (1975, Chapter IV, Section 5) could be interpreted as providing indirect evidence for the opposite conclusion. In any event, the time-series studies directed at capital utilization are few and basically descriptive (e.g., Kim and Kwon 1977; Foss 1963). There is, of course, a substantial body of literature on the concept and measurement of capacity utilization, which includes short-run capital utilization among other things; but this literature is of limited interest for our present purposes because of its short-run macroeconomic orientation. A recent discussion of the literature on capacity utilization is available (Winston 1977a).

on the subject (Marris 1964, Chapter 7; Winston 1971). Because these two studies illustrate the general nature of the problems faced by subsequent investigators, they will be discussed first. The remaining studies can be placed into the following two categories: those based on the use of continuous measures of utilization and those based on discrete measures of utilization. Because the choice of different utilization measures leads to some important differences between the two sets of studies, the two categories will be considered separately. The studies based on discrete measures of utilization will be taken up last because they are more closely related to the work presented in the next two chapters.

5.1 Early empirical studies

Marris's statistical tests were based on the following two implications of the theory (as restated in our terminology): If we consider two firms similar in most respects except that one works shifts and the other does not, Proposition 1 of Chapter 1 implies that the observed basic ratio of profits to wages will be higher for the shift-working firm; that is, $rK^2/w_1L_1^2 - rK^1/w_1L^1 > 0$. Under similar conditions, both the analysis of a constant-β technology [Chapter 3, equation (3.9)] and the analysis of a semi-U technology (Chapter 3, Figure 3.1) imply that the observed relative-size ratio will be higher for the shift-working firm (i.e., $X^2/X^1 > 1$). Marris's results for a set of British establishments, drawn from the 1951 Census of Production, provide evidence in favor of (or, more accurately, fail to reject) these two implications of the theory, but they shed little light on the determinants of shift-work.

Marris also tested the hypothesis that size is a determinant of shift-work by regressing, across industrial classifications, the average shift-work ratio (the percentage of operatives working shifts) on the average net output per establishment. Although this regression may be partially justified on the basis of Proposition 6B of Chapter 3, the appropriate independent variable would have been the level of output under single-shift operation (X^1), not an average of X^1 and X^2. Because the shift-work ratio should be positively correlated with the profitability of shift-work, the positive and statistically significant correlation found by Marris can be explained by the reverse causation that runs from the shift-work ratio to X^2, for the analysis in Chapter 3 suggests that as the cost ratio decreases (the profitability of shift-work increases), X^2/X^1 increases [see Chapter 3, equation (3.9) or Figure 3.2A]. As will be seen later, a similar problem affects most of the subsequent literature surveyed here.

Winston (1971) was the first to test the theory using a continuous index of utilization in a regression context. He used mid-1960s data for 26 industrial sectors from what is now Pakistan. His best results ($R^2 \simeq 0.90$) were obtained using six variables to explain a utilization index based on two and one-half shifts as the standard; if operating rates were higher than this standard, the actual operating rates were used as the standard. The six variables were the following: lagged competing imports as a percentage of total supply; lagged exports; the ratio of real value of assets to value added unadjusted for capacity use; average annual production per firm in the industrial sector; the number of firms; the value added per unit of labor. The free-form specification of these independent variables was used. His size variable introduced the same reverse-causation mechanism that we found in Marris's work. This mechanism can be used to explain the positive and statistically significant coefficient (at the 1% level) in Winston's regression. In addition, his measure of capital intensity had a number of problems, some of which were pointed out by Acheson and Willmore (1974). From our perspective, Winston measured $P_K K^1/(w_1 L^1 + rK^1)$ in the single-shift sectors and $P_K K^2/[w_1(2 + \alpha)L_1^2 + rK^2]$ in the double-shift sectors; thus the unobservable-variable problem analyzed in Chapter 4 (Section 4.4) was also present (for simplicity, we are assuming r and w to be the same across sectors). Once more, a similar problem affects the subsequent literature.

To summarize, these two early empirical studies provided evidence of a positive association between ex-post size and ex-post capital intensity with shift-work, but in neither case can this evidence be given a causal interpretation. This evidence is consistent with the implications of the theory developed in earlier chapters, but no more can be said.[2]

5.2   Studies based on continuous dependent variables

The second set of studies is related mainly to a World Bank project on capital utilization.[3] The World Bank studies relied on surveys of

[2] This evidence is also consistent with other explanations of capital utilization. For instance, in their comment on Winston's study, Acheson and Willmore (1974) used organization theory to provide alternative explanations.

[3] Very recently (October 1979) a book-length manuscript that brings together the results of this project has become available (Bautista et al. 1979). The

plants in four countries:[4] Colombia (1970, 1973), Israel (1972), Malaysia (1972), and the Philippines (1972–3). Several indexes of utilization were constructed, three of which will be discussed here:[5] U_1 was the proportion of time a plant was operated during the year. If different sections were operated different proportions of time, the responses were weighted by the respondent's answer to the question of what proportion of the plant this section represented. The weights were interpreted by these authors as representing the proportion of capital used by a section of the plant. U_2 was U_1 adjusted by the proportion of a section or of the plant that was in operation during the year. This adjustment was interpreted as representing variations in speed. U_3 was a subjective measure obtained by asking the respondent at what percentage of full capacity he operated the previous year.

From our point of view, a question arises: Are the variations in these indices across firms or industries due to short-run factors or long-run factors?[6] Clearly, even in a cross section, variations in U_3 will be influenced mainly by short-run considerations. Variations in U_1 and U_2, on the other hand, will be considerably affected by variations in long-run factors that determine the firm's decision with respect to shift-work at the time of the investment decision. U_1 may be freer of short-run influences than U_2, but in practice the two measures are quite similar, as Table 5.1 shows. Moreover, the regression results are very similar for the two measures. To conclude, if long-run factors are important sources of variation in U_1, they should also be important sources of variation in U_2.

The regression results reported by Hughes et al. (1976, Table 8) are based on the following (free-form) regression equation:

$$\ln U_2 = \beta_0 + \beta_1 \ln X_1 + \beta_2 \ln X_2 + \beta_3 \ln X_3 + \beta_4 \ln X_4 \qquad (5.1)$$

where X_1 is the observed capital–labor ratio for the day shift, with capital valued at replacement cost; X_2 is the size of the plant measured in terms of total blue-collar workers; X_3 is the capital/wage-rental

empirical results presented in this manuscript are essentially the same as those in the earlier work cited here.

[4] The Colombian 1970 survey was not a part of the project, but it was analyzed by the same author, and it leads to similar results (Thoumi 1975, p. 93). A convenient summary of the main results from the other four surveys is available (Hughes et al. 1976).

[5] The description of these measures is based on the Colombian questionnaire (Thoumi 1975, Annex 3).

[6] A detailed discussion of this question is undertaken, for example, by Betancourt (1977, Section IV).

Table 5.1. *Average utilization indices in manufacturing*

	Colombia	Israel	Malaysia	Philippines
M_{U_1}	81.4	46.5	74.9	64.9
S_{U_1}	19.7	12.0	24.7	19.9
M_{U_2}	78.9	43.1	70.8	60.0
S_{U_2}	22.0	12.5	27.2	20.1

Note: M is mean utilization in manufacturing. S is standard deviation of utilization in manufacturing.
Source: Hughes et al. (1976, Table 1).

ratio measured in terms of the opportunity cost of owning $1 worth of capital to the firm and hourly daytime wages; X_4 is the night-shift premium as a percentage of the daily wage.

Six regressions were run: one using within-country averages for each four-digit ISIC category, with pooling of the four countries (244 observations); one using across-country industry averages for each four-digit ISIC category (74 observations); one regression for each country using the within-country industry averages for each four-digit ISIC category in that country. The results were quite similar for all six regressions: The coefficients of X_1 and X_2 had t ratios greater than 2.33 in every regression; the coefficients of X_3 and X_4 had t ratios less than 1.61 in every regression. The values of $\overline{R}^2$ ranged from 0.36 to 0.41 for the regressions based on within-country averages; $\overline{R}^2 = 0.54$ for the regression based on across-country averages. The range of β_1 was $0.18 < \beta_1 < 0.23$; the range of β_2 was $0.16 < \beta_2 < 0.28$.

Although they are based on better data, these results suffer from problems similar to those affecting the results of Winston and Marris. That is, the positive association between size (X_2), as measured in these studies, and utilization can be explained by the reverse causation running from utilization to size; and the positive association between capital intensity (X_1), as measured in these studies, and utilization can also be explained by the reverse causation running from utilization to observed capital intensity (Proposition 1). Again, we must conclude that the empirical evidence is broadly consistent with the implications of the theory of earlier chapters, but no causal interpretation is available.

The results on X_3, the factor-price ratio, can be interpreted as follows: The discussion of Proposition 4 in Chapter 2 shows that this variable has only an indirect effect on shift-work through its effect on the capital–labor ratio chosen under single-shift operation (hence on the capital share under single-shift operation); the sign of this indirect effect can be positive or negative depending on the elasticity of substitution. Variations in the observed capital–labor ratio across firms are due to both variations in technological characteristics (e.g., δ in the CES production function) and variations in the wage-rental ratios faced by the firms. Thus it is not surprising that inclusion of the capital/wage-rental ratio to explain utilization in a regression where the capital–labor ratio is also included leads to statistically insignificant results.[7] It is also interesting that when running the same regressions for a given industry (which can be broadly interpreted as keeping technology constant while allowing factor prices to vary across countries) these authors obtained statistically insignificant results at the 5% or 10% level in twenty-eight of thirty regressions for at least one of these two variables and in ten of thirty regressions for both of them (Hughes et al. 1976, Table 9). To conclude our discussion of the factor-price ratio, the theory suggests that the appropriate independent variable in all the regressions would be rK^1/w_1L^1, not the two ratios r/w_1 and K^1/L^1 introduced as separate independent variables.[8]

Finally, we come to the shift differential. The authors expected, as the theory predicts (Proposition 3), this variable to have a negative impact on utilization, but the data did not confirm their expectations. One explanation is discussed in detail in one of the individual studies (Morawetz 1975). That is, for plants working a single shift, the shift-differential question is hypothetical, and often it is necessary to impute a shift differential to the firm based on an estimate for the industrial branch; therefore, if workers in the shift-work industries bargain successfully over shift differentials, the negative correlation between the shift differentials and utilization will be weakened. Although this explanation is quite plausible, the discussion of Proposi-

---

[7] An insightful way of looking at this issue is provided by one of the systems defined in Chapter 4 (Section 4.4); that is, equations (4.7) and (4.16). If, for simplicity, we assume that there is no error in equation (4.16), then that equation implies that $k_i^0 = \delta_0[(w/r)_i^0]^\sigma$. In this situation the introduction of w/r or r/w as an additional independent variable in 4.7 would lead to severe multicollinearity. As a matter of fact, if the elasticity of substitution were unity and δ_0 were constant, the multicollinearity would be perfect, and the regression model would break down. Under general assumptions, the multicollinearity will still be present, and it can easily lead to statistically insignificant results for one or both of the independent variables.

[8] Of course, the authors did not use K^1/L^1 for the firms that work shifts; instead, they used the equivalent of K^2/L_1^2, which is what gave rise to the simultaneity problem discussed in connection with their capital-intensity variable X_1.

tion 3 in Chapter 1 suggests an additional explanation for this result. Namely, it was shown that the higher the shift differential, the higher the observed capital intensity for the firms that work shifts. Thus the observed capital-intensity variable should be positively correlated with the measured shift differential for those firms that work shifts, thereby weakening the estimated impact of the shift differential on utilization, or even changing its sign. As a matter of fact, in the latter situation it is quite possible that elimination of observed capital intensity from the regression will make the effect of the shift differential take on the right sign.[9]

To summarize, the simultaneous-equation bias introduced by the observed variables used for X_1 and X_2 prevents a causal interpretation of the results obtained for these two variables by Hughes et al. (1976); similarly, the simultaneous-equation bias with respect to capital intensity clouds the interpretation of the results for the shift differential; finally, the inappropriate specification of the wage-rental-ratio variable (i.e., separately from the capital-labor ratio) also clouds the interpretation of the results for this variable. Because the same or similar problems arise in the individual-plant data regressions reported in the country studies (Bautista et al. 1979, Chapters 5–8), we shall not discuss these studies in detail. Instead, we end our discussion of these studies by selectively reporting some additional findings that are of interest in the present context.

First, in two of these studies (Colombia, Israel) an attempt was made to explain the capacity index (U_3) using the same explanatory variables that were successful (in terms of adjusted $\bar{R}^2$) for U_1 and U_2. The $\bar{R}^2$ in the best regression fell from 0.5503 for U_2 (0.5734 for U_1) to 0.0361 for U_3 in Israel, and the comparable decrease for Colombia was from 0.3965 (0.3769) to 0.075. These results lend support to the long-run interpretation of the main sources of variations in the utilization indices U_1 and U_2.

Second, in some of the individual studies an intercept dummy was used for continuous-process industries (e.g., Morawetz 1975) or for seasonal variation in output (e.g., Lim 1976). As indicated in Chapter 1, Section 1.3, a continuous process increases the profitability of shift-work, which leads to higher observed capital intensity for continuous-process plants. Similarly, the arguments in Chapter 3, Section 3.4, show that if the elasticity of substitution is less than unity, seasonality increases the capital share under single-shift operation, an increase that in turn raises the profitability of shift-work and the observed capital intensity of the shift-work firm with seasonal varia-

[9] Visco (1978) developed the necessary and sufficient conditions for this result to occur in the general case.

tions in output. Therefore, inclusion of continuous-process plants or seasonal plants in a sample exacerbates the simultaneity problem with respect to observed capital intensity, unless slope (capital-intensity) dummies are included for the plants with continuous processes or seasonal fluctuations in output.

Finally in the country study for the Philippines (which became available to us as Chapter 8 of Bautista et al. 1979) there was explicit recognition of the dependence of factor proportions on the factor-price ratio. Nevertheless, the simultaneity problem between the choice of a level of utilization and the choice of factor proportions was not recognized. For instance, three regressions were reported in the Philippine chapter (8-10) that purported to explain the capital–labor ratio on the first shift in terms of the factor-price ratio unadjusted for utilization, value added unadjusted for utilization, and a continuous-process dummy. From the point of view of estimation, all three regressions suffer from the simultaneity problem discussed with respect to equation (4.19) in Chapter 4; that is, the factor-price ratio needs to be adjusted for the level of utilization. In addition, as stressed in our discussion in this chapter, high levels of utilization will lead to high levels of value added and high values of the capital–labor ratio. Hence, the positive and significant coefficients reported in these three regressions for the value-added term are quite likely to be biased.

To conclude this section, mention must be made of Lecraw's study (1978), which is based on data from 200 firms in Thailand. He used two continuous measures of utilization as dependent variables. Conceptually, these measures corresponded to the time- and intensity-adjusted measure (U_2) of the World Bank studies. One of the measures was a desired level of utilization at the time of the investment (D), which was reported by the interviewer at the time of the interview; the other was a profit-maximizing level of utilization (P), which was calculated by Lecraw on the basis of ex-ante data gathered from the interviews. His independent variables fell into two categories: the economic ones, which included the four described in this section for the World Bank studies plus the time at which the firm made its investment, scaled from 1 (1962) to 13 (1974); the noneconomic ones, which included projected profits from single-shift operation expressed as a rate of return on equity, the number of firms in the four-digit industry, the projected growth rate of sales in percentage per year, and three categorical or dummy variables to capture the perceived risk of multishift operation (high–low), the type of ownership (other LDCs, Thai and other foreign), and the type of management (owner-nonowner). Finally, Lecraw also included firms with continuous processes and seasonal fluctuations in output as part of his sample.

Lecraw's empirical findings with respect to the economic variables are very similar to the ones noted here for the World Bank studies. Moreover, our interpretation of these studies is equally applicable to Lecraw's study. From this perspective, his work can be said simply to provide additional evidence for the existence of a positive association between observed capital intensity and measures of utilization, as well as between observed size and measures of utilization. The only new result in this regard is the finding of a positive association between utilization and the time of investment. This finding suggests, according to Lecraw, that new technologies require higher levels of utilization than old technologies.

What distinguishes Lecraw's work is his empirical investigation of the role of non-profit-maximizing managerial behavior in determining capital idleness. He conducted several experiments based on his calculation of the profit-maximizing level of utilization (P). One implication of our research for this calculation is that the profit-maximizing level of utilization for every firm will depend on the assumptions one makes about the degree of economies of scale and the possibilities of ex-ante substitution. Yet Lecraw made no explicit assumptions about either one of these characteristics of the production function. Therefore, although we find these experiments interesting, we are skeptical of any results based on the calculated dependent variable. On the other hand, Lecraw also conducted a number of experiments based on the desired level of utilization, and the results from these experiments raise some novel issues.

The sample of firms was split into two groups: those with low profits (i.e., those with less than a 25% ratio of projected profits from one-shift operation to equity); those with high profits (i.e., those with more than a 25% rate of return). For each sample a multiple regression was run to explain the level of desired utilization. Both the economic variables and the noneconomic variables were used as independent variables in terms of what we have labeled a free-form specification. The economic variables seemed to have a greater impact on utilization than the noneconomic variables in the low-profits group. Lecraw's interpretation of these results stems from the argument that if a firm can earn high profits on the basis of single-shift operation, high profits allow managers to engage in a wide variety of non-profit-maximizing activities that will affect the level of utilization chosen. Nevertheless, other interpretations can be put forth. For instance, some variables classified as noneconomic can easily be given economic interpretations. One of these noneconomic variables is the number of firms in an industry, and it can be argued that this variable is directly related to (and thus is a proxy for) the elasticity of demand in the industry. The profit-maximizing theory of Chapter 3 suggests that the higher the elasticity of demand in the industry, the higher the profits from high utilization. Therefore, the positive and statistically significant association that Lecraw found between this "noneconomic" variable and the desired level of utilization is quite consistent with profit maximization. Be that as it may, it is clear that the implications of non-profit-maximizing behavior by the firm for capital utilization could provide a fruitful area for further research.

5.3 Studies based on discrete dependent variables

We conclude this chapter with a review of the three studies based on discrete dependent variables.[10] It is convenient to start with the empirical tests for seventy-three plants in Kenya conducted by Baily (1976). A unique characteristic of her study is that she obtained data at the process level rather than at the plant level (see Chapter 1, Section 1.3, for a discussion of the multiprocess case). Grouping the processes according to the number of shifts, she calculated for each shift the mean values of $P_K K^1/w_1 L^1$, $P_K K^2/w_1 L_1^2$, and $P_K K^3/w_1 L_1^3$ (in our notation) and tested the differences in the means of the three groups. Again, this test simply confirms the basic implication of the theory, but a causal interpretation is not warranted. In all fairness to Baily it must be added that she related these observed capital-intensity measures to critical ratios (E_{21} and E_{32}) that depended on differential shift costs and that she hypothesized were not systematically related to the capital intensity of the process. But her hypothesis is not reasonable because at least one of the main factors in these critical ratios, the shift differentials a and b, will be systematically related to observed capital intensity for the firms that work shifts. The discussion of Proposition 3 in Chapter 1, already mentioned in the previous section, shows that there is a positive correlation. Moreover, whereas for this very reason she excluded continuous processes from the sample, she did not exclude firms with known seasonal fluctuations. Her second test was affected by the same basic problem: her assumption that the stochastic components in the measures of observed capital intensity and the critical ratios were not related is not valid, for the same reasons as before.

The second study using a discrete measure of utilization was based on a survey of manufacturing firms in Peru (Abusada 1975). Abusada's results are of interest for two reasons: They have a bearing

[10] In the 1978 revision of his 1975 study, Thoumi defined a discrete dependent variable to which he applied logit analysis. His results are similar to the ones obtained with the continuous dependent variable. Thus we shall not explicitly review his results here.

on the same issues emphasized thus far in this chapter, and they have a bearing on the specification of the dependent variable and the measures of predictive performance discussed in Sections 4.2 and 4.6, respectively, in Chapter 4. To preserve continuity, we take up first the issues relating to the measurement of the independent variables. Abusada used a free-form specification of the independent variables. He included the following variables: observed capital intensity, its square, size, a continuous-process dummy, and five other variables, plus fifteen industry dummies. The use of observed capital intensity and a continuous-process dummy led to the same simultaneity problems already discussed, once more preventing a causal interpretation of the results. In order to correct the reverse-causation problem with respect to size, Abusada tried to measure size on the first shift for the shift-working firms (i.e., X_1^2 and X_1^3). This was a step in the right direction, but it was not likely to remove the reverse-causation problem in Abusada's work because of the crude nature of his correction.[11] In any case, Abusada's measures of size and capital intensity generated coefficients with the "right" sign and "statistically significant" t ratios in most specifications.

At this point we pause to provide a broader interpretation of the role of size in empirical work. Size is introduced as a causal factor to explain utilization for two entirely different reasons: as a proxy for the degree of economies of scale at the process level and as a proxy for managerial problems in organizing shift-work. The semi-U technology assumption, which leads to proposition 6B of Chapter 3, provides a rationale for introducing size for the first reason; but the constant-β technology assumption (Chapter 3, Section 3.2) allows us to show that the degree of economies of scale can have an impact on shift-work even when size does not belong in a regression as a causal factor. In either case, however, higher utilization implies larger size in terms of the total level of output produced, and the reverse-causation problem is present. Thus, if one is interested solely in the second reason for introducing size as a causal factor, as was Abusada, it is far better to seek a proxy other than size for the organizational problems associated with shift-work. For instance, Thoumi successfully used a dummy variable for corporate–noncorporate ownership[12] that presumably

[11] He divided value added by 1.6 for the double-shift firms and by 2.2 for the triple-shift firms. These two numbers came from the average numbers of production workers in the second shift and the combined second and third shifts, respectively, relative to the single shift in the UNIDO sample of factories in five countries.

[12] This result was first obtained by Thoumi for the 1970 Colombian sample (Thoumi 1975, p. 93)

Table 5.2. *Predictive measures for Abusada's logits*

Statistical model	$\bar{I}$	I_A	I_R	$\bar{I}_R$
Trinomial	0.321	0.282	0.293	0.261
Two and three the same	0.323	0.311	0.314	0.299
Two eliminated	0.438	0.354	0.386	0.370

captured an important aspect of this phenomenon, and the same dummy was useful in World Bank studies for Colombia, the Philippines, and Malaysia, though not for Israel (Hughes et al. 1976, p. 19).

A second aspect of Abusada's work that is of interest for our purposes concerns the estimation techniques that Abusada applied to his data. He first fitted a trinomial logit model to the data. Because his results for one of the two trinomial equations were not satisfactory, he fitted two binomial logits to the data; in one of them he assigned zeros to the observations that chose either two or three shifts; in the other one he dropped the two-shift observations from the sample. The same independent variables were used in all three cases. The discussion in Section 4.2 in the previous chapter provides an interpretation of these three estimation procedures. It also suggests that the model that treats two shifts and three shifts as the same should predict better than the trinomial because the restriction it imposes on the data is preferable to the one imposed by the trinomial through the axiom of independence of irrelevant alternatives.

Abusada used the measure of information developed in our earlier work ($\bar{I}$), but as noted in Section 4.6, this measure is not satisfactory for comparing models with different alternatives or with widely different distributions of observations among the alternatives. It is easy, however, to use the information in Abusada's paper to calculate the measures developed in the preceding chapter. The results are presented in Table 5.2. With all four measures the trinomial logit exhibits the worst performance. But it becomes far more noticeable with respect to treating two shifts and three shifts as the same in terms of the three measures introduced in Chapter 4. The drop in performance for all three models in going from $\bar{I}$ to I_A stems from subtracting the information contained in the sample proportions; the increase in going from I_A to I_R stems from dividing by the maximum amount of information that the independent variables could have explained; the drop in going from I_R to $\bar{I}_R$ stems from correcting for degrees of freedom, which affects trinomial logit the most. With all four measures the predictive performance is superior for the binomial model that drops the two-shift observations than for the one that treats them as the same, and to this topic we shall return when discussing our own results in Chapter 7.

The last of the studies based on a discrete dependent variable is our own earlier empirical work (Betancourt and Clague 1978). We fitted two theoretical models to the plant data for each of four countries (France, India, Israel, and Japan); one of the models was based on the constant-β technology, the other on the semi-U technology. Each model was estimated using a restricted-form specification and a free-form specification for the independent variables. Two shifts and three shifts were treated as the same by assigning a value of unity to the dependent variable in both cases. Both OLS and binomial logit analysis were used as estimation techniques.

Let us consider first the size variable. Conceptually we relied on the use of size in the first shift, X_1^2 or X_1^3, as a proxy for the level of output the factory would have produced if built for single-shift operation, X^1. Because our rationale for including size was economies of scale at the process level, in the actual measurement of size we attempted to capture the true variable (X^1) through a number of adjustments that we believed would eliminate the reverse-causation problem, at least in the restricted-form specification. The details of these adjustments are discussed in the next chapter (Section 6.4); here we merely report and interpret the results. For the two developed countries (France, Japan) we cannot reject the hypothesis that our measure of size is not associated with shift-work.[13] This result holds for both the restricted-form specification and the free-form specification of the independent variables. For the two less-developed countries (India, Israel), on the other hand, we reject the hypothesis that the same measure of size is not associated with shift-work. This finding also holds true for both the restricted-form specification and the free-form specification of the independent variables and with both estimation techniques. Nevertheless, the association between size and shift-work is considerably stronger with the free-form specification in Israel.

What is our interpretation of these results? First, the constant-β technology model of Chapter 3 is the one applicable to the developed countries, since size does not play a causal role in these countries. Second, our adjustments to the size variable successfully eliminate the reverse-causation problem. Finally, the semi-U technology model of Chapter 3 is the one relevant for the less-developed countries. But in Israel there are other factors correlated with our measure of size that

---

[13] Incidentally, if we had not corrected our measure of size, we would have found an association between size and shift-work.

are responsible for the considerably stronger association between size and utilization in the free-form specification. These factors are eliminated in the restricted-form specification of the independent variables. Of course, there may be other interpretations, but a measured evaluation of our interpretation as well as any alternatives must be based on the information provided by the detailed discussion of our procedure in the next chapter. What should be clear at this point is that our results provide empirical evidence that raises further questions (besides those that derive from the theoretical reasoning) about interpreting the association between size and shift-work found in the other studies reviewed here as implying a causal relationship. We suspect that in all cases the causal relationship is considerably weaker than is implied by the results of these studies, and we also suspect that in several instances there is no causal relationship.

Let us now consider the capital-intensity variable. We did exclude continuous-process industries and plants with known seasonal fluctuations from our samples. In the free-form specification, however, we used the observed capital-to-wages ratio on the first shift; thus our results suffer from the same simultaneity problem as the other studies. In the restricted-form specification, on the other hand, we assumed for all plants in a country the same value of the elasticity of substitution, and we appropriately corrected the observed capital intensity for the shift-working firms. Thus we estimated the true variable, capital intensity under single-shift operation. Nevertheless, we chose to present only the results for the restricted-form specification under the assumption of a Leontief production function because "the CES Cost Ratio was empirically inferior to the Leontief one in every comparison" (Betancourt and Clague 1978, p. 212, footnote 2). The analysis in Section 4.4 shows that if the production function is not Leontief and the bias is positive, one should expect precisely this result! Our results for the Leontief cost ratio suffer from the same simultaneity bias as all other studies, except when the ex-ante production function is Leontief,[14] an assumption that is hard to swallow.

By way of conclusion, we note that the identification of the two reverse-causation problems stressed in this chapter was greatly facilitated by recent developments in both the theory of capital utilization and econometric methodology. Thus it is easy to understand why they have gone largely unnoticed in the literature. Because of the situation described here, a substantial part of the next chapter is devoted to the development of empirical measures that are free from these two problems.

---

[14] Of course, in this case there is no simultaneity bias due to using observed capital intensity in any of the other studies reviewed here.

CHAPTER 6

Empirical implementation

In this chapter we take the final step in bridging the gap between the theory and the data. Thus the first subject for discussion will be the nature of the primary data base used in the study and the data-cleaning process (Section 6.1). The subsequent four sections are devoted to discussion of the measurement of each of the four variables identified in earlier chapters as being major determinants of the shift-work decision: capital intensity (Section 6.2), the elasticity of substitution (Section 6.3), the degree of economies of scale (Section 6.4), and the shift differential (Section 6.5). The empirical specifications of the working-capital hypotheses introduced in Chapter 2, Section 2.4, constitute the subject of Section 6.6. In the last section we put together the discussion of the previous ones, and we conclude by setting out in tabular form the models to be implemented empirically with our data.

Before addressing the topics just outlined, we should indicate some general characteristics of the subsequent sections. One way of viewing the discussion to be undertaken here is simply as the specification of the independent variables in terms of the actual data available in our samples. Thus, the distinction between the restricted-form specification and the free-form specification of the independent variables, introduced in Chapter 4, plays an important role in the subsequent arguments. With respect to the restricted-form specification, one of the main results of our efforts in this chapter is a set of empirical constructs that correspond to the cost ratios of Part I of this book. Also, as noted at the end of Chapter 5, our efforts in this chapter are directed toward elimination of the unobservable-variable, or reverse-causation problem, with respect to capital intensity and the level of output. Finally, it is worth noting that one set of results presented in this chapter is of interest for other problems besides the analysis of shift-work or capital utilization. Namely, we obtain estimates of the elasticity of substitution using the appropriate specification of the estimation problem in the presence of shift-work; these estimates are substantially higher in most industries than the ones obtained by ignoring the presence of shift-work (Section 6.3, Table 6.1). The

general reader who is not interested in the estimation of the elasticity
of substitution or the details of our empirical procedures may want to
move on to Section 6.7, where we summarize the models to be
confronted with the data in the next chapter.

6.1   The data base

The primary data source for this study is a survey of industrial
establishments carried out and published by UNIDO (1967-8). Data
were collected for several countries. In particular, we concentrate our
efforts on the data published in the first two volumes, which cover five
countries (France, India, Israel, Japan, and Yugoslavia).[1] These first
two volumes provide us with a most welcome variety of countries: two
developed (France and Japan) and two less developed (India and
Israel).

An exact description of the criteria for selecting establishments and
industries is available in the original publication (pp. 5-6). Nonetheless, it is worth noting at this point a characteristic of the available data
that is directly relevant to our study. That is, the sample selection was
done by local experts on the basis of whether or not the establishment
and industry met desirable criteria for inclusion in a reference work on
which to base industrial programming. Thus the selection criteria
lead, in our opinion, to an overrepresentation of large and well-run
factories; therefore, the sample tends to overstate the prevalence of
shift-work. Some empirical evidence for this statement is available in
the case of France. For example, the average number of production
workers divided by the number of production workers on the first shift
is estimated by Denison (1967, p. 173) as 1.11. The corresponding
figure in our French sample is 1.23. Hence, the sample in each country
should not be viewed as representative of the whole industrial sector
for that country.

There is a great wealth of material available in this body of data.
Complete documentation is available in the introductory notes to the
published volumes, but it is desirable to describe here the information
available that is used directly in this study. The published information

[1] The data for Yugoslavia will not be analyzed in this book for two reasons.
First, the data require a somewhat different treatment than the data for the
other four countries. Second, and more important, the models that explain
shift-work in a labor-managed system are somewhat different from the ones
used for the capitalist enterprise (see the concluding remarks to Chapter 3
for a discussion of this point and the pertinent references).

includes the number of production workers on each shift, total wages paid to production workers, and the book value of machinery and of buildings. The industrial classification at one further level of disaggregation than the ISIC three-digit classification is provided for each establishment (forty-eight different industries are covered). Information on value added and seasonal employment is also furnished for every establishment, as well as the desired level of inventories for finished goods and work in process. This information constitutes the input from the primary data base into the empirical analysis.[2]

As is usual with most econometric work, the data were not collected primarily for empirical analysis of the theoretical issue of interest. Nevertheless, sufficient information on the variables of interest is available to permit the development of empirical constructs that correspond to some of the theoretical determinants of the decision to work shifts, particularly if one is willing to supplement the primary data base with secondary sources. It should also be noted that in some respects the data are quite good. For example, an aspect of our data-cleaning procedure was to check the reliability of the data by using them to estimate five typical regressions in the analysis of the elasticity of substitution. In four of them, the logarithm of the capital–labor ratio variously defined was regressed on the logarithm of the wage–rental ratio variously defined; in the other regression, the traditional approach of regressing the logarithm of value added per worker on the wage rate was employed. The results are comparable to others available in the literature that used different data but the same definitions of the variables (Grieves 1973).

The actual sample size for each country used in this study differs from the published sample size for various reasons. Some plants, such as sugar and ice cream factories, exhibit pronounced seasonality in

---

[2] The UNIDO data contain information on total electricity use and on the nominal capacity of electric motors and furnaces. Hence, in principle one could construct a survey measure of utilization based on electricity consumption. However, such a measure is not likely to be very reliable for two reasons. First, the capacity of electric motors installed as obtained from survey data will be influenced by the subjective perceptions of the respondents as well as by the theoretical problems in defining the concept of installed capacity of electric motors (Morawetz 1976). Second, to construct the numerator of the utilization index properly, one needs the amount of electricity consumed by electric motors, not the total amount of electricity consumption, which is the information usually available. Incidentally, the overlooking of this distinction renders invalid the consistency checks reported by Morawetz (1976, footnote 8).

their operation. As mentioned in the last section of the previous chapter, seasonality affects observed capital intensity, and as discussed in Chapter 3, it also affects capital intensity under single-shift operation. Hence, these plants were excluded from the samples. In other cases it was not possible to match the UNIDO classification with the U.S. industrial classification; this problem prevented the construction of several variables used in the analysis (e.g., rates of return and the degree of economies of scale). In three cases the peculiarity of the factories' data led to their elimination. These considerations reduced the initial samples for the four countries from 316 establishments to 284.

Another issue in the cleaning up of the data was the treatment of all those firms belonging to the continuous-process industries. Although economies of prime costs constitute one of the main factors (if not the main factor) inducing shift-work in certain industries, the cost savings from continuous operation are very difficult to measure. Also, as mentioned in Chapter 5, including these industries in the samples accentuates the simultaneity or unobservable-variable problem with respect to capital intensity. These two considerations led us to exclude such industries from the samples. Without detailed knowledge of the production process of each industry, however, the researcher is not always able to determine in which industries economies of prime costs are present. Fortunately, the Norwegian Central Bureau of Statistics (1960) provides, in connection with the Norwegian labor legislation, a classification of industries according to types of shift-work: completely continuous shift-work, twenty-four-hour continuous shift-work (in which the factory shuts down for Sundays and holidays), and two-shift operation. An industry in which 29% or more of the workers were engaged in completely continuous shift-work was classified as a fully continuous-process industry. This initial classification was then supplemented by, and checked against, the available industry studies (Marris 1964, Chapter 9) in deciding which establishments to eliminate from the samples.[3] With this procedure the remaining 284 plants for the four countries were reduced to 231 plants, which is the sample size actually used in our earlier work (Betancourt and Clague 1978).

The sample of 231 plants provided the point of departure for the empirical analysis in this study. Empirical implementation of the working-capital hypotheses, however, required the elimination of five

[3] The following industries were classified as fully continuous (UNIDO classification): 250, 251, 271, 311, 332, 339 part (asbestos cement), 342 part (aluminum smelting), 300.

additional plants that did not have information on the inventory variables. Thus the main results presented in Chapter 7 are based on a total of 226 plants, which are distributed as follows: 75, India; 52, Japan; 50, France; 49, Israel.

6.2   Capital intensity

Capital intensity has been identified in the theoretical chapters as one of the major determinants of shift-work (see Proposition 4). In the restricted-form specification the appropriate measure of capital intensity is the capital share under single-shift operation, θ; in the free-form specification there is some flexibility with respect to the measure of capital intensity that one uses in the empirical analysis. We shall use the capital–labor ratio under single-shift operation, or more precisely $P_K K^1 / L^1$. Two different types of measurement problems arise with respect to capital intensity, and we shall consider each of them separately.

The first problem to be discussed affects only the capital share. This share is defined as follows: $\theta = rK^1/(rK^1 + w_1 L^1)$. It is more convenient, however, to work in terms of the ratio of the capital share to the labor share; that is,

$$\frac{\theta}{1 - \theta} = \frac{rK^1}{w_1 L^1} = \frac{(i + d)P_K K^1}{w_1 L^1} \tag{6.1}$$

The cost of owning a unit of the capital stock for a year, r, contains two terms not available in the data; that is, the annual rate of return (i) and the rate of depreciation (d). Our procedure was to approximate i by the U.S. pre-tax cost of capital in the corresponding two-digit U.S. industrial classification. In order to do so, we adjusted the after-tax rates of return (i') from Collins and Preston (1968) by the U.S. corporate tax rate, and to this estimate of i we added the annual depreciation (d) calculated from

$$d = 1/\sum_{s=1}^{T}(1 + i')^{T-s} \tag{6.2}$$

where T is the life of the asset, which was taken to be forty-five years for buildings and various periods for machinery following the guidelines of the U.S. Treasury (1964).[4] Thus, for factories working only

---

[4] The calculated profit rates are based on the "one-hoss-shay" assumption and on the assumption that the tax-allowable depreciation corresponds to the one calculated by the formula. Because depreciation allowances are in reality more generous, our procedure tends to underestimate on this

one shift, the ratio in (6.1) can be easily calculated using the published information on the book value of machinery and buildings and the total wages paid to production workers, together with our estimates of $i + d$. Of course, the measure of capital intensity in the free-form specification $(P_K K^1/L^1)$ can also be easily calculated for the single-shift firms from the published information on the book value of buildings and machinery and the number of production workers on the first shift.

The second measurement problem affects both measures of capital intensity; namely, for the firms that work two or more shifts we observe actual capital intensity $(P_K K^2/L^2_1)$ rather than what capital intensity would have been under single-shift operation $(P_K K^1/L^1)$. As indicated in Chapter 4, if we know the values of the elasticity of substitution and the shift differential, we can estimate for both specifications of the independent variables the theoretically appropriate concept by using relation (4.4) for the double-shift firms and a similar relation for the triple-shift firms. Consequently, we followed precisely this procedure, but an additional adjustment was necessary to take account of multiple processes.

If all factories were single-process factories, or if our data were available at the process level, no further adjustment would be necessary. Nevertheless, factories do consist of more than one process, and our data are available at the plant level. As the theoretical discussion in Chapter 1 reveals, it can be economically attractive to operate some processes under shift-work and other processes under single-shift operation. Moreover, the empirical evidence suggests that this practice is not uncommon (Baily 1974, p. 93). Therefore, the adjustment embodied in (4.4) is appropriate only for that portion of the capital stock that is employed under shift-work. Although our data do not contain this information directly, there is sufficient information to provide a fairly accurate estimate of this proportion. For instance, for those firms that work two shifts, the fraction of the capital stock employed on the second shift was estimated as follows:

$$\frac{K^2_2}{K^2_1} = \frac{L^2_2}{L^2_1} + \frac{L^2_2}{L^2_1}\left(1 - \frac{L^2_2}{L^2_1}\right) \tag{6.3}$$

account, but since physical depreciation is faster than the one-hoss-shay assumption implies, our procedure tends to overestimate on this account. It is interesting that the profit rates calculated under our assumptions are almost identical with those derived under the "two-bucket" method employed in the Maryland inter-industry forecasting model (Reimboldt and Almon 1972).

Equation (6.3) implies that the fraction of the capital stock employed on the second shift depends positively on the ratio between direct production workers in the second shift and direct production workers in the first shift (L_2^2/L_1^2), that it is always greater than this ratio,[5] and that it will never exceed unity. The adjustment in (4.4) was applied only to this fraction of the capital stock. A similar adjustment was made for the third shift.

With these adjustments, we now have empirical constructs for capital intensity that correspond to the theoretically appropriate concepts under both the restricted-form specification and the free-form specification of the independent variables. However, in order to carry out these adjustments we need to estimate the elasticity of substitution, and to this task we now turn.

6.3   Elasticity of substitution

In order to place the arguments that follow in their proper perspective, we must stress at the outset the precise nature of the concept we are interested in and the reasons why we are interested in this concept at this stage. Throughout this book we have been focusing on the ex-ante elasticity of substitution between factor services. One reason for our current interest in this concept is that we need to measure capital intensity under single-shift operation, as mentioned in the previous section. But this ex-ante elasticity of substitution between factor services is also one of the determinants of capital utilization in its own right (Proposition 5). Thus, we have another powerful reason for measuring this concept.[6] Finally, we are interested in measuring this concept at the plant level, which is the one that corresponds to the availability of our data.

It would be extremely desirable to have a reliable set of estimates of σ for each of our factories (or, at least, each of our industries) available in the literature. Unfortunately, despite the substantial amount of research on the topic in the last fifteen years or so, there remains a great deal of uncertainty not only about the values of σ in particular industries but also about the typical or average value of σ in manufac-

[5] Incidentally, this property is desirable because the theory suggests that the more-capital-intensive processes are the ones that will be used in the second shift.

[6] We are also interested in this concept because of the role it plays in determining the impact of shift-work on employment and capital requirements, but this topic will be discussed in Chapter 9.

turing generally. As a matter of fact, our discussion in Section 4.4 added yet another reason for questioning the validity of existing estimates (namely, their failure to incorporate the phenomenon of shift-work). Thus we shall construct our own estimates. Although we think these estimates are more reliable than the existing ones, it would be foolish to claim that they are devoid of problems. Therefore, before reviewing briefly the literature to justify our claim, we shall indicate at this point an important consequence for our purposes of the likely biases in our estimates of the ex-ante elasticity of substitution.

As we shall argue shortly, if our estimates of σ are biased, they will tend to be biased upward. Therefore it is desirable to note an immediate consequence of an upward bias in the estimate of σ on our estimation of the probability of shift-work. In the free-form specification there will be a definite effect on the capital–labor ratio used as an independent variable. The higher is σ, the lower will be the estimated value of the capital–labor ratio under single-shift operation for shift-work firms. That is, the adjustment in (4.4) will be larger. Because the adjustment is not applied to single-shift firms, this upward bias in σ tends to reduce the strength of any positive correlation between the capital-intensity variable and shift-work. In the restricted-form specification there will be a similar effect through the capital share. That is, the estimated capital share under single-shift operation will be smaller the larger is σ, a fact that increases the value of the cost ratio for shift-working firms. Thus an upward bias in σ will weaken any negative correlation between the cost ratio and shift-work. To put it differently, one consequence of an upward bias in σ is to bias our results against establishing a relationship between shift-work and the conceptually appropriate measures of capital intensity.

6.3.1 Brief review of the literature

The econometric estimates of σ have come under heavy criticism recently, but there is no need to review these criticisms in detail here.[7] The following general points are sufficient to place our procedure in the literature. Time-series estimates would seem to be especially dubious because of the difficulties in separating technical progress from capital–labor substitution and in distinguishing between long-run and short-run adjustments. In any event, cross-sectional estimates

---

[7] Several detailed reviews of the problems in estimating σ and related issues are available (e.g., O'Herlihy 1972; Acharya 1974; Roemer 1975; Gaude 1975; Morawetz 1976; White 1978).

are the ones appropriate for our purposes, given the concept we are trying to measure. The great bulk of the cross-sectional estimates have relied on a relationship between value added per man and the wage rate. For instance, this relationship can be expressed in our notation as follows:[8]

$$\log(X^1/L^1) = \beta_0 + \beta_1 \log X^1 + \beta_2 \log(N_l w_1/P^1) + u_l \tag{6.4}$$

where $\beta_2 = \sigma$ and $N_l = (1 + n_l^{-1})/(1 + n_P^{-1})$, with n_l being the elasticity of labor supply and n_P being the elasticity of demand for the product. The criticisms of the cross-sectional econometric estimates of σ have been almost exclusively directed against the estimates obtained from the formulation in (6.4) or some of its variants. One major criticism of this formulation is that it ignores the simultaneous-equation character of input demand functions and production functions (Desai 1977, pp. 128–31). Yet there is an alternative formulation, suitable for implementation with cross-sectional data, that avoids this problem. It relies on a relationship between the capital–labor ratio and the wage-rental ratio.[9] Because this is the formulation we shall use, as indicated in Chapter 4, our detailed remarks will focus exclusively on this approach.

An equation analogous to (6.4), but in terms of the capital input, also follows from the CES production function; that is,

$$\log(X^1/K^1) = \beta_0' + \beta_1 \log X^1 + \beta_2 \log(N_k r/P^1) + u_k \tag{6.5}$$

where $N_k = (1 + n_k^{-1})/(1 + n_P^{-1})$ and n_k is the elasticity of supply of capital. By subtracting (6.5) from (6.4) and collecting terms, we obtain

$$\log\left(\frac{K^1}{L^1}\right) = (\beta_0 - \beta_0') + \beta_2 \log\left(\frac{N_l}{N_k}\frac{w_1}{r}\right) + u_l - u_k \tag{6.6}$$

which is a slight generalization of equation (4.13). A comparison of (6.6) with either (6.5) or (6.4) shows that (6.6) eliminates the simultaneity problem with respect to the level of output, which affects both (6.4) and (6.5).[10] Although this feature is very attractive, of course, a balanced evaluation of the approach in (6.6) requires a discussion of the data and econometric problems that may affect its use.

---

[8] Our presentation follows that of Gaude (1975, p. 39).

[9] For an early statement of the advantages of this formulation, see the work of Moroney (1970).

[10] To keep matters simple, we have been ignoring the additional problems in estimating (6.4) introduced by the existence of shift-work. Briefly put, the existence of shift-work accentuates the simultaneity problem.

An econometric problem arises in both (6.6) and (6.4), albeit in somewhat different forms. This problem is introduced by the lack of perfect competition in factor markets [the lack of perfect competition in product markets affects (6.4) but not (6.6)]; that is, by the term $N_l/N_k = (1 + n_l^{-1})/(1 + n_k^{-1})$ in (6.6). If there is perfect competition in both factor markets, $N_l/N_k = 1$, and (6.6) collapses to (4.13). In the absence of perfect competition, there can be a bias in estimating (4.13) when (6.6) is applicable. If the elasticity of supply in both factor markets is constant across firms, the estimates of the slope, $(\beta_2 = \sigma)$ in (4.13), will not be biased. If these elasticities vary across firms, there will be a bias that will be positive if the correlation between N_l/N_k and the wage-rental ratios is positive. In regressions across firms within the same industry, but in different countries, which are the ones relevant to our study, the variations in both ratios will tend to be determined by variations in the wage rate and in the elasticity of supply of labor across countries. If in low-wage countries the elasticity of labor supply is high, the bias will tend to be positive.

Perhaps the main reason for the infrequency with which this approach has been employed in the literature is that data problems arise with respect to both the value of the capital stock and the rate of return to capital. In our case we are fortunate to have good data on the value of the capital stock at the plant level. Although rate-of-return data at the plant level are simply not available, the lack of these data is far less serious when observations are available for firms in the same industry but in countries with widely different wage rates, as is the case in our samples. As indicated earlier, wage-rate variations will dominate the variations in the factor-price ratios.

There remains the problem of the quality of labor. In the capital-labor approach, equation (6.6) or (4.13), as in the labor-productivity approach, equation (6.4), variations in labor quality that are correlated with wage rates tend to bias the estimated σ values toward unity (Moroney 1970, pp. 292–3). It seems reasonable to say, however, that the effect of labor quality on the capital–labor ratio approach is likely to be substantially less important than its effect on the labor-productivity approach, at least in our context. Labor quality biases our estimates only to the extent that workers in low-wage countries are assigned fewer machines because they cannot handle as many machines as the workers in high-wage countries.

The considerations elaborated in the preceding three paragraphs constitute the main sources of difficulties in the application of the capital–labor ratio approach to the estimation of σ in the absence of shift-work. As argued in Chapter 4, Section 4.4, the existence of shift-work will introduce a bias in the estimates of σ obtained by this approach [as in equation (4.19), for example], unless the dependent and independent variables are measured consistently with equation (4.16), in which case (4.16) and (4.13) will be equivalent. As far as we know, none of the studies available in the literature has measured the relevant variables consistently with (4.16).

To illustrate the problem, we consider four fairly different studies that relied on the capital–labor ratio approach. Arrow et al. (1961) reported a study actually undertaken by Bickel involving U.S. and Japanese two-digit or three-digit manufacturing sectors; σ was estimated from the two points for the United States and Japan using the relation

$$\frac{(K/L)_{\text{U.S.}}}{(K/L)_J} = \left[\frac{(w/r)_{\text{U.S.}}}{(w/r)_J}\right]^{\sigma} \qquad (6.7)$$

Neither the capital–labor ratio nor the wage–rental ratio was adjusted for the existence of shift-work. The average value of σ was about 0.9. Another study using the same relation, but comparing Peru and the United States, was undertaken by Clague (1969). In this study, capital intensity was measured on the first shift (e.g., K^2/L_1^2 for a double-shift firm). Hence, this variable was correctly measured, but the measured wage-rental ratio did not adjust the cost of capital services for the intensity of utilization. The average value of σ in Clague's study was quite low; that is, $\sigma = 0.2$ for one set of U.S. data and $\sigma = 0.5$ for another set of U.S. data. A somewhat different study using relation (6.7) was undertaken by Pack (1975). Although he followed Clague in measuring capital intensity on the first shift and in not adjusting the cost of capital services for the intensity of utilization, he used only firms on the efficiency frontier to estimate σ from (6.7). His estimates of σ were extremely high; they averaged substantially above unity. Finally, Moroney (1970) ran regressions [the ones implied by (6.7)] for two-digit manufacturing sectors across states of the United States. He did not adjust either the capital–labor ratio or the wage–rental ratio for the existence of shift-work. The average σ by this method was 0.328. Thus the estimates of σ varied widely even when the conceptual approaches were basically the same, and the procedure is subject to the same biases with respect to shift-work.[11]

---

[11] It is worthwhile to mention briefly a major implication of our analysis for a related group of studies. Concern with the need for appropriate or intermediate technologies has led to a number of microeconomic studies that discuss, among other subjects, the possibilities for substitution in particular processes [e.g., Boon (1964), a number of studies in the work

6.3.2   *Estimation of σ with the UNIDO data*

Our estimation of σ was based on the fitting of equation (4.16) for each
of seventeen different industries in the UNIDO data. To repeat, (4.16)
is equivalent to (4.13), and under perfect competition (4.13) is
equivalent to (6.6); that is, $N_l/N_k = 1$. Our first task was to measure
the price of capital services r' rather than the price of owning the
capital stock for a year (i.e., to adjust r by the degree of capital
utilization or shift-work). It is the price of capital services that is
consistent with the application of (4.16) to the data, and it is this
adjustment that has been neglected in the prior literature.

   As was the case in other studies, we had no data on variations in r
within an industrial category, but we had information on the amount
of shift-work for each plant. Therefore we set r and r' equal to unity
for plants working a single shift. When production workers were
evenly divided across shifts, we set $r' = r/2 = 1/2$ for double-shift
factories and $r' = r/3 = 1/3$ for triple-shift factories.[12] The existence
of multiple processes, however, leads to different numbers of workers
in the different shifts, as indicated in our discussion of capital intensity.
Consequently, in these cases we estimated the proportion of the capital
stock used on each shift in the same manner as in the previous section.
Knowledge of this proportion allowed us to estimate the amount of
capital used solely during the day shift (D), the amount of capital used
during both the day shift and the evening shift (E), and the amount of
capital used during all three shifts (N). The price of capital services
was then calculated from the following weighted average:

edited by Bhalla (1975), and the recent work of the Strathclyde group
(Forsythe et al. 1977)]. Similarly, concern over the role of multinationals in
development has led to studies comparing the technology used by these
firms in the host and home countries [e.g., Morley and Smith (1977a,b)]. A
common feature of both sets of studies is that they indicate the existence of
substitution possibilities in varying degrees, not necessarily based on the
measurement of σ; but they frequently go on to point out that other factors,
besides factor prices, seem important in determining capital intensity. In
particular, these studies usually single out a positive association between
size and capital intensity. A major implication of our theoretical analysis of
shift-work is that high utilization leads to both high capital intensity and
large size (in terms of value added). Thus it is impossible to provide
meaningful interpretation for these associations unless the phenomenon of
shift-work, or capital utilization, is explicitly taken into consideration.

[12] Note that this procedure assumes the absence of wear-and-tear depreciation.

$$r' = \frac{D(r) + E(r/2) + N(r/3)}{D + E + N} = \frac{D(1) + E(1/2) + N(1/3)}{D + E + N} \quad (6.8)$$

To illustrate, if in a double-shift plant production workers are evenly divided across the two shifts, D and N will equal zero, and (6.8) will collapse to $r' = r/2 = 1/2$, which is precisely the desired outcome for a situation in which no adjustment for multiple processes is necessary.

Table 6.1 presents the results of fitting (4.19) and (4.16) to our data. The dependent variable was the same in both cases. That is, it was the observed capital–labor ratio in the first shift measured as the ratio of the book value of machinery and buildings to the number of production workers on the first shift. The wage-rate variable was the same in both cases (i.e., the average wage rate measured as the total wages of production workers, including fringe benefits, divided by the number of production workers, which is the conceptually appropriate variable). The difference in the two equations arose in the measurement of the price of capital. The left-hand-side results were obtained by setting $r' = r = 1$, following the procedure used by Clague (1969) and Pack (1975); the right-hand-side results were obtained using r' as calculated from (6.8), which is the conceptually appropriate variable. The estimates from fitting (4.16) were almost always higher than the estimates from (4.19); the weighted average of σ values for the former was 0.917, whereas the weighted average of σ values for the latter was 0.762. The higher estimates for (4.16) are due to the tendency of shift-work to be more common in the low-wage country (India) than in the high-wage countries (France, Japan).

By and large, the estimates obtained from fitting (4.16) were more precise (had higher t ratios) than those obtained from fitting (4.19). The predictive performance of (4.16) was also superior to that of (4.19) in fourteen of seventeen cases; this superiority was often quite noticeable, and in twelve of fourteen cases it exceeded 10%. All the estimates from fitting (4.16) had the right sign. Finally, the null hypothesis that σ is zero was rejected for the overwhelming majority of the industries in Table 6.1 at the 1% level of significance. On the other hand, the null hypothesis that σ is unity could not be rejected for the overwhelming majority of industries in the table at the 1% level of significance.

To sum up our discussion, we feel justified in our earlier claim that our estimates of σ, from fitting (4.16), are more reliable than the ones in the existing literature for two reasons. First, the capital–labor ratio approach is not subject to the simultaneity problem that besets the labor-productivity approach. Second, even in the capital–labor ratio

Table 6.1. *Estimates of the elasticity of substitution*

Industry[a]	(4.19) Regressions			(4.16) Regressions		
	$\overline{w}/r$	$\overline{R}^2$	R^2	$\overline{w}/r'$	$\overline{R}^2$	R^2
Dairy	0.360	0.2756	0.3481	0.380	0.2398	0.3158
NOBS = 11	(0.164)			(0.187)		
Food	0.345	−0.0781	0.0759	0.621	0.2468	0.3544
NOBS = 8	(0.492)			(0.342)		
Grain	1.129	0.7955	0.8141	1.367	0.8793	0.8903
NOBS = 12	(0.195)			(0.152)		
Spinning	0.917	0.3869	0.4011	1.041	0.4246	0.4380
NOBS = 44	(0.173)			(0.182)		
Knitting	0.931	0.3203	0.3498	1.169	0.3602	0.3880
NOBS = 24	(0.271)			(0.313)		
Leather	1.172	0.3930	0.4797	1.308	0.4588	0.5361
NOBS = 8	(0.498)			(0.497)		
Rubber	1.010	0.4358	0.4985	1.184	0.6618	0.6994
NOBS = 10	(0.358)			(0.274)		
Oils and fats	0.832	0.2846	0.3740	1.056	0.6379	0.6831
NOBS = 9	(0.407)			(0.272)		
Paint	0.876	0.6693	0.7024	0.9843	0.7656	0.7891
NOBS = 11	(0.190)			(0.170)		
Medical, soap	0.581	0.3096	0.3590	0.807	0.6512	0.6761
NOBS = 15	(0.215)			(0.155)		
Brick	0.755	0.3259	0.3778	0.617	0.3294	0.3810
NOBS = 14	(0.280)			(0.227)		
Ferrous	0.824	0.2356	0.2902	1.065	0.5367	0.5698
NOBS = 15	(0.357)			(0.257)		
Nonferrous	0.410	0.0210	0.0862	0.814	0.2331	0.2843
NOBS = 16	(0.356)			(0.345)		
Metal products	0.873	0.4231	0.4327	1.027	0.6142	0.6206
NOBS = 61	(0.130)			(0.105)		
Nonelectrical						
Machinery	0.703	0.3340	0.3507	0.807	0.4715	0.4847
NOBS = 41	(0.153)			(0.133)		
Electrical						
Machinery	−0.292	−0.0030	0.0425	0.127	−0.0415	0.0059
NOBS = 23	(0.302)			(0.360)		
Concrete	1.082	0.3618	0.4017	1.204	0.3141	0.3570
NOBS = 17	(0.341)			(0.417)		

Note: Standard errors are given in parentheses below the estimated coefficients.
[a]The industry regressions include the Yugoslav plants in the industry as well as plants that were eliminated for the analysis of shift-work because of inability to match the UNIDO industrial classification with the U.S. classification.

approach our estimates account for the phenomen of shift-work in the estimation, whereas the existing ones do so incompletely if at all. Although our approach is not entirely free of problems, as discussed earlier, these problems are also present in other studies using the capital–labor ratio approach. Moreover, if these problems bias our estimates, it is likely that the bias is upward, and we have indicated the main consequence of an upward bias for our empirical analysis of shift-work.

6.4   Economies of scale

The degree of economies of scale was first identified as an important determinant of shift-work under cost minimization in Chapter 1 (Proposition 2), and the analysis of profit maximization in Chapter 3 provided us with two different models to describe the impact of the degree of economies of scale on the shift-work decision: the constant-β technology and the semi-U technology. As emphasized in Chapter 5, however, these two models have very different implications for the role of size as a determinant of shift-work. We shall present here an empirical procedure for implementing these two models with our data. This procedure is almost identical with the one used in our earlier work (Betancourt and Clague 1978) that favored the constant-β technology in France and Japan and the semi-U technology in India and Israel.

As noted in Chapter 3, the cost ratio can be thought of in terms of two components; that is,

$$CR(X^1) = CR^*\phi(X^1) \tag{6.9}$$

where CR^* is the cost ratio under constant returns to scale and the specification of $\phi(X^1)$ depends on the assumption one makes about the technology. For empirical purposes it is convenient to define the relation

$$\phi(X_i^1) = (1 + e_{cx}^2)/2 \tag{6.10}$$

where e_{cx}^2 is the proportionate increase in average costs generated by cutting in half the level of output under single-shift operation.[13] The

---

[13] There is, of course, a corresponding definition for the triple-shift cost ratio (CR^1 in Chapter 2); namely, $\phi^1(X_i^1) = (1 + e_{cx}^3)/3$, where e_{cx}^3 is the proportionate increase in average costs generated by cutting by two-thirds the level of output under single-shift operation.

implications of the theory with respect to (6.10) can be summarized in the following way: With a constant-β technology, e_{cx}^2 and e_{cx}^3 will be constant, although not at the same value. As indicated in Chapter 3, under this assumption $\phi(X^1) = 2^{-1/\beta}$, and thus size plays no causal role in the shift-work decision. With a semi-U technology, however, e_{ex}^2 and e_{cx}^3 will decline as the optimal level of output under single-shift operation increases; hence the cost ratio will decline as X^1 increases.

The empirical literature on economies of scale contains two types of estimates: engineering estimates and interview estimates. The engineering estimates (e.g., Haldi and Whitcomb 1967; Moore 1959) provided the initial inspiration for the assumption of a constant-β technology. These estimates indicated that the average cost curve keeps falling within the range of observed plant size. We implemented this model in the restricted-form specification by assuming e_{cx}^2 and e_{cx}^3 to be constant at values of 0.10 and 0.15, respectively. The former value is a rough average of the available industry estimates, and it happens to coincide with the value for the soap industry; the latter estimate was chosen, somewhat arbitrarily, to make the increases in costs of cutting output by two-thirds 50% higher than the increases in costs from cutting output by one-half. In the free-form specification this model does not require a measure of size to be used as an explanatory variable.

The interview estimates (e.g., Bain 1956; Pratten 1971) provided the initial impetus for the definition of the semi-U technology[14] because of their implication that the average cost curve flattens out at some level of output. This model was implemented in the restricted-form specification by making e_{cx}^2 and e_{cx}^3 functions of a measure of size with the following general properties: e_{cx}^2 and e_{cx}^3 are set to zero at a high enough level of the measure of size; e_{cx}^2 and e_{cx}^3 are forced to decline continuously up to that level. In the free-form specification this model was implemented by introducing the measure of size and its square as explanatory variables.

Before defining the empirical measure of size used to implement the semi-U technology, and the specific functional forms adopted for e_{cx}^2 and e_{cx}^3, a few general remarks are necessary. First, the argument that shift-work is more likely to be profitable under a semi-U technology

---

[14] A recent study by Scherer et al. (1975) that was based on interviews provided evidence for some industries that is consistent with the main implication of the engineering estimates about the shape of the average cost curve.

the higher the level of output under single-shift operation (Proposition 6B of Chapter 3) includes other dimensions of the shift-work decision besides the degree of economies of scale. For instance, it encompasses demand characteristics, including market structure, and their interactions with economies of scale. Our empirical procedures are aimed at incorporating solely one aspect of this proposition into the estimation, namely, the effect of a high level of output (X^1) in lowering the degree of economies of scale and thus increasing the profitability of shift-work [lowering $CR(X^1)$]. Clearly, the restricted-form specification accomplishes this objective far more effectively than the free-form specification. Finally, it is worth stressing that there is an unobservable-variable problem with respect to the level of output under a semi-U technology that is similar to the one previously discussed with respect to capital intensity. That is, we observe X^1 for the firms that work a single shift, but we observe X^2 or X^3 for the shift-working firms. The theory tells us that X^2 and X^3 for shift-working firms will be larger than X^1 would have been, but we do not know how much larger. Conceptually, our approach is based on the use of X_1^2 or X_1^3 (i.e., size per shift) as a proxy for X^1.

We are now ready to discuss the actual measurement of size in our data. Our size variable is a relative size variable, RS. The base for this relative size measure is the size of the first shift of a U.S. plant in the 30th percentile of the same four-digit U.S. industry classification as the UNIDO firm. Thus our size varible variable accounts for differences across industries in the optimal size of plant. Our analysis is directed to data that consist of samples of firms across different industries for each country. Therefore this normalization was necessary to avoid large differences in the values of the size variable due to variations in characteristics across industries that have nothing to do with the problem at hand. Moreover, unless the error in using X_1^2 as a proxy for X^1 is correlated with the minimum optimal size of plant across industries, this procedure tends to attenuate the simultaneity problem; to put it in a slightly different manner, our procedure should reduce the size of the error in using X_1^2 as a proxy for X^1, particularly in the restricted-form specification.

The relative size of the ith UNIDO firm was measured as follows:

$$RS_i = \frac{L_i^1}{L_{30}} \frac{VA_i^1}{VA_{30}} \tag{6.11}$$

where L_{30} and VA_{30} refer to employment and value added on the first shift of the U.S. firm in the 30th percentile and L_i^1 and VA_i^1 refer to employment and value added on the first shift of the UNIDO firm;

thus, for shift-working firms these variables are the proxies for what the optimal levels of X^1 and L^1 would have been under single-shift operation. Total employment and value added for the U.S. firm were obtained by interpolating from the distribution of firms by size in the Census of Manufactures. Employment and value added on the first shift were obtained by multiplying total employment and value added by the ratio of workers in the first shift to total workers, as given in the BLS Industry Wage Survey (e.g., O'Connor 1970). Employment on the first shift was directly available for the UNIDO firms. Value added on the first shift for the UNIDO shift-working firms was obtained by multiplying the value-added figures for the plant by the ratio of workers on the first shift to total workers in the plant.

Relative size (RS_i) was measured as a geometric average of relative employment and relative value added because these two measures seem to contain opposing biases. Because efficiency tends to be lower in countries other than the United States (i.e., output per unit of total input is smaller), the UNIDO factories will appear smaller when measured by relative value added than when measured by an index of labor and capital input. Inasmuch as the degree of economies of scale depends, at least in part, on the size of total input rather than on total output, the relative size of the UNIDO factories would be understated by the use of relative value added alone. On the other hand, the use of relative employment alone would clearly overstate the relative size of the UNIDO factories, since both labor per unit of capital and labor per unit of output are higher than in the United States. To conclude this discussion, we present in Table 6.2 a distribution of plants in our data according to the relative-size variable.[15]

Finally, we come to the precise specification of the relationship between e_{cx}^2 (and e_{cx}^3) and relative size. We use the following relationship:

$$e_{cx}^2 = a^2 + b^2 \log RS_i \tag{6.12}$$

The value of a^2 was set at 0.10; hence, if relative size equals 1, $e_{cx}^2 = 0.10$. The value of b^2 was obtained by assuming that $e_{cx}^2 = 0$ at a value

---

[15] It is perhaps worth noting in connection with this table that intercountry comparisons of size that include Japan are subject to pitfalls. In particular, the system of lifetime employment and the concomitant widespread use of subcontracting would lead Japanese firms to show smaller sizes than comparable firms in other countries. Thus the dramatic difference between France and Japan revealed by Table 6.2 should be interpreted with regard for this lack of comparability.

Table 6.2. *Distribution of plants by relative size*

Country	RS < 2		RS > 2	
	n	f	n	f
France	26	0.50	26	0.50
Japan	42	0.81	10	0.19
India	59	0.78	17	0.22
Israel	38	0.75	13	0.25

Note: The number of firms in a country sample that belong to the relative-size category is represented by n; f is the proportion of firms in a country sample that belong to the relative-size category.

of relative size equal to four, and e_{cx}^2 was constrained to have a minimum value of zero. We adopted this formulation for our empirical work in this book because it provides a convenient way of defining e_{cx}^3 as a function of relative size in a manner consistent with the definition of e_{cx}^2. That is,

$$e_{cx}^3 = a^3 + b^3 \log \mathrm{RS}_i \qquad (6.13)$$

where a^3 was chosen to equal 0.15 and b^3 was chosen so that e_{cx}^3 in (6.13) becomes zero at a relative size equal to six (and, of course, e_{cx}^3 was constrained to remain at zero for values of RS larger than six). Incidentally, in our earlier work (Betancourt and Clague 1978) b^2 was chosen so that $e_{cx}^2 = 0.05$ at RS = 4. A sensitivity analysis of the effect of the new specification in this book has revealed that it improves predictive performance in India and Israel and worsens predictive performance in France and Japan.

To conclude this section, we stress the following point: Our previous empirical work favored the constant-β (semi-U) technology for France and Japan (India and Israel) under both the restricted-form specification and the free-form specification; the empirical work presented in this book should be viewed as taking those results as a maintained hypothesis.[16] Thus, we shall not be testing any new hypotheses

---

[16] We did, of course, check to see if any of the changes in our procedures in the previous sections, or the one just discussed, altered these results, but the same conclusions held.

empirically with respect to economies of scale. Nevertheless, the rather lengthy discussion in this section has been necessary because the role of economies of scale must be taken into account in ascertaining, for example, the empirical importance of the simultaneity problem with respect to capital intensity.

6.5   Shift differentials

The wage differentials for the second (evening) shift and the third (night) shift are important variables in terms of the theory developed in Part I. For instance, they play a direct role as determinants of the shift-work decision (Proposition 3). Moreover, they also affect the measurement of the impact of other variables on the shift-work decision (e.g., the correction for the simultaneity problem with respect to capital intensity that was developed in Section 6.2). Unfortunately, these variables are not available in our data; thus we have developed a procedure (to be explained in detail later) to compensate for this important shortcoming of our data. It is certainly our hope that data-gathering efforts in the future will generate information on these variables. In this regard we want to stress that information on these differentials is necessary for those firms that do not work shifts as well as for those that do. But even if it is possible to obtain this information on a reliable basis only for the firms that work shifts, it is worthwhile to do so because of the role of the differentials in the appropriate measurement of capital intensity.

The absence of information on the shift differentials helps illustrate the complementarity of the two approaches to the specification of the independent variables identified in Chapter 4 (Section 4.3). With respect to the direct effect of the shift differentials on shift-work, the absence of information on these variables creates the possibility of biases due to omitted variables in the free-form specification, unless these excluded variables are uncorrelated with the included ones or with utilization. One could argue that the World Bank results discussed in Chapter 5 provide evidence that indeed the shift differentials are uncorrelated with utilization, but it was also noted in Chapter 5 that this result can be explained by a positive correlation between the observed capital–labor ratio per shift and the shift differentials. Therefore, the possibility of bias in our estimates due to this source cannot be dismissed. In the restricted-form specification a value for the differentials must be assumed in order to calculate the cost ratios. This assumption leads to an error-in-the-variables problem that differs from the classical one in that the downward-bias conclusion need not hold. This difference arises because the cost ratio is a nonlinear function of the elementary variables. Because there is no reason to expect that the magnitudes (or even the signs) of the biases will be the same in both specifications of the independent variables, the absence of information on the differentials illustrates one of the advantages of using both specifications in our empirical work.

Our procedure in selecting a value for the shift differential (α) was to calculate the two-shift Leontief cost ratio [CR in equation (2.5)] for various values of α and to count the numbers of correct and incorrect predictions, defining a correct prediction as a cost ratio greater than 1 when the firm did work shifts and less than 1 when the firm did not work shifts. The value of e_{cx}^2 was set at 0.10 in the calculation of the cost ratio. The smallest percentages of incorrect predictions were obtained for $\alpha = 0.12$ in Israel, $\alpha = 0.20$ in France, $\alpha = 0.45, 0.50$, and 0.75 in Japan, and $\alpha = 0$ in India. The values of α that minimize the percentage of incorrect predictions were selected, except for India, where a value of 0.03 was chosen instead of the actual minimum of zero.

Given different values of α, the Leontief cost ratio of three shifts to two shifts, $CR(32) = CR^1/CR$ [CR^1 given by equation (2.12)], was calculated, and the number of incorrect predictions was counted for the subsample of firms working either two or three shifts. The value of e_{cx}^3 was set equal to 0.15. Just as in the case of α, the values of b that minimized the percentage of incorrect predictions were selected (under a constraint forcing b to be greater than or equal to unity); thus, in India and Israel $b = 1$, and in France $b = 1.5$. In Japan, where the percentage of incorrect predictions was the same for every b, b was simply set equal to unity.

In the absence of data on shift differentials, the procedure just described seems to be an appropriate way of selecting α and b. It leads to values of the shift differential, α, for each country that correspond to one's prior expectations. It also has the particular advantage of not creating a direct association between the values of α and capital intensity under shift-work. The criterion used for selecting α and b is different from the measures of predictive performance used in evaluating models (either R^2 or the information measures). The Leontief cost ratios used in selecting α and b are also different from the CES cost ratios relevant for our empirical work. Thus, we hope to have avoided the introduction of systematic biases in our results through our procedure for selecting α and b.

*6.6   Working-capital hypotheses

In Chapter 2, Section 2.4, we analyzed the role of working capital in
the shift-work decision under alternative assumptions. One formulation of working-capital requirements, embedded in equation (2.14),
led to the conclusion that working capital had no effect on the
shift-work decision. This formulation was termed the zero-effect
hypothesis, and if we limited our discussion to this hypothesis we
would be ready to bring together the arguments of the previous
sections into the models implemented empirically. Nevertheless, an
alternative formulation was suggested, embedded in equation (2.15),
in which working capital did have an effect on the shift-work decision
through its impact on the capital share and thus on the cost ratio. In
this section we implement this effect of working capital on the capital
share under two alternative hypotheses about the nature of the capital
market: a perfectly competitive capital market and a segmented capital
market.

We shall consider the restricted-form specification first. Thus the
starting point of our argument is equation (2.20), which is repeated
here for convenience:

$$\theta^* / (1 - \theta^*) = [\theta / (1 - \theta)](1 + IP)^{\sigma - 1} \qquad (6.14)$$

In order to calculate (6.14) empirically, we need information on θ, σ,
P, and I for every firm. The first two variables can be calculated as
described in Sections 6.2 and 6.3. P is the average period of financing
required for labor (and capital) costs. It is the sum of the periods of
turnover for inventories of work in process and of finished goods plus
the average period of credit extended to customers. The periods of
turnover can be calculated from the information in our plant data on
the desired level of inventories for these two categories and on value
added. We have no information on the average period of credit
extended to customers; therefore, for simplicity, we assumed that it
was zero.[17] The calculation of the interest rate, however, depends on
the assumption one makes about the capital market.

In a perfectly competitive capital market the interest rate faced by
all the firms in a given country will be the same, but for implementing
(6.14) a specific value must be assumed. Our procedure was to obtain
for each country the bank rate, or discount rate, from the publications

---

[17] If $\sigma < 1$, this procedure leads to an overestimate of the capital share (θ^*); if
$\sigma > 1$, it leads to an underestimate of the capital share (θ^*).

of the International Monetary Fund (1964); this rate was then adjusted by subtracting the rate of inflation over the period 1962-6 and by adding 3% to cover the costs and profits of financial intermediation. The resulting figure provided an estimate of the minimum real interest rate on working capital in each country. This minimum was 0.75% for India, 5.66% for Israel, 4.76% for France, and 4.86% for Japan. The real interest rate assumed to prevail under the assumption of a perfectly competitive capital market (I) was set at 150% of the minimum (i.e., 1.25% for India, 8.49% for Israel, 6.24% for France, and 7.29% for Japan).

Under the segmented-capital-market hypothesis the interest rate faced by any one firm will be viewed as independent of its working-capital requirements. Nevertheless, the interest rates faced by different firms may vary depending on the segment of the capital market in which a firm operates. Thus, in implementing this hypothesis empirically, it is necessary to identify or postulate criteria by which firms are assigned to different segments of the capital market.[18] Moreover, in order to implement (6.14), it is also necessary to relate these different segments of the capital market to a rate of interest. Extensive research into the details of this segmentation for each of our countries is beyond the scope of our inquiry, but it seems reasonable to postulate that the segment of the capital market in which the firm operates will be closely associated with the market power possessed by the firm. Firms with substantial market power will usually be able to operate in those segments of the capital market with lower interest rates.

In order to capture the relationship just described, we used value added as a proxy for market power, and we defined the interest rate facing the firm to be the following function of value added:

$$I(\text{VA}) = A/(\text{VA})^{1/2} \qquad (6.15)$$

The relation in (6.15) was subjected to two constraints: The interest rate could not fall below the minimum defined in connection with the implementation of the hypothesis of a perfectly competitive market, and the interest rate could not rise above a maximum of 40% for any firm. The parameter A was chosen to assure that most values of the interest rate would not be at the minimum value or the maximum value. This criterion resulted in the following values: $A = 25$ in India, Israel, and France; $A = 4$ in Japan. The resulting value of $I(\text{VA})$ for

---

[18] Thoumi (1975) provided examples of these criteria for Chile and Colombia, as well as additional references to this literature.

each plant was inserted in (6.14) in order to calculate the capital share under this hypothesis.

In the free-form specification of the independent variables the hypothesis of a perfectly competitive capital market was implemented by introducing the period-of-turnover variable (P), defined earlier, into the regressions as an additional explanatory variable. The segmented-capital-market hypothesis was implemented by introducing both P and $I(\text{VA})$ as additional explanatory variables.

To conclude this section, we explicitly address a possible problem with our choice of value added as a variable for the implementation of the segmented-capital-market hypothesis. The theory in Chapter 3 and the interpretation of the literature in Chapter 5 suggest a reverse-causation mechanism in which the profitability of shift-work leads to large size. We do not think this reverse causation will operate in our restricted-form specification of the independent variables. First, we are entering value added into the empirical analysis through the specific functional form in (6.15). The nature of this functional form is to reduce the strength of any reverse-causation mechanism by mapping the magnitudes of value added into the dimensions of an interest rate. Second, this interest rate is allowed to affect the main independent variable only through its impact on the capital share (and thus on the cost ratio), as specified in (6.14). Hence, if σ is less than unity, large size increases the share, but if σ is greater than unity, large size decreases the share. This feature of the relation makes it very difficult, if not impossible, for the reverse-causation mechanism to be of significance in the restricted form specification. In the free-form specification, we chose to use $I(\text{VA})$ rather than VA directly to reduce the possible reverse causation. Nevertheless, only the first of the two mechanisms just cited is at work in breaking down the reverse causation under the free-form specification; therefore, we are less certain that the results with this specification are entirely free from this problem.

6.7   Models implemented empirically

The information provided by the detailed procedures described in the previous sections allows us to construct the substantive models that will be confronted with the sample data for each of the four countries in both the restricted-form specification and the free-form specification of the independent variables. The presentation of these models thus provides a fitting summary to the somewhat lengthy and frequently intricate arguments of this chapter. To facilitate the exposition, we shall present the restricted-form specification models in terms of the cost ratio for three shifts versus one shift, CR^1.

In the terminology developed in Chapter 4, Section 4.5, the index (Y_i) that is a function of the independent variables can now be written as follows: Under the restricted-form specification, we have

$$Y_i = \beta_0 + \beta_1 CR_i^1 \tag{6.16}$$

where

$$CR_i^1 = [3 + (1 + b)\alpha]\{\theta_i[3 + (1 + b)\alpha]^{\sigma_i - 1} + (1 - \theta_i)\}^{1/(1 - \sigma_i)} \phi^1(X_i^1) \tag{6.17}$$

Recall that $\phi^1(X^1) = (1 + e_{cx}^3)/3$, where e_{cx}^3 is a function of relative size [see equation (6.13)]. Under the free-form specification we have

$$Y_i = \gamma_0 + \gamma_1(K/L)_i^1 + \gamma_2(RS)_i + \gamma_3(RS)_i^2 + \gamma_4 P_i + \gamma_5 I(VA_i) \tag{6.18}$$

where the most general specification of the independent variables has been chosen for our present purposes. The implementation of any specific substantive model is undertaken by imposing the appropriate assumptions on (6.16) [through (6.17)] and on (6.18) (through the setting of one or more parameters to zero) and by calculating the relevant variables as described in Sections 6.2 through 6.6.

The set of models and specifications implemented with our data is summarized in tabular form (Table 6.3) for the reader's convenience. In using this table it is desirable to keep in mind the following considerations: For any one country there are only three alternative substantive models, which are defined by the working-capital hypotheses. Each one of these three alternative models can be implemented under either the restricted-form specification or the free-form specification. In the former, the impact of the alternative models on the cost ratio (6.17) operates strictly through the calculation of the capital share under single-shift operation, θ, as indicated in the table. In the free-form specification these alternative models operate through the variables that are included or excluded from the index Y_i as indicated in the appropriate cells in the table. In this connection it is worth noting that the expected signs of the coefficients of P and $I(VA)$ are ambiguous because they depend on whether $\sigma \gtrless 1$; the results of Section 6.3 indicate that in the sample of plants for any one country, some will have values of σ greater than unity, whereas others will have values of σ less than unity. Finally, the model used to describe economies of scale in the sample for any one country is being treated as a maintained hypothesis for the reasons discussed in Section 6.4.

Table 6.3. *Models implemented empirically: specification of independent variables*

Working-capital hypotheses	Restricted-form[a] CR^1		Free-form	
	Developed countries[b] ($e^3_{cx} = 0.15$)	Developing countries[c] ($e^3_{cx} = a^3 + b^3 \log RS_i$)	Developed countries[b]	Developing countries[c]
H.1 Zero effect	$\theta = rK^1/(rK^1 + w_1L^1)$	$\theta = rK^1/(rK^1 + w_1L^1)$	K^1/L^1	K^1/L^1, RS, RS²
H.2 Perfectly competitive market	$\theta^* = rK^1/[rK^1 + w_1L^1(1 + IP)]$ I is constant	$\theta^* = rK^1/[rK^1 + w_1L^1(1 + IP)]$ I is constant	K^1/L^1, P	K^1/L^1, RS, RS², P
H.3 Segmented market[d]	$\theta^* = rK^1/[rK^1 + w_1L^1(1 + IP)]$ $I = I(VA)$	$\theta^* = rK^1/[rK^1 + w_1L^1(1 + IP)]$ $I = I(VA)$	K^1/L^1, P, $I(VA)$	K^1/L^1, RS, RS², P, $I(VA)$

Note: RS is relative size. P is period of financing.

[a] In the restricted-form specification the independent variable in all models is CR^1, the cost ratio for three shifts versus one shift. The entries in the body of the table merely indicate the assumptions under which this cost ratio is calculated.

[b] The constant-β technology underlies the estimation for the developed countries (France, Japan).

[c] The semi-U technology underlies the estimation for the developing countries (India, Israel).

[d] With this hypothesis the interest rate (I) is specified to be an inverse function of value added (VA), which is viewed as a measure of market power.

At this point we are ready to confront the theory developed in Part I with the UNIDO data through the use of the estimation framework developed in Chapter 4 and the procedures presented in this chapter. In the next chapter we present the results of this confrontation.

PART III

Results

CHAPTER 7

Individual-country results

This part of the book is transitional in nature, for we conclude some of the strands in the arguments presented in previous parts, and we broaden the scope of our inquiry into other directions. One issue that stands out above all others in this context is the validation of the theory. The theoretical analysis of Part I identified clearly the main causes or determinants of shift-work at the level of the firm, but the discussion of estimation and the review of the empirical literature in Part II revealed the difficulty of undertaking appropriate empirical tests that will corroborate or deny the existence of these causal relationships. The individual-country results presented in this chapter bring together these two aspects of the issue by providing evidence on the validity of the theory after correcting for the econometric problems that cloud the interpretation of previous results. In Chapter 8 we move on to other dimensions of the topic. There we present evidence on the extent to which the theory previously developed explains differences in shift-work among the countries in our UNIDO data, and we summarize the available evidence on the extent and the main characteristics of shift-work in various countries. This summary provides some motivation for the subsequent discussion in Part IV, which focuses on the effects of shift-work at the economy-wide level as well as at the firm level.

Our main objective in the present chapter is, of course, to ascertain whether or not the theory is consistent with the data once the bias due to the unobservable-variable problem is eliminated. In Section 7.1 we accomplish this objective. In addition, the results of this section illuminate another issue that underlies the discussion in Part II, for they provide a quantitative indication of the improvement in predictive performance that results from the bias due to the unobservable-variable problem with respect to capital intensity. Thus they are helpful in evaluating the empirical results available in the prior literature. The two sections that follow Section 7.1 are more limited in scope. In Section 7.2 we present evidence on the extent to which the working-capital considerations discussed in Chapter 2, Section 2.4, affect the shift-work decision. In Section 7.3 we present results that help clarify several methodological issues discussed in Part II. As the reader can surmise, these two sections cover somewhat specialized topics; therefore the reader who is not interested in working-capital considerations or econometric methodology may want to proceed directly from Section 7.1 to the concluding remarks of Section 7.4.

7.1   Capital intensity, elasticity of substitution, and the unobservable-variable problem

In our previous discussion a great deal of emphasis has been placed on the bias that arises from the use of observed measures of capital intensity in ascertaining the existence of a statistical relationship between capital intensity and shift-work. Therefore, our first task is to obtain results that are free from this bias. These results will allow us to perform an appropriate statistical test of the hypothesis that a relationship exists between shift-work and its determinants in the four countries for which we have data. Although the possibility of bias arises in both the restricted-form specification and the free-form specification of the independent variables, it is convenient to begin with the restricted-form specification.

In order to construct the cost ratio (CR^1) used as the main independent variable in the statistical analysis, we followed the procedures described in Chapter 6. The model implemented in this section corresponds to the one in the first row of Table 6.3 (i.e., the zero-effect-of-working-capital hypothesis). In Table 7.1 we present the results of estimating equation (6.16) with logit analysis. The entries in the body of the table for each country provide the results of this estimation under two alternative assumptions about substitution possibilities. In one instance we assumed that the elasticity of substitution was zero. Hence, we used the observed measures of capital intensity in calculating the cost ratio. In the other instance we assumed that the elasticity of substitution for a firm in a country sample coincided with the point estimate of the elasticity of substitution, presented in Chapter 6, for the industry to which the firm belonged. This estimate was then used to obtain the "true" measure of capital intensity, or the capital share under single-shift operation, and the elasticity of substitution for the calculation of the cost ratio in (6.17). Thus for each country there are two sets of estimates in Table 7.1 that correspond to one or the other of these two alternative assumptions about σ.

A comparison of the statistical results under these two assumptions provides an indication of the extent of the bias introduced by using

Table 7.1. *Bias in observed measures of capital intensity: logit analysis of (6.16)*

Country	Intercept	$CR^{1\,a}$	L^b	I_A^c	$\dfrac{I_R^c}{(\bar{I}_R)^c}$
France ($N = 50$)					
$\sigma_i = \sigma = 0$	7.697	−8.737	17.84	0.2518	0.2607
	(2.437)	(2.536)			(0.2403)
$\sigma_i = \hat{\sigma}_i$	2.550^d	−3.562	3.08	0.0491	0.0508
	(1.947)	(2.102)			(0.0310)
Japan ($N = 52$)					
$\sigma_i = \sigma = 0$	8.336	−8.164	16.74	0.2182	0.2279
	(3.001)	(2.656)			(0.2125)
$\sigma_i = \hat{\sigma}_i$	∴683	−5.524	8.60	0.1146	0.1196
	(2.100)	(2.117)			(0.1020)
India ($N = 75$)					
$\sigma_i = \sigma = 0$	6.483	−6.575	17.56	0.1701	0.1762
	(1.710)	(1.876)			(0.1649)
$\sigma_i = \hat{\sigma}_i$	3.615	−3.425	5.07	0.0501	0.0519
	(1.392)	(1.606)			(0.0389)
Israel ($N = 49$)					
$\sigma_i = \sigma = 0$	8.619	−8.147	20.41	0.2771	0.2830
	(2.428)	(2.380)			(0.2677)
$\sigma_i = \hat{\sigma}_i$	7.333	−7.211	15.28	0.2000	0.2043
	(2.172)	(2.263)			(0.1874)

Note: Standard errors are given in parentheses below their respective coefficients.
[a] The three-shifts-versus-one-shift cost ratio (CR^1) was calculated under the hypothesis of zero effect of working capital (H.1), as described in Chapter 6.
[b] Observed value of $-2 \ln \lambda$, where λ is a likelihood-ratio statistic; that is, $\lambda = L(\hat{w} \mid \beta_1 = 0)/L(\hat{\Omega})$. $\chi_1^2 (1\%) = 6.63$, $\chi_1^2 (5\%) = 3.84$, $\chi_1^2 (10\%) = 2.71$, where χ_1^2 refers to the chi-square variable with one degree of freedom.
[c] These measures of predictive performance were defined in Chapter 4: equations (4.26), (4.27), and (4.28).
[d] Statistically insignificant t ratio at the 5% level, using a one-sided t test.

observed measures of capital intensity rather than the "true" ones in the restricted-form specification. The easiest way of comparing the two sets of results for each country is in terms of the measures of predictive performance. The drop in the amount of information explained by the theory once we account for the bias is quite substantial for all four countries, but it seems especially large for France and India. In every country the absolute values of both coefficient estimates decrease as a result of the removal of the reverse-causation problem.

The results in Table 7.1 for $\sigma_i = \hat{\sigma}_i$ are also of interest in themselves, because they provide the first opportunity to test the theory of shift-work in a context where an attempt has been made to account for the unobservable-variable problem. The results are encouraging. The coefficient of the cost ratio has the expected sign in every country. A one-sided t test at the 5% level of significance rejects the null hypothesis that the cost ratio has no impact on shift-work in every country. The likelihood ratio test of the same null hypothesis rejects this hypothesis at the 10% level in every country and at the 5% level in every country but France. It is worth stressing that in France and Japan the cost ratio varies among firms in the sample because of variations in θ_i or σ_i; in India and Israel, on the other hand, the cost ratio varies among firms as a result of variations in these two variables as well as variations in relative size (RS_i).

In Table 7.2 we present similar results corresponding to the free-form specification. This table provides a reference against which to evaluate the likely impact of the bias on the results available in the existing literature. It also provides useful information to complement the discussion in the previous paragraph. Two estimated relationships are presented in Table 7.2 for every country. One of these relationships is based on the observed capital–labor ratio (k^0); the other relationship uses the estimated elasticity of substitution (and the assumed shift differential) to calculate the "true" capital–labor ratio, k^*. To repeat, because the empirical analysis of Chapter 6, Section 6.3, rejects the hypothesis that the elasticity of substitution is zero, $k = k^*$ is the conceptually appropriate specification, and the results for $k = k^0$ are biased and correspond to the estimates in the prior literature reviewed in Chapter 5. No working-capital variables were introduced in either relationship.

There is a substantial drop in predictive performance after removal of the bias, but the drop is now more noticeable for France and Japan than for India and Israel; this result is to be contrasted with the restricted-form result, where the drop was larger for France and India than for Japan and Israel.[1] Parenthetically, the coefficient of the capital–labor ratio is noticeably lower in three of the countries for $k = k^*$ than for $k = k^0$, and it is slightly higher for $k = k^*$ than for $k = k^0$ in Israel. Our analysis of the bias for a simple case in Chapter 4, Section 4.4.1, is consistent with these results. That analysis led us to expect the following for a situation where $k = k^0$: If the bias is positive, the

---

[1] This result suggests that the elasticity of substitution plays a role in explaining shift-work in Japan but not in India.

Table 7.2. *Bias in observed measures of capital intensity: logit analysis of (6.18)*

Country	Intercept	Capital intensity	RS	RS^2	L^a	I_A^b	I_R^b $(\bar{I}_R)^b$
France ($N = 50$)							
$k = k^0$	-1.816 (0.551)	0.015 (0.006)	—	—	7.10 (1)	0.0871	0.0902 (0.0713)
$k = k^*$	-0.552^c (0.464)	-0.004^c (0.008)	—	—	0.33 (1)	0.0067	0.0069 (-0.0138)
Japan ($N = 52$)							
$k = k^0$	-2.536 (0.695)	0.779 (0.301)	—	—	16.506 (1)	0.2044	0.2134 (0.1977)
$k = k^*$	-2.056 (0.661)	0.674 (0.316)	—	—	7.34 (1)	0.0862	0.0900 (0.0718)
India ($N = 75$)							
$k = k^0$	-0.841^c (0.527)	0.069 (0.033)	0.641^c (0.649)	-0.006^c (0.161)	20.84 (3) / 6.78 (2)	0.2195	0.2273 (0.1947)
$k = k^*$	-0.557^c (0.514)	0.046 (0.026)	0.741^c (0.738)	-0.007^c (0.197)	15.66 (3) / 9.25 (2)	0.1708	0.1769 (0.1421)
Israel ($N = 49$)							
$k = k^0$	-4.152 (1.439)	0.126 (0.048)	3.843 (1.446)	-0.770 (0.303)	36.76 (3) / 14.99 (2)	0.5383	0.5498 (0.5198)
$k = k^*$	-3.776 (1.384)	0.129 (0.052)	3.554 (1.233)	-0.649 (0.234)	30.16 (3) / 18.68 (2)	0.4361	0.4455 (0.4085)

Note: Standard errors are given in parentheses below their respective coefficients.

^{a}Observed value of $-2 \ln \lambda$, where λ is a likelihood-ratio statistic and the number in parentheses indicates the number of restrictions imposed (always starting with the last column entry in the table). For instance, in Israel $-2 \ln \lambda (r) = 18.68$ (2) in one case, and $\lambda = L(\tilde{\omega} \mid \gamma_2 = \gamma_3 = 0)/L(\hat{\Omega})$ in this example. $\chi_1^2 (5\%) = 3.84$, $\chi_2^2 (5\%) = 5.99$, $\chi_3^2 (5\%) = 7.81$, where χ_n^2 refers to a chi-square variable with n degrees of freedom.

^{b}These measures of predictive performance were defined in Chapter 4.

^{c}Statistically insignificant t ratio at 5% level, using a one-sided t test.

measure of predictive performance will be higher than in the unbiased case; if the bias is negative, the measure of predictive performance can be higher or lower than in the unbiased case. Because the previous empirical literature relied solely on the use of observed measures of capital intensity, our results suggest that measures of predictive performance reported in this literature overestimate the true explanatory power of the theory,[2] and often by a substantial amount.

The results in Table 7.2 for $k = k^*$ are of interest in themselves for reasons similar to those presented for $\sigma_i = \hat{\sigma}_i$ in the analysis of the restricted form specification. A striking result is that in the free-form specification the sign of the coefficient of capital intensity for France contradicts the expectations of the theory, although the null hypothesis that the population parameter is zero cannot be rejected at the 5% level. Nevertheless, the coefficient of capital intensity in the other three countries has the expected sign, and the same null hypothesis is rejected at the 5% level, using a one-sided t test. In India and Israel, where the maintained hypothesis calls for the introduction of relative size and its square as independent variables, the relationship between size and shift-work is strengthened as a result of using the "true" measure of capital intensity. This change is most easily seen as follows: The probability value at which one rejects the null hypothesis that the coefficients of the two size variables are zero decreases substantially for $k = k^*$ relative to $k = k^0$. The substantive results with respect to relative size, however, are not affected by the use of the "true" capital intensity rather than the observed capital intensity. In both cases relative size enters nonlinearly into the explanation of shift-work for India and Israel.

Although a considerable amount of effort is required for implementing the restricted-form specification of the independent variables, there are benefits to be derived from this effort in terms of enhanced confidence in our results. The restricted-form results for each of the four countries provide substantial support for the main elements of the theory developed in Part I as an explanation of shift-work, and the free-form results yield a similar but weaker conclusion, except for France, where the theory is not supported by the data with this specification. Furthermore, in both cases the use of observed measures of capital intensity leads to a substantial overestimate of the predictive performance of the theory in every country.

---

[2] The evidence based on the R^2 values from the OLS estimation yields similar results.

*7.2   Working-capital hypotheses

The working-capital hypotheses were implemented under both the restricted-form specification and the free-form specification of the independent variables, as described in Chapter 6. The results for the restricted-form specification, which are presented in Table 7.3, will be considered first.

For the reader's convenience, the first entry for each country in Table 7.3 (H.1) merely reproduces the result in Table 7.1 for $\sigma_i = \hat{\sigma}_i$, which corresponds to the hypothesis of zero effect of working capital. The entries next to H.2 and H.3 for each country correspond to the hypothesis of a perfectly competitive capital market and to the hypothesis of a segmented capital market, respectively. As summarized in Table 6.3, the only difference between the three hypotheses in the restricted-form specification is in the calculation of the capital share under single-shift operation, which is in turn used to calculate the cost ratio (CR^1).

The main characteristic of the results in Table 7.3 is the miniscule difference in the coefficient estimates that arises as a consequence of making substantially different assumptions about the way working capital affects firm behavior. Although this result may initially seem surprising, it is what one would expect in light of the discussion in Chapter 2 and the estimates of σ in Section 6.3. In Chapter 2 (Section 2.4) we showed that if the elasticity of substitution equals unity, working capital will have no effect on shift-work, because it will not affect the capital share under single-shift operation. This conclusion holds regardless of the nature of the working-capital market (i.e., for both H.2 and H.3). The average value of the estimated elasticity of substitution for all the firms in our samples is 0.917. Thus the negligible differences in the results are quite consistent with what would be expected from the theory, given that the estimated values of σ are close to unity.[3] For whatever they are worth, the equally minuscule differences in predictive performance favor the segmented-capital-market hypothesis (H.3) in Japan, India, and Israel and the zero-effect hypothesis (H.1) in France.

In Table 7.4 we present the results of implementing these three alternative hypotheses with the free-form specification for each country. Once more, the first row of the table for each country merely reproduces the results presented earlier (Table 7.2). The next two

---

[3] Even when $\sigma = 0$ the quantitative importance of the effect of working capital on the cost ratio has been questioned (Chapter 2, Section 2.4).

Table 7.3. *Working-capital hypotheses: logit analysis of (6.16)*

Country	Intercept	CR^{1a}	L^b	I_A^c	I_R^c $(\bar{I}_R)^c$
France ($N = 50$)					
H.1	2.550^d	-3.562	3.08	0.0491	0.0508
	(1.947)	(2.102)			(0.0310)
H.2	2.542^d	-3.552	3.07	0.0489	0.0506
	(1.946)	(2.100)			(0.0308)
H.3	2.545^d	-3.556	3.07	0.0490	0.0507
	(1.946)	(2.101)			(0.0309)
Japan ($N = 52$)					
H.1	4.683	-5.524	8.68	0.1146	0.1196
	(2.100)	(2.117)			(0.1020)
H.2	4.685	-5.526	8.62	0.1149	0.1199
	(2.099)	(2.116)			(0.1023)
H.3	4.694	-5.536	8.65	0.1154	0.1205
	(2.100)	(2.117)			(0.1029)
India ($N = 75$)					
H.1	3.615	-3.425	5.07	0.0501	0.0519
	(1.392)	(1.606)			(0.0389)
H.2	3.617	-3.427	5.07	0.0501	0.0519
	(1.392)	(1.607)			(0.0389)
H.3	3.651	-3.464	5.16	0.0509	0.0537
	(1.398)	(1.612)			(0.0408)
Israel ($N = 49$)					
H.1	7.333	-7.211	15.28	0.2000	0.2043
	(2.172)	(2.263)			(0.1874)
H.2	7.335	-7.212	15.30	0.2003	0.2046
	(2.172)	(2.263)			(0.1877)
H.3	7.338	-7.214	15.32	0.2006	0.2049
	(2.173)	(2.262)			(0.1880)

Note: Standard errors are given in parentheses below their respective coefficients.
[a]The cost ratio for three shifts versus one shift was calculated in three different ways by using the values of θ, summarized in Table 6.3, that correspond to the three working-capital hypotheses.
[b]Observed value of $-2 \ln \lambda$, where λ is a likelihood-ratio statistic. $\chi_1^2 (5\%) = 3.84$.
[c]These measures of predictive performance were defined in Chapter 4.
[d]Statistically insignificant t ratio at the 5% level, using a one-sided t test.

rows for each country present the results of implementing the hypothesis of a perfectly competitive market and the hypothesis of a segmented market, in that order. In the free-form specification the different hypotheses are implemented through the introduction of additional variables in the equation to be estimated. Specifically, H.2 is implemented by introducing the period of turnover, P, and H.3 is implemented by introducing both the period of turnover and the interest variable, $I(VA)$.

For both France and Japan a two-sided t test at the 10% level fails to reject the null hypothesis of a zero value for the population parameters that correspond to the two working-capital variables.[4] Similarly, the likelihood-ratio test fails to reject the null hypothesis that the coefficients of P or of both P and $I(VA)$ do not belong in the logit equation at the 5% level. In sum, the free-form results are consistent with the restricted-form results for France and Japan (i.e., working-capital considerations are inconsequential for the shift-work decision).

For India the results are somewhat harder to interpret. A two-sided t test rejects the null hypothesis that the interest variable does not affect shift-work at the 10% level, but it does not reject the hypothesis at the 5% level; and the likelihood-ratio test cannot reject the null hypothesis that both P and $I(VA)$ do not belong in the logit equation (H.3) at the 5% level. The introduction of the interest variable for India has the effect of lowering the t ratios for capital intensity and relative size; it also lowers predictive performance, corrected for degrees of freedom $(\bar{I}_R)$, relative to the zero-effect hypothesis (H.1). For Israel, by contrast, the statistical results are unequivocal in favoring the segmented-capital-market hypothesis (H.3) relative to the other two.[5] To conclude, for India these free-form results are consistent with the restricted-form results regarding the lack of importance of working-capital considerations for the shift-work decision, but the same conclusion does not hold for Israel.

There is no doubt that one's confidence in a particular conclusion is enhanced when both specifications of the independent variables support the same conclusion. When there is a conflict, however, we tend to favor the conclusion supported by the restricted-form results. In this particular case, our favoritism is due to the following considerations: The interest-rate variable under the segmented-capital-market hypothesis (H.3) is based on total value added for the firm. Hence, the presence of a simultaneity problem with respect to the level of output

[4] For simplicity, the table indicates statistical insignificance with a one-sided test, but the appropriate test for the working-capital variables is a two-sided test because their expected sign is ambiguous, as indicated in Section 6.7.
[5] The results presented for H.2 in Israel are not strictly comparable because of the omission of the squared relative-size term.

Table 7.4. Working-capital hypotheses: logit analysis of (6.18)

Country	Intercept	k^*	RS	RS²	P	I(VA)	L^a	I_A^b	I_R^b $(\bar{I}_R)^b$
France (N = 50)									
H.1	-0.552^c (0.464)	-0.004^c (0.008)	—	—	—	—	0.33 (1)	0.0067	0.0069 (−0.0138)
H.2	−1.219 (0.638)	-0.002^c (0.008)	—	—	2.834^c (1.77)	—	2.75 (1)	0.0329	0.0341 (−0.0070)
H.3	-0.426^c (1.047)	-0.002^c (0.008)	—	—	2.099^c (1.897)	-8.629^c (9.617)	3.72 (2)	0.0546	0.0565 (−0.0050)
Japan (N = 52)									
H.1	−2.056 (0.661)	0.674 (0.316)	—	—	—	—	7.34 (1)	0.0862	0.0900 (0.0718)
H.2	−2.148 (0.774)	0.671 (0.315)	—	—	0.903^c (3.831)	—	0.05 (1)	0.0879	0.0918 (0.0547)
H.3	-2.077^c (1.441)	0.662 (0.357)	—	—	0.788^c (4.308)	-0.226^c (3.890)	0.06 (2)	0.0878	0.0917 (0.0349)
India (N = 75)									
H.1	-0.557^c (0.514)	0.046 (0.026)	0.741^c (0.738)	-0.007^c (0.197)	—	—	15.66 (3)	0.1708	0.1769 (0.1421)
H.2	-0.795^c (0.598)	0.046 (0.027)	0.763^c (0.605)	-0.018^c (0.147)	1.427^c (2.010)	—	0.53 (1)	0.1744	0.1806 (0.1338)
H.3	1.455^c (1.340)	0.025^c (0.028)	-0.317^c (1.010)	0.141^c (0.258)	2.451^c (2.150)	−8.888 (4.649)	4.45 (2)	0.1925	0.1994 (0.1414)

Israel ($N = 49$)

H.1	-3.776	0.129	3.554	-0.649	—	—	30.16 (3)	0.4361	0.4455
	(1.384)	(0.052)	(1.233)	(0.234)					(0.4085)
H.2[d]	-1.293[c]	0.088	-0.132[c]	—	2.208[c]	—	12.33 (3)	0.1833	0.1872
	(1.908)	(0.036)	(0.155)		(5.117)				(0.1330)
H.3	3.676[c]	0.191	3.990	-0.918	-2.970[c]	-53.936	8.36 (2)	0.5860	0.5986
	(2.941)	(0.086)	(1.860)	(0.399)	(7.870)	(26.280)			(0.5519)

Note: Standard errors are given in parentheses below their respective coefficients.
[a] Observed value of $-2 \ln \lambda$, where λ is a likelihood-ratio statistic and the number in parentheses indicates the number of restrictions imposed (always starting with the last column entry in the table).
[b] Measures of predictive performance defined in Chapter 4.
[c] Statistically insignificant t ratio at the 5% level, using a one-sided t test.
[d] Introduction of the square term led to nonconvergence of the iterative procedure.

must be considered; that is, we are using a function inversely related to
X^3, X^2, or X^1 as one of our independent variables. Whereas the
functional form chosen may dampen the reverse-causation problem, it
may not completely eliminate this problem in the free-form specification, as indicated in Section 6.6. Moreover, reverse causation is likely
to be more severe for Israel than for the other three countries because
the proportion of firms that work three shifts is much larger in Israel
than in the other three countries.[6] The arguments of Section 3.3
suggest that the difference between X^1 and X^2 or X^3 for any one firm
will be larger the greater the profitability of shift-work, and the
presence of a large number of firms working three shifts suggests a
high profitability of shift-work. These considerations indicate that the
causation running from shift-work to large value added [and a low
$I(VA)$] is stronger for Israel than for the other countries and is thus
responsible for the seeming strength of the interest variable in Israel.

To conclude, working-capital considerations play a largely inconsequential role in the long-run decision to work shifts. The theory
suggests this conclusion, and the empirical evidence supports it, with
one exception. This exception is, in our judgment, largely due to a
spurious correlation introduced by a severe reverse-causation problem
in Israel.

*7.3   Methodological issues

In this section we present results that cast some light on issues that are
important from the point of view of econometric methodology. In doing
so, however, we also provide evidence on the robustness of our
substantive results. The items to be discussed fall into the following
general categories: the appropriate independent variable in the
restricted-form specification; samples restricted by eliminating a class
of observations; estimation by the multinomial logit method; estimation
by ordinary least squares.

The results presented in Sections 7.1 and 7.2 for the restricted-form
specification were obtained by using the cost ratio for three shifts
versus one shift (CR^1) as the independent variable. The perceptive
reader may wish to know why we did not use the cost ratio for two
shifts versus one shift (CR), or perhaps both of them. When the
elasticity of substitution is high, the decision-making process can be
viewed as sequential (Section 2.3), and the appropriate basis for the

[6] The proportions of firms working three shifts in the four countries are as
follows: France 0.22, Japan 0.10, India 0.40, and Israel 0.53.

first step in the sequence is the cost ratio for three shifts versus one shift. Because our estimates of σ in Chapter 6 tended to be on the high side, we chose to use CR^1. However, there are two reasons that we should not rely solely (or even mainly) on this argument. First, we view our sequential procedure only as an approximation, because the conditions for sequentiality to hold for every observation are somewhat restrictive. Second, a very important source of differences between the two cost ratios (the shift differentials) takes on the same value for every observation in our empirical implementation. Thus the results of using CR with our data should be similar to the results based on CR^1. The results indeed corroborate this conjecture for all the combinations of models and assumptions employed in this chapter.[7] Furthermore, we also estimated a model for each country with the three-shift cost ratio (CR^1) introduced separately as an additional explanatory variable. The results (not presented here) exhibited the classic symptoms of multicollinearity: There were unusually large magnitudes for the coefficient estimates; the coefficient of CR and CR^1 always had opposite signs; t tests on the individual parameters led to statistically insignificant results, whereas a joint test on the whole relationship led to statistically significant results.

A related issue arises from our approach to the specification of the dependent variable (Section 4.2). We have argued that an informal test of our sequential approach to estimation would be provided by a comparison of the results obtained by treating two shifts and three shifts as the same in the first step of a sequence and the results obtained by dropping from the sample the observations of firms that worked either two or three shifts. In Table 7.5 we present the results obtained when the two-shift observations are dropped from the sample.[8] In this table the first row for each country is comparable to the corresponding row in Table 7.3. All corresponding coefficient estimates are within at least one standard deviation of one another, and in most cases they are

---

[7] Incidentally, the magnitudes of the coefficients for the two cost ratios are not directly comparable. In going from one cost ratio to the other, a difference in dimension, comparable to the scaling of variables, is introduced. Thus the similarity of results refers to the substantive hypotheses accepted or rejected by the data and to the predictive performance of the models in each country. Because no new insights can be derived from these results, they are not presented here.

[8] We dropped the two-shift observations rather than the three-shift observations because in three of the four countries (Japan being the exception) the resulting samples were larger.

Table 7.5. *Two-shift observations eliminated: logit analysis of (6.16)*

Country	Intercept	CR^1	L^a	I_A^b	I_R^b $(\bar{I}_R)^b$
France ($N = 45$)					
H.1	2.247^c	-3.649^c	2.55	0.0564	0.0627
	(2.169)	(2.365)			(0.0409)
Japan ($N = 41$)					
H.1	3.913^c	-5.922	3.54	0.0900	0.1203
	(3.222)	(3.362)			(0.0977)
India ($N = 54$)					
H.1	3.172	-3.495	3.41	0.0273	0.0273
	(1.717)	(1.999)			(0.0086)
Israel ($N = 43$)					
H.1	8.229	-8.504	16.87	0.2301	0.2317
	(2.512)	(2.693)			(0.2130)

Note: Standard errors are given in parentheses below their respective coefficient estimates.
[a]Observed value of $-2 \ln \lambda$, where λ is a likelihood-ratio statistic. χ_1^2 (5%) = 3.84; χ_1^2 (10%) = 2.71.
[b]These measures of predictive performance are defined in Chapter 4.
[c]Statistically insignificant t ratio at the 5% level, using a one-sided t test.

considerably closer than that. The same conclusion about the lack of importance of working-capital considerations emerges from the results for this restricted sample (the results for the other two working-capital hypotheses, H.2 and H.3, are not shown in Table 7.5 for reasons of space). Finally, in terms of predictive performance, dropping the two-shift observations produces a slight increase in $\bar{I}_R$ for France and Israel and a slight decrease in $\bar{I}_R$ for Japan and India.[9]

These results do not provide a formal test of the appropriateness of specifying the dependent variable in the full sample by treating two shifts and three shifts as the same with respect to one shift; nevertheless, they certainly demonstrate that the results are not very sensitive to the exclusion of the two-shift firms, and therefore they provide substantial informal support for the appropriateness of this approach

[9] It is possible, of course, to undertake similar informal comparisons of the two samples before removal of the bias due to the use of observed capital intensity and/or in terms of the free-form results; once more, however, we avoid being repetitive by merely reporting that in these comparisons the main substantive conclusions are the same in both samples.

Table 7.6. *Single-shift observations eliminated: logit analysis*

Country	Intercept	Slope	L^a	$I_A{}^b$	$\dfrac{I_R{}^b}{(\bar{I}_R)^b}$
France H.1 ($N = 16$)					
CR(32)	2.211^c	-1.496^c	0.02	0.0008	0.0008
	(10.65)	(11.18)			(-0.0706)
k^*	-0.152^c	0.022^c	0.47	0.0226	0.0235
	(1.460)	(0.033)			(-0.0463)
Japan H.1 ($N = 16$)					
CR(32)	-2.429^c	1.759^c	0.05	0.0260	0.0271
	(7.424)	(7.264)			(-0.0424)
k^*	-0.471^c	-0.122^c	0.31	0.0184	0.0191
	(0.800)	(0.245)			(-0.0510)
India H.1 ($N = 51$)					
CR(32)	-3.827^c	4.636^c	1.350	0.0077	0.0077
	(3.639)	(4.026)			(-0.0126)
k^*	0.407^c	-0.002^c	0.06	0.0006	0.0006
	(0.349)	(0.010)			(-0.0204)
Israel H.1 ($N = 32$)					
CR(32)	8.079^c	-7.175^c	0.94	0.0311	0.0384
	(7.060)	(7.575)			(0.0063)
k^*	0.525^c	0.034^c	2.00	0.0660	0.0815
	(0.824)	(0.029)			(0.0509)

Note: Standard errors are given in parentheses below their respective coefficient estimates.
[a]Observed values of $-2 \ln \lambda$, where λ is a likelihood-ratio statistic. χ_1^2 (10%) = 2.71.
[b]These measures of predictive performance are defined in Chapter 4.
[c]Statistically insignificant t ratio at the 5% level, using a one-sided t test.

to the estimation problem. Further support for this position can be derived from the two experiments to be reported next.

Our approach to the estimation problem, by itself, does not suggest any implications for the results obtained by dropping the single-shift observations from a sample. This restricted sample merely provides the information for estimating the second step in our sequence. We report the results of this second step in Table 7.6. In the restricted-form specification we used the ratio of costs of the triple-shift system to the costs of the double-shift system as our main explanatory variable;[10] that is, we used CR(32) = CR^1/CR. In the free-form specification, we

[10] We used the cost ratios corrected for the simultaneity problem with respect to capital intensity. In other words, the cost ratios were based on $\sigma_i = \hat{\sigma}_i$.

Table 7.7. *A comparison of predictive performance*

Statistical model	Country	I_A	I_R	$\bar{I}_R$
Intercept, k^*				
Trinomial logit	France	0.0058	0.0064	−0.0368
	Japan	−0.1042	n.a.[a]	n.a.[a]
Two and three the same	France	0.0067	0.0069	−0.0138
	Japan	0.0862	0.0900	0.0718
Intercept, k^*, RS, RS^2				
Trinomial logit	India	−0.0001	n.a.	n.a.
	Israel	0.1825	0.2020	0.1436
Two and three the same	India	0.1708	0.1769	0.1421
	Israel	0.4361	0.4455	0.4085

[a]Not applicable because the information derived from the statistical analysis is less than the information available in the sample proportions.

used the true measure of capital intensity, k^*. Two of the four coefficients for the cost ratio have "wrong" (positive) signs and the same holds true for the capital–labor ratio. Both specifications of the independent variables are quite unsuccessful in explaining the choice of two shifts versus three shifts. In a sense, this result is not surprising because of the absence of information in our data about the shift differentials for every firm. Clearly these differentials play a critical role in the choice between two shifts and three shifts. For instance, as indicated in Section 2.3, a sufficiently low value of b (the ratio of the night-shift differential to the evening-shift differential) ensures the inferiority of the double-shift system. In any event, the empirical choice between two shifts and three shifts is not explained in these four countries by the variables that we have been able to measure.

Another experiment performed on our data was the fitting of a multinomial logit. We limited ourselves to the free-form specification of the independent variables. In one specification we introduced the "true" capital–labor ratio and a constant in each of the two multinomial logit equations. The results confirm what one would expect on the basis of the previous results in this section. For instance, in every country at least one coefficient (and often both coefficients) of the capital–labor ratio was not significantly different from zero at the 5% level, with a one-sided t test. In every country but Israel, one of the coefficients of the capital–labor ratio had the "wrong" sign. In Table 7.7 we compare the predictive performance of the trinomial logit

Table 7.8. *Results of OLS estimation: (6.16)*

Country	Intercept	CR[1]	R^2	$\overline{R}^2$
France ($N = 50$)				
H.1 $\sigma_i = \sigma = 0$	1.847	-1.528	0.3285	0.3145
	(0.320)	(0.315)		
$\sigma_i = \hat{\sigma}_i$	1.019	-0.742	0.0604	0.0408
	(0.404)	(0.422)		
H.3 $\sigma_i = \hat{\sigma}_i$	1.018	-0.741	0.0602	0.0406
	(0.404)	(0.423)		
Japan ($N = 52$)				
H.1 $\sigma_i = \sigma = 0$	1.822	-1.331	0.3009	0.2869
	(0.331)	(0.287)		
$\sigma_i = \hat{\sigma}_i$	1.388	-1.062	0.1605	0.1438
	(0.354)	(0.343)		
H.3 $\sigma_i = \hat{\sigma}_i$	1.388	-1.062	0.1613	0.1445
	(0.354)	(0.343)		
India ($N = 75$)				
H.1 $\sigma_i = \sigma = 0$	1.598	-1.102	0.2062	0.1953
	(0.216)	(0.253)		
$\sigma_i = \hat{\sigma}_i$	1.242	-0.688	0.0649	0.0521
	(0.255)	(0.306)		
H.3 $\sigma_i = \hat{\sigma}_i$	1.248	-0.694	0.0659	0.0531
	(0.256)	(0.306)		
Israel ($N = 49$)				
H.1 $\sigma_i = \sigma = 0$	1.851	-1.282	0.3547	0.3409
	(0.242)	(0.252)		
$\sigma_i = \hat{\sigma}_i$	1.794	-1.270	0.2797	0.2644
	(0.274)	(0.297)		
H.3 $\sigma_i = \hat{\sigma}_i$	1.794	-1.270	0.2803	0.2650
	(0.273)	(0.297)		

Note: Standard errors are given in parentheses below their respective coefficient estimates.

results with that of the results obtained by treating two shifts and three shifts as the same with respect to one shift. These comparisons uniformly and without the slightest doubt favor the approach we have adopted over the trinomial logit. For France and Japan, the comparisons are undertaken in terms of a free-form specification that relies only on a constant and the capital–labor ratio; for India and Israel, the comparisons are undertaken in terms of a free-form specification that relies on a constant, the capital–labor ratio, relative size, and its square as explanatory variables. Similar conclusions with respect to the comparison are obtained, however, by adding the working capital variables or by making the comparisons using observed measures rather than "true" measures of capital intensity. A noteworthy feature of Table 7.7 lies in the results for Japan and India with the trinomial model. The predictions of the model for these two countries contain misinformation rather than information. As a matter of fact, for these two countries the information (misinformation) contained in the predictions using the sample proportions is greater (smaller) than that provided by the predictions of the model!

Finally, we turn to the results of estimating the same relationships as in Sections 7.1 and 7.2 with ordinary least squares. Let us consider first the restricted-form specification (Table 7.8). These estimates are to be compared to those available in Tables 7.1 and 7.3. Just as in the case of logit analysis, there is a substantial drop in predictive performance when we use the conceptually appropriate measure of capital intensity (the results for the row where $\sigma = \hat{\sigma}_i$) instead of observed capital intensity ($\sigma_i = \sigma = 0$). Along the same lines, working-capital considerations have a negligible impact on the statistical results (compare the second and third rows for each country in Table 7.8). Last but not least, these OLS results also provide evidence that the theory is consistent with the data after the removal of the simultaneity problem with respect to capital intensity.

OLS estimation with the free-form specification of the independent variables also leads to conclusions similar to those of the corresponding logit analysis. Because of space limitations, these OLS estimates will not be presented here. The differences between the two sets of estimates in the free-form specification are differences in degree, not in kind; by and large, they stem from the tendency of the OLS estimates to have somewhat higher t ratios than the corresponding logit estimates. Moreover, the main substantive conclusions to be derived from the results using the free-form specification of the independent variables are the same with both estimation methods.

7.4   Concluding remarks

From the arguments in the previous three sections, three very firm conclusions emerge with respect to the substantive topic under investigation.

First, the simultaneity problem with respect to capital intensity leads to very serious biases in the statistical analysis of the shift-work decision. Although the sign of the bias with respect to the capital-intensity coefficient was theoretically and empirically ambiguous, the overstatement of predictive performance by the use of observed measures of capital intensity was empirically observed in every instance where a comparison was possible. Moreover, the empirically observed degree of overstatement was of substantial magnitude in almost every instance.

Second, the working-capital considerations exposed in Section 2.4 were not found to be empirically useful in explaining the shift-work decision.

Third, and most important, the main elements of the theory developed in Part I were not rejected by the data for each of the four UNIDO countries. A noteworthy aspect of this result is that it was obtained after removal of the simultaneity problem with respect to capital intensity.

In order to place these conclusions, particularly the last one, in perspective, we need to add a few brief remarks. In the testing of the theory we have placed special emphasis on the cost ratio. This emphasis can be justified by three general considerations: This concept captures the four main elements identified as important in explaining shift-work under cost minimization (Chapters 1 and 2, Propositions 2 through 5); it is in principle amenable to empirical measurement; it allows us to detect how and why we "explain" shift-work. Nonetheless, the theoretical analysis in Chapter 3 suggests that there are other considerations, in addition to the ones captured by the cost ratio, that affect the profitability of shift-work. Incidentally, this argument holds for both the constant-β technology and the semi-U technology. For instance, one would certainly expect the difference in profits between the two systems [e.g., equation (3.7)] to be more closely associated with shift-work than the cost ratio, but it is almost impossible to measure a concept that requires information on each firm's demand curve. Considerations such as this one (and there are others) partly justify our assertion that the results of this chapter provide strong empirical support for the main elements of the theory developed in Part I, specifically those captured in the cost ratio, despite the relatively low values obtained for our measures of predictive performance in most cases.

Among the tasks left by our results for future empirical research on shift-work, there is one that deserves the highest priority, namely, application of the procedures developed in Part II to bodies of data that contain direct information on the shift differentials. Additional information bearing further evidence of the importance of these differentials will be presented in the next chapter. Before turning our attention to these results, however, we conclude this chapter by noting an important methodological issue raised by the results presented in Section 7.3. We have shown that the results of the most popular estimation method for the analysis of qualitative dependent variables, multinomial logit, are decidedly inferior to the results obtained in the first step of a sequential estimation procedure that is derived from an economic analysis of our choice problem. If the number of choice alternatives is small, let us say four or less, or if one has reason to question the axiom of independence of irrelevant alternatives, the results presented here suggest that the development of a sequential estimation procedure should be seriously considered as an alternative to the multinomial logit method.

CHAPTER 8

International comparisons

As we mentioned in the previous chapter, the individual-country results do not shed much light on one issue, namely, the existence of an inverse relationship between the level of the shift differentials and shift-work (Proposition 3). Our within-country analysis provides no information on this relationship because of the absence of direct information on these differentials. Nevertheless, the analysis of inter-country differences in shift-work will allow us to overcome to some degree this absence of information and to provide indirect evidence on the existence of such a relationship. Moreover, this analysis will also broaden the scope of our inquiry. From the confines of the causes of shift-work in the context of the theory of the firm, we move into the realm of the implications of shift-work for the firm and the economy.

A useful starting point in our present endeavor is a brief discussion of the existing literature on capital utilization and the level of economic development (Section 8.1). This discussion sets the stage for the econometric analysis of differences in shift-work among the countries in our UNIDO data (Section 8.2); moreover, it also provides the setting for a review of the available evidence on the extent and main characteristics of shift-work in various countries (Section 8.3). Our concluding remarks (Section 8.4) highlight several issues raised by the results in this chapter. These issues will be taken up in Part IV.

8.1 Capital utilization and the level of economic development

Two important conclusions are available in the literature on this subject. These conclusions have been quite clearly stated by Kim and Winston (1974): On the empirical side, there exists a positive relationship between capital utilization and the level of economic development; on the theoretical side, one should expect a negative relationship between capital utilization and the level of economic development. Not surprisingly, these conclusions are frequently referred to in subsequent work (e.g., Kim and Kwon 1977; Lecraw 1978). In this section we argue that the first conclusion is based on a measure of capital utilization that is extremely unreliable; in addition, we show here that the UNIDO data support the existence of a negative relationship rather than a positive relationship between utilization and development. In this section we also generalize the theoretical argument that led Kim and Winston to their second conclusion, and we show that on the theoretical side the sign of the relationship between utilization and development is likely to be ambiguous.

Kim and Winston came to their empirical conclusion on the basis of comparisons among Pakistan, South Korea, and the United States. The comparisons were based on Foss's measure of utilization (Kim and Winston 1974, p. 377), which was defined in terms of the relationship between electricity consumption and the rated capacity of electric motors over the year. The estimates reported by Kim and Winston were Pakistan 14%, South Korea 13–17%, and United States 23%. These estimates were remarkably low, although broadly consistent with the conclusion of a positive empirical relationship between utilization and development.

Morawetz (1976) analyzed the theoretical underpinnings of electricity-based measures of capital utilization. His analysis led to the conclusion that there are severe downward biases in these measures of capital utilization. More specifically, he argued that the severity of these biases depends directly on the difference between the theoretical rated capacity and maximum feasible consumption and on the share of non-electric-powered equipment in total equipment. It is worth noting that both sources of bias will be sensitive to the technological characteristics of different industrial processes; hence the extent of the bias is likely to vary when the sectoral composition of output varies. Morawetz (1976) also presented some empirical estimates of the bias for Israel by comparing the electricity measure with a time and intensity measure derived from survey data (defined as U_2 in our Chapter 5). The electricity measure indicated an all-industry utilization rate of 15%, whereas the survey estimate indicated a comparable utilization rate of 43%. Furthermore, the rankings of industrial branches by the two utilization measures were substantially different; for instance, the rank correlation across industrial branches was 0.56, and the null hypothesis of zero correlation could not be rejected at the 1% level. To conclude, Kim and Winston's empirical conclusion, derived entirely from electricity-based measures of capital utilization, is open to serious question.

It is useful at this point to emphasize the distinction between planned capital utilization and actual capital utilization. Actual utilization may fall below planned utilization because of machinery breakdowns, power failures, delivery failures on the part of suppliers, and other unforeseen events. One would expect the shortfall of actual from planned utilization to be greater in the developing countries than in developed countries. The electricity measure of utilization may be capturing some of these phenomena. Our interest throughout this book, however, is primarily in the determinants of planned capital utilization. As we shall discuss in the next paragraph, this variable is also the one to which Kim and Winston directed their theoretical analysis.

Kim and Winston reached their theoretical conclusion by a two-step argument. First, they established the factors determining the level of utilization in terms of a condition (equation 9 in their article) that could be derived by imposing the assumption of constant returns to scale on the Leontief cost ratio.[1] Second, they tried to establish a relationship between these factors and the level of economic development, measured in terms of per capita income (y). In light of the theory developed in Part I, we can recast their first step in somewhat more general terms by postulating

$$u = u\,[\theta, \alpha, \sigma, \phi(X)\,] \tag{8.1}$$

where the symbols remain the same as in previous chapters. Moreover, we can recast their second step by letting the arguments in (8.1) be functions of the level of per capita income. The relationship between the level of capital utilization (u) and the level of per capita income (y) can then be ascertained by determining the sign of

$$\frac{du}{dy} = \frac{\partial u}{\partial \theta}\frac{\partial \theta}{\partial y} + \frac{\partial u}{\partial \alpha}\frac{\partial \alpha}{\partial y} + \frac{\partial u}{\partial \sigma}\frac{\partial \sigma}{\partial y} + \frac{\partial u}{\partial \phi(X)}\frac{\partial \phi(X)}{\partial y} \tag{8.2}$$

One way of summing up the Kim-Winston analysis in terms of (8.2) is as follows: They ignored the last two terms in (8.2); they established that $\partial u/\partial \theta > 0$ and $\partial u/\partial \alpha < 0$ from the Leontief cost ratio; they presented arguments implying that $\partial \theta/\partial y < 0$ and $\partial \alpha/\partial y > 0$; on this basis, they concluded that $du/dy < 0$ (i.e., there should be a negative relationship between capital utilization and the level of economic development). An important purpose of the discussion that follows is to show that $du/dy \gtreqless 0$. That is, the relationship between utilization and development that can be extrapolated from the results of the theory of the firm is ambiguous.

First, let us note the signs of the following partial derivatives: $\partial u/\partial \theta > 0$; $\partial u/\partial \alpha < 0$; $\partial u/\partial \sigma > 0$; $\partial u/\partial \sigma(X) < 0$. These signs follow

---

[1] Equation (2.5) in Chapter 2 gives the Leontief cost ratio; constant returns to scale imply that $\phi(X) = \frac{1}{2}$ in this equation.

from Propositions 2 through 5, which were established in Chapters 1 and 2, and they require no further comment. Next we consider the relationship between capital intensity and development $(\partial\theta/\partial y)$. Kim and Winston asserted that this relationship is negative on the grounds that the price of capital relative to the price of labor decreases as development increases, a phenomenon that will decrease the capital share (θ) if the elasticity of substitution is less than unity. If the elasticity of substitution is greater than unity, however, their argument implies that the relationship between capital intensity and development is positive. Most of the estimates of σ presented in Table 6.1 are consistent with the null hypothesis that σ is unity. Hence, we would be hesitant to assert that the first term in (8.2) is unambiguously negative. Kim and Winston also argued that $\partial\alpha/\partial y > 0$ because the shift differential reflects the disutility of working at abnormal hours and daytime work is a normal good. Although this argument is plausible, we shall note in Chapter 12 that the level of α depends importantly on a society's traditions with respect to the time patterns of work and social life. If societies become less tradition-bound as they modernize, the level of α might even decline as income increases. The available evidence on the magnitude of α in rich and poor countries is also thoroughly ambiguous, as we shall document in Chapter 12. The third term in (8.2) is also of uncertain sign, because there is no compelling reason to argue that the elasticity of substitution depends positively, negatively, or not at all on the level of per capita income. Finally, if one makes the reasonable assumption that the level of output of the typical firm increases with the per capita income of the country, then with a semi-U technology $\partial\phi(X)/\partial y < 0$. Therefore, a case could be made that the fourth term is positive.

To reiterate, the analysis of shift-work and the theory of the firm does not yield any definite results on the relationship between capital utilization and the level of economic development. What the theory of the firm clearly suggests is that capital utilization is negatively related to the cost ratio, but arguments in favor of the cost ratio bearing a stable relationship to the level of economic development require so many caveats as to render them useless. For additional caveats, besides the ones discussed here, see the work of Thoumi (1975, revised 1978, Appendix 6).

We conclude this section by presenting the evidence that the UNIDO data provide on this issue (Table 8.1). Two features of the table are noteworthy. First, the ranking of Israel and Japan in terms of per capita income will conflict with the judgment of many observers on the relative levels of development of the two countries at that time

Table 8.1. *Capital utilization and its determinants and the levels of economic development in UNIDO countries*

Country	u^a	θ^b	$(\alpha^1)^c$	σ^d	$\phi(X)^e$	$(CR^1)^f$	y^g
India	0.680	0.385	0.03	0.82	0.595	0.818	129
Japan	0.308	0.295	0.45	0.99	0.575	1.018	1,021
Israel	0.653	0.320	0.12	0.94	0.590	0.898	1,528
France	0.320	0.304	0.30	0.91	0.575	0.942	2,503

[a]u is the proportion of firms that work shifts in the UNIDO sample.
[b]θ is the average capital share under single-shift operation, calculated as described in Section 6.2.
[c]α^1 is the value of the nighttime shift differential selected in Section 6.5.
[d]σ is the average value of the elasticity of substitution according to the estimates described in Section 6.3.
[e]$\phi(X)$ is the average value of relation (6.10) for each country. For France and Japan this value is the same for every firm because of the assumption of a constant-β technology.
[f]CR^1 is the average value of the three-shifts-versus-one-shift cost ratio, which was used to estimate the model with a zero-effect-of-working-capital hypothesis (H.1) for each country. For France and Japan CR^1 was calculated under the assumption of a constant-β technology.
[g]y is real gross domestic product per capita in 1963 (measured in 1973 U.S. dollars) taken from Table 1-2 of Kindleberger and Herrick (1977).

(1963), and that ranking is currently reversed by a substantial margin. Second, if one views Japan and France as developed countries and India and Israel as developing ones, the data in column 7 notwithstanding, a comparison of columns 1 and 7 suggests the existence of an inverse empirical relationship between capital utilization and the level of economic development, a relationship that is fully consistent with the behavior of the cost ratio. Instead of pursuing this type of argument further, we turn now to the following question: To what extent is the theory of the firm, captured in our measured cost ratio, capable of explaining intercountry differences in shift-work?

8.2   An econometric analysis of shift-work differences among the UNIDO countries

Our point of departure is the same as in Chapter 7. We are interested in estimating the probability that the factory works shifts, and logit analysis will be the estimation technique. The independent variable will be the cost ratio (CR^1) for three shifts versus one shift. This cost ratio is calculated for each country in the manner described in Chapter 6. In light of the results of Chapter 7, the analysis will be restricted to the cost ratio that incorporates the hypothesis of zero effect of working capital (H.1). Thus the only difference between the analysis here and the analysis in Chapter 7 lies in our pooling of the four country samples.[2] Consequently, the main questions of specification that arise in this section are the following: Should we expect the relationship between shift-work and the cost ratio to be the same in every country? Should we expect the intercept of this relationship to vary because of country-specific factors? Finally, should we also expect the slope of this relationship to vary with country-specific factors?

The empirical specifications consistent with the preceding questions are, respectively:

$$Y_i = \beta_0 + \beta_1 CR^1 \qquad \text{(6.16 repeated)} \qquad\qquad (8.3)$$

$$Y_i = \beta_0 + \beta_1 CR^1 + \beta_2 D_I + \beta_3 D_{IN} + \beta_4 D_{IS} \qquad\qquad (8.4)$$

$$Y_i = \beta_0 + \beta_1 CR^1 + \beta_2 D_I + \beta_3 D_{IN} + \beta_4 D_{IS}$$
$$+ \beta_5 D_I CR^1 + \beta_6 D_{IN} CR^1 + \beta_7 D_{IS} CR^1 \quad (8.5)$$

where Y_i is an index of independent variables as before, and D_j indicates a dummy variable for country j. For example, D_{IS} is a variable that takes on the value 1 if an observation in the pooled sample is from Israel and the value of 0 otherwise. France is the base country in (8.4) and (8.5). That is, β_0 and β_1 are the population parameters for France; the other parameters measure differences between the intercept or slope parameter for France and the intercept or slope parameters for the other countries.

The results of implementing (8.3) through (8.5) are presented in panel A of Table 8.2. To repeat, the cost ratio for each factory is the same as that used in Chapter 7, and of course the shift differentials vary across countries. Equation (8.5) in panel A shows that the data do not support the specification that implies different slopes among the countries. That is, using the likelihood-ratio test, it is not possible to reject the joint null hypothesis that each of the three slope coefficients (β_5, β_6, and β_7) is equal to zero at the 5% level of significance. Similarly, using an individual t test, it is not possible to reject the null hypothesis that each of these slope coefficients equals zero at the 5% level of significance. These results suggest that for each country an

[2] Incidentally, one advantage of our development of the theory in terms of the cost ratio is that no dimensionality or measurement problems arise at this stage with respect to international comparisons.

Table 8.2. *Cross-country logit analysis*

Model	Japan				India		Israel		I_R^a $(\bar{I}_R)$	L^b
	β_0	β_1	β_2	β_5	β_3	β_6	β_4	β_7		
A. Shift differentials vary across countries										
(8.3)	4.954	−5.396							0.0902	45.38 (1)
	(0.848)	(0.913)							(0.0853)	
(8.4)	3.677	−4.801	0.296[c]		1.116		1.380		0.1227	13.26 (3)
	(0.933)	(0.966)	(0.460)		(0.417)		(0.459)		(0.1068)	
(8.5)	2.550[c]	−3.562	2.133[c]	−1.962[c]	1.065[c]	0.136[c]	4.783[c]	−3.649[c]	0.1305	2.47[d] (3)
	(1.947)	(2.102)	(2.864)	(2.983)	(2.393)	(2.645)	(2.917)	(3.088)	(0.1036)	
B. Shift differentials identical across countries										
(8.3)	4.072	−4.553							0.0488	28.46 (1)
	(0.844)	(0.936)							(0.0441)	
(8.4)	3.503	−4.833	−0.050[c]		1.524		1.619		0.1181	28.82 (3)
	(0.921)	(0.997)	(0.447)		(0.416)		(0.465)		(0.1021)	
(8.5)	2.674[c]	−3.879	2.773[c]	−3.245[c]	0.752[c]	0.824[c]	4.622[c]	−3.240[c]	0.1293	3.51[d] (3)
	(2.046)	(2.319)	(3.155)	(3.591)	(2.438)	(2.739)	(2.976)	(3.220)	(0.1014)	

Note: Standard errors are given in parentheses below their respective coefficients.

[a] Measures of predictive performance defined in Chapter 4.

[b] Observed value of $-2 \ln \lambda$, the likelihood-ratio statistic. The numbers in parentheses are the numbers of restrictions tested. For equation (8.5) the restrictions are $\beta_5 = \beta_6 = \beta_7 = 0$.

[c] Statistically insignificant t ratio at the 5% level, using a one-sided t test.

[d] Statistically insignificant restrictions at the 5% level.

increase in the cost ratio has approximately the same impact on the probability that a factory works shifts. Parenthetically, the estimates of the intercepts and slopes for each country implied by (8.5) are the same as those obtained individually in Chapter 7, a fact that can be easily checked by comparing the estimates for France in Table 8.2 with the corresponding ones in Table 7.1 or 7.3.

A very clear-cut result emerges from panel A in Table 8.2. The specification supported by the data is the one that allows the intercepts to vary across countries (8.4). For instance, it scores highest on the measures of predictive performance corrected for degrees of freedom $(\bar{I}_R)$. Furthermore, using the likelihood-ratio test, we reject the joint null hypothesis of zero differences in the intercepts $(\beta_2 = \beta_3 = \beta_4 = 0)$ at the 1% level of significance. An individual t test on India and Israel also rejects, at the 1% level, the null hypothesis that the intercept for each of these countries is the same as that for France. By contrast, in a similar t test, it is not possible to reject, at the 5% level, the null hypothesis that the intercept parameters are the same in Japan and France.[3] An interpretation of these results is that the cost ratio is capable of explaining within-country variations as well as between-country variations in shift-work, but there are country-specific factors that are also helpful in explaining intercountry variations in levels of shift-work. These country-specific factors differ substantially between the developed countries (France, Japan) and the developing ones (India, Israel), but they are similar within each of these two categories.

At last we are ready to consider the evidence provided by the analysis of intercountry differences regarding the relationship between the shift differentials and shift-work. The results in panel A of Table 8.2 rely on a cost ratio that is calculated with different shift differentials for each country. Thus, part of the explanatory power of the cost ratio in these regressions is due to variations across countries in these differentials. Table 8.1 reveals that the shift differentials selected are lower in the developing countries (India, Israel), where utilization is high, than in the developed countries, where utilization is low (France, Japan). Hence, in order to ascertain the degree to which these variations in the assumed shift differentials are useful in explaining shift-work differences across countries through their impact on the cost ratio, we performed the following experiment: We set the shift differentials equal to each other at a value of 0.136 (i.e., $\alpha^1 = \alpha =$

---

[3] A similar test between India and Israel cannot reject the null hypothesis that their intercept coefficients are the same at the 5% level of significance.

0.136). We then calculated the cost ratio in exactly the same manner as described in Chapter 6, with one exception: Wherever the shift differentials appeared in a calculation, the new common value was inserted in place of the old different ones. The results of estimating equations (8.3) through (8.5) with the cost ratio calculated in this fashion are presented in panel B of Table 8.2.

What do the results show? We must note first that the substantive conclusions arising from the results in panel B are the same as those already discussed in connection with panel A. Hence they will not be discussed again. Instead, we focus on comparisons between panels A and B. In every one of the three feasible comparisons the measures of predictive performance are higher in panel A than in panel B, a result that implies that there is a gain in explanatory power from allowing the shift differentials to vary across countries in the manner we chose in Chapter 6. Nevertheless, the increase in predictive performance is quite substantial with specification (8.3) but of limited magnitude with specifications (8.4) and (8.5). Our interpretation of these findings is that the substantial improvement in predictive performance in (8.3) provides indirect evidence of the existence of the relationship between the shift differentials and shift-work suggested by the theory. The fact that the improvements in predictive performance are small in magnitude for the other two specifications is quite consistent with this interpretation, because allowing the intercepts to differ across countries tends to capture the effects that the differentials may have had. In particular, notice the increases (decreases) in the values of the intercept-related estimates for India and Israel (Japan) in going from panel A to panel B; that is, compare β_3 and β_4 (β_2) in panels A and B of Table 8.2.

An alternative but also illuminating way of assessing the impact of variations in the shift differentials across countries is provided by another experiment that is based on the following considerations: If the theory captures the essence of the shift-work decision and the variables are measured correctly, the probability of shift-work when the cost ratio equals unity should be 0.5. Therefore we can calculate for each country, from the results for (8.4) or (8.5), the probability of shift-work when the cost ratio is unity under the two alternative assumptions for the shift differentials [i.e., that the shift differentials differ across countries (panel A results) or that the shift differentials are the same across countries (panel B results)]. When the shift differentials are allowed to vary across countries (e.g., in the manner indicated in Table 8.1), the theory (Proposition 3) suggests that the ability to explain or predict shift-work should be greater than when the shift

Table 8.3. *Probability of shift-work when cost ratio equals unity*

Country	Equation (8.5)		Equation (8.4)	
	Different α	Same α	Different α	Same α
France	0.267	0.231	0.245	0.209
Japan	0.301	0.158	0.304	0.201
India	0.547	0.592	0.498	0.548
Israel	0.531	0.544	0.564	0.572

Note: The entries in the body of the table are the probabilities of working shifts in each country, calculated according to (8.6). The slope and intercept estimates were obtained from the results presented in Table 8.2 by adding the French intercept or slope estimate to the corresponding one for every other country.

differentials are forced to be the same across countries. Thus, we should expect the predictions for each country based on the estimates from panel A to be closer to 0.5 than the corresponding predictions based on the estimates from panel B. For each country, when the cost ratio is unity, the probability of shift-work is

$$P(S_i = 1) = e^{\beta_{0j} + \beta_{1j}} / (1 + e^{\beta_{0j} + \beta_{1j}}) \qquad (8.6)$$

where the subscript j varies across the countries, the subscript 0 indicates an intercept coefficient, and the subscript 1 indicates a slope (cost ratio) coefficient.

The results are presented in Table 8.3. For every country the predictions based on the results that allow the shift differentials to differ are closer to 0.5 than the ones based on the results that force the shift differentials to be the same. This conclusion holds for every country and with either specification of the dummy variables (8.4) or (8.5). Hence, we have additional indirect support in favor of the existence of an inverse relationship between the shift differentials and shift-work. Therefore, incorporating this relationship into the inter-country analysis not only improves the amount of correct information in the whole sample ($\bar{I}_R$) but also improves our ability to predict correctly at specific points (i.e., where the cost ratio for a country equals unity). It is worth stressing that these two criteria do not necessarily lead to the same conclusion. For instance, in Chapter 7 we found that by using the cost ratios for each country separately, we predicted best (in terms of $\bar{I}_R$) over the whole sample in Japan and Israel, and we predicted worst in France and India (Table 7.3). Yet, using the same cost ratio, we predicted best at the point where the cost ratio equals unity in India and Israel, and we predicted worst in France and Japan [Table 8.3, the first column under equation (8.5)].

An inverse relationship between the shift differentials and shift-work is useful in interpreting the available evidence on the extent and main characteristics of shift-work in the next section; more important, it is a valuable result for the analysis of the implications of shift-work in Part IV. Therefore the provision of indirect evidence in favor of the existence of this relationship is a welcome stepping stone for our subsequent arguments.

8.3   Available evidence on the extent and main characteristics of shift-work in various countries

In Section 8.1 we gave several reasons for our serious reservations about the use of electricity-based measures for international comparisons of capital utilization. Continuous measures derived from the surveys performed in connection with the World Bank studies (Hughes et al. 1976) are indeed appropriate, but they are available for only four countries. Therefore in this section we shall rely on three different measures that are based on the number of shifts. These measures will allow us to engage in international comparisons using almost all the existing empirical information on shift-work. Parenthetically, variations in these measures across countries are indicative of variations in the intended long-run levels of capital utilization, but they cannot be interpreted as indicative of variations in capacity utilization or of the difference between actual and planned utilization. These measures are defined as follows:

$$S = \frac{1}{N} \sum_{i=1}^{N} S_i \tag{8.7}$$

$$S_K = \sum_{i=1}^{N} S_i w_i(K) \qquad \sum_{i=1}^{N} w_i(K) = 1 \tag{8.8}$$

$$S_L = \sum_{i=1}^{N} \sum_{k=1}^{3} L_{ki} / \sum_{i=1}^{N} L_{1i} \tag{8.9}$$

S_i, the number of shifts in plant i, can take on the value 1, 2, or 3. $w_i(K)$ is the ratio of the capital stock in plant i to the total capital stock in the sample. L_{ki} is the number of production workers on the kth shift in the ith plant. N is the number of plants in the sample.

The first measure (S) is a simple average of the numbers of shifts worked by plants in a sample. It has a tendency to overstate the degree

Table 8.4. *Extent of shift-work: UNIDO countries*

Country	Date	S_L	S	S_K
France	1964	1.23	1.65	1.95
India	1964	2.00	2.28	2.79
Israel	1964	1.40	2.34	2.80
Japan	1964	1.16	1.51	2.26
Yugoslavia	1963	1.59	2.77	2.93

Source: UNIDO (1967–8).

of capital utilization for multiple-process plants that work shifts on some processes but not on others. Because the capital-intensive processes will be the ones operated under shift-work (Chapter 1, Section 1.3), the degree of overstatement involved in the use of the measure S may not be too severe. The second measure (S_K) is a weighted average of the numbers of shifts in the sample, each plant's number of shifts being weighted by that plant's share in the total capital stock of the sample. This weighting scheme is conceptually appropriate for estimating the average rate of capital utilization in a country (provided the sample is representative in terms of size of factory and rate of utilization by size, a point to which we shall return later). S_L is simply the ratio of the total number of production workers in the sample to the sum over the plants of production workers on the first shift.[4] In multiple-process plants the ratio of night workers to day workers may seriously understate the proportion of the capital stock being operated at night, since the capital-intensive processes will be the ones operated at night. Thus the measure S_L is subject to severe downward bias as a measure of capital utilization. Incidentally, the severity of the bias is directly related to the level of the shift differentials: The higher the differentials, the more capital-intensive are shift-work processes (relative to the other processes).

Table 8.4 presents the results of calculating the three measures for each of the UNIDO countries. From this table one can derive an indication of the relationships among the three measures. Because we are not able to calculate all three measures for every other country for which we have some information, Table 8.4 will also be a convenient

[4] This statistic is defined in terms of production workers, but if only total workers were available, we used total workers. This practice may account for some of the differences between Tables 8.4 and 8.5.

reference standard for the measures we do present in Table 8.5. Nevertheless, some caution must be exercised in the comparisons of levels in the two tables, because in the UNIDO samples large and well-run factories are by design overrepresented, a fact that leads to overstatement of the amount of shift-work in these countries (see Chapter 6, Section 6.1).

As indicated in our earlier work (Betancourt and Clague 1976b), most of the capital stock in the UNIDO samples is utilized quite intensively. Even in the two countries where shift-work is not as prevalent when measured by S, the mean number of shifts weighted by the capital stock (S_K) is around 2, and in the other three countries it is very close to 3. Nonetheless, a somewhat different picture emerges from looking at the employment ratio, S_L. It is perhaps significant, however, that the drop in going from S to S_L is smallest in India, where we believe the shift differential to be the smallest of the four countries.

We have attempted to gather evidence comparable to that in Table 8.4 from the available sources for other countries and dates. Information on shift-work, however, is rather scarce, and it is difficult to ensure that the bodies of information obtained from different sources are comparable. Hence, inferences drawn directly from Table 8.5, where we summarize the evidence from other studies, should be made cautiously and after consulting the original sources. The estimates in Table 8.5 were selected as reasonably representative of the manufacturing sector of the country concerned. Nevertheless, large firms may be overrepresented in many of these sources, particularly in the ones

Table 8.5. *Extent of shift-work: other available evidence*

Country	Source	Date	S_L	S	S_K
United States	U.S. Department of Commerce, Bureau of Census, Survey of Plant Capacity	1973[a]	—	2.1	—
		1974[a]	—	1.8	—
		1975[a]	—	1.9	—
		1976[a]		1.9	
		1977[a]		1.9	
United States	U.S. Department of Labor (1978)[b]	1977	1.22	—	—
		1977	1.14		
United States	Denison (1967)[c]	1960	1.30	—	—
Belgium		1960	1.11	—	—
Denmark		1960	1.11	—	—
France		1960	1.11	—	—
Germany		1960	1.11	—	—

Table 8.5 *(cont.)*

Country	Source	Date	S_L	S	S_K
Netherlands		1960	1.11	—	—
Norway		1960	1.11	—	—
United Kingdom		1960	1.11	—	—
Italy		1960	1.19	—	—
France	Maurice (1975)[d]	1963	1.11	—	—
United Kingdom		1964	1.10	—	—
Japan		1968	1.07	—	—
United Kingdom	NBPI (1970)[e]	1968	1.13	—	—
Colombia	Thoumi (1975, revised 1978)[f]	1973	—	1.61	—
Israel	Hughes et al. (1976)[g]	1972	—	1.57	—
Malaysia	Hughes et al. (1976)[g]	1972	—	2.24	—
Philippines	Hughes et al. (1976)[g]	1972–3	—	1.88	—
USSR	Kabaj (1965)	1927	1.46	—	—
USSR		1932	1.73	—	—
Poland	Kabaj (1965)	1950	1.42	—	—
Poland		1956	1.69	—	—
Yugoslavia	Yugoslav Yearbook[h]	1971	1.53	—	—
Brazil	Schydlowsky (1979)[i]	1974	—	2.04	—
Costa Rica		1974	—	1.56	—
Peru		1971	—	1.56	2.42
Venezuela		1974	—	1.40	2.01
Kenya	Baily (1976)[j]	1971	—	1.30	2.24
Nigeria	Winston (1977b)[k]	1976	—	2.18	—
Morocco	Phan-Thuy (1979)[l]	1978		1.45	

[a]Fourth-quarter average for U.S. manufacturing.

[b]The upper number refers to manufacturing; the lower number refers to total nonfarm wage and salary workers.

[c]Calculated from the estimates of percentages of workers on the evening and night shifts reported by Denison (p. 173).

[d]Calculated from the appendix tables using the Denison procedure explained in the text.

[e]National Board for Prices and Incomes. Calculated from Table W using the Denison procedure.

[f]Calculated from Table No. 23 in 1978 revision.

[g]Calculated from Hughes (Table 1) by assuming that the estimate of the discrete measure bears the same relationship to the estimate of the continuous measure as in Colombia, where the discrete estimate of the measure of utilization was directly available.

[h]Calculated using the Denison procedure.

[i]S was calculated from Table I-1, S_K from Table I-4.

[j]Baily's units of observation are processes.

[k]Calculated from Table II-2.

[l]Calculated from Table IV-1 by assigning values of 1.5 and 2.5 to those factories reporting between one and two shifts per day and between two and three shifts per day, respectively.

for developing countries.[5] The analysis in Chapter 3 implies that overrepresentation of large firms leads to overestimates of shift-work.

Before discussing the estimates in Table 8.5, we should make several comments about procedures. Because the data for European countries and Japan typically include in "shift-workers" those working on the day shift, those day workers must be excluded from total shift-workers to obtain estimates of S_L. We have followed Denison (1967) in assuming that half of those engaged on double-shift systems and one-third of those engaged on triple-shift systems are employed on the day shift; because these are probably underestimates, the resulting measure of S_L is apt to be slightly overstated. In this context, we should also note that Denison's U.S. estimate of S_L is based on Bureau of Labor Statistics (BLS) surveys of standard metropolitan areas, where large factories are overrepresented; hence it is not comparable to the 1977 estimates reported in Table 8.5 that include the entire country.

Another source of noncomparability is that the reported average in Table 8.5 for the unweighted number of shifts in the United States (S) is actually based on an employment-weighted distribution of plants by the number of shifts. Because employment size tends to be positively correlated with shift-work, the figures listed in the table are probably somewhat overstated estimates of S. In this connection it is worth noting that from additional data in the surveys of plant capacity we can calculate the (employment-weighted) average number of hours per week for the sample plants. These averages for the years 1973 through 1977 were 89, 76, 82, 82, and 85 hours.

Despite the qualifications suggested by the previous remarks, several interesting conclusions can be drawn from Tables 8.4 and 8.5. First, as has been noted by many observers, shift-work is somewhat more common in the United States than in Western Europe.[6] Consequently, comparisons between the United States and less-developed countries (Kim and Winston 1974) give a misleading picture of the relationship between shift-work and economic development. Second, and more generally, the tables reveal a wide variety of shift-work experience among both developed and less-developed countries; there is obviously a great deal of room for social choice with respect to the

[5] An interesting discussion of this issue with respect to Nigeria and Malaysia is available in the work of Winston (1977b, Appendix).

[6] Kan and Prais (1978) have reexamined the data on shift-work in Britain, the United States, and Germany, and although they have revised Denison's estimates, they reaffirm the statement made in the text.

extent of shift-work. In particular, no relationship between the amount of shift-work and the level of economic development is discernible from these tables.[7]

Third, we observe in Table 8.5 that several European countries of very different sizes have extremely similar measures of S_L. Moreover, Japan, a country of large size, has the lowest measure of S_L. Because we know that average factory size is rather well correlated with market size as measured by a country's GDP (Scherer 1973; Pryor 1973), these figures on S_L pose something of a puzzle for those who believe that economies of scale constitute an important obstacle to shift-work in developed countries. The data presented here, as well as our findings for France and Japan, are consistent with the hypothesis that scale barriers are unimportant in developed countries. Also interesting in this context is the fact that among the Latin American countries for which Schydlowsky reported data, the highest level of shift-work occurred in Brazil (Table 8.5).[8] This observation is consistent with our finding that scale barriers to shift-work were important in the two less-developed countries in our sample (India and Israel).

The fourth and final observation we shall make about Tables 8.4 and 8.5 is that they indicate that the industrial capital stock of a country tends to be utilized rather heavily, whereas only a minority of industrial workers are exposed to shift-work. Thus, although the lowest value of S_K in the two tables is 1.95 for France, the value of S_L is well below 2 in all countries except India. An interesting aspect of these results is that they can be related to the two main characteristics of shift-work or stylized facts of capital utilization. To reiterate, the theory of the firm in Part I suggested, and every study reviewed in Chapter 5 corroborated, the following: a positive association between observed capital intensity and shift-work; a positive association between observed size and shift-work. The relationships among the three summary measures in Tables 8.4 and 8.5 bring out these two characteristics of shift-work or capital utilization.[9] In every possible comparison, $S_L < S < S_K$. The first of these inequalities is suggested by

[7] A more detailed analysis of this issue for the four countries in the World Bank study (Israel, Malaysia, Colombia, and the Philippines) leads to the same conclusion (Thoumi, 1975, revised 1978, pp. 89–91).

[8] However, Schydlowsky (1979, p. 313) warned that the higher level of shift-work in Brazil may be due to the higher representation of large enterprises in the Brazilian sample.

[9] Incidentally, there is additional descriptive evidence on these two characteristics of shift-work that will not be explicitly reviewed here (e.g., Winston 1977b; Betancourt 1977; Phan-Thuy 1979; Schydlowsky 1979).

the first characteristic; the second of these two inequalities is suggested by both of these characteristics.

To conclude this section, we shall discuss the scanty evidence on whether or not the extent of shift-work or capital utilization is increasing. Several time-series studies, conveniently summarized by Kim and Kwon (1977, Table 2), have revealed an increasing trend in utilization over time: Foss (1963) and Jorgenson and Griliches (1967) for the United States (1929-55 and 1954-62); Heathfield (1972) for the United Kingdom (1955-68); Kim and Kwon for South Korea (1962-71). All of these studies relied on electricity-based measures of utilization, and although the findings are interesting in their own right, one might question whether or not they provide solid evidence of an increasing trend in hours of use of the capital stock or in the extent of shift-work. In a similar vein, the National Board for Prices and Incomes (1970) reported that there was an upward trend in the extent of shift-work in the United Kingdom, but a reexamination of the basic data by Kan and Prais (1978) indicated that the evidence is also consistent with the proposition that no change in the extent of shift-work occurred during the period 1951-68.

Although the studies just cited suggest an upward trend in shift-work, they fail to provide conclusive evidence for this trend. There is, however, solid evidence of an upward trend in shift-work in the United States from the BLS surveys of manufacturing plants for the period 1960-74 (O'Connor 1970; U.S. Department of Labor 1975). Additional evidence was furnished by Taubman and Gottschalk (1971), whose series for the average work week of capital in U.S. manufacturing revealed a 5% increase in utilization from 1952 to 1968; moreover, as Denison (1974, p. 56) pointed out, this series together with a similar one for the average work week of labor indicated that the prevalence of shift-work may have increased toward the end of the period. There is also some evidence for other market economies. For instance, the National Board for Prices and Incomes (1970) reported increases in the proportions of workers engaged in shift-work in The Netherlands (1949-63) and France (1957-63). For various periods during the postwar years, Sloane (1978) reported a noticeable increase in shift-work for most Western European countries, especially France and West Germany, and minor changes in shift-work for a few countries (e.g., The Netherlands and Japan). His information was based on a personal communication for Mr. K. H. Horn of the International Labour Office. Finally, Thoumi (1975, revised 1978, pp. 79-85), in his analysis of Colombian data, provided some evidence of substantial increases in capital utilization over the period 1945-74; furthermore, the evidence of increases in capital utilization from 1961 to 1970 is especially convincing because of the quality and comparability of the underlying measurements.

The experience of the socialist countries with respect to shift-work is markedly different from that of the market economies. As can be seen from Table 8.5, substantial increases in shift-work took place in Russia and Poland during the periods 1927–32 and 1950–6, respectively. These increases differed from the others noted here because, as stressed by Kabaj (1965), they were the results of a conscious policy to augment capital utilization during these periods. According to the same authority, this policy was also employed by other socialist countries during the early postwar period. Interestingly enough, in a very recent study, Kabaj (1978, p. 86) noted a minor reversal of the upward trend for most socialist countries in the late postwar period, roughly from the mid-1960s to the mid-1970s. Not much should be made of this reversal, because the more recent levels of shift-work in the socialist countries are still substantially above those in the market economies. For instance, the most recent figure reported for Poland in 1976 was 1.63, which is slightly lower than the figure for 1956 but considerably higher than the level reported for any market economy in Table 8.5.

On the basis of all the studies discussed in the previous paragraphs, we find it eminently reasonable to conclude that one of the main characteristics of capital utilization is its upward trend in a variety of countries during the postwar period. This conclusion from the country studies cited previously is substantially strengthened by the results obtained from a unique industry study that was undertaken by GATT for cotton textiles. The information from this study was utilized by Kabaj (1978, pp. 31–7) to calculate a measure of shift-work, the shift coefficient,[10] that exhibited the following behavior: In the spinning activity the average shift coefficient increased from 1.44 in 1953 to 2.04 in 1964 for fifteen developed countries and from 1.85 to 2.38 for ten developing countries over the same period; in the weaving activity the average shift coefficient increased from 1.41 in 1953 to 1.98 in 1964 for the fifteen developed countries and from 1.65 to 2.03 for the ten developing countries. The cotton textile industry provided remarkably solid evidence of a significant increase in capital utilization for a wide variety of countries during the 1953–69 period.

[10] Conceptually, the shift coefficient is defined for this purpose as the ratio of the number of machine hours worked in all shifts to the number of machine hours worked in the first shift.

8.4 Concluding remarks

The conventional wisdom on the relationship between capital utilization and economic development is, first, that theoretical considerations lead one to expect high rates of capital utilization in countries where capital is scarce and per capita incomes are low and, second, that the facts are the opposite of what one would expect. We have argued that when we expand the theoretical model to include all the relevant considerations, the relationship between economic development and capital utilization is thoroughly ambiguous. Moreover, our review of the empirical evidence from the UNIDO countries and from many other countries revealed no discernible relationship between the rate of utilization and the level of development.

The intercountry regressions from the UNIDO sample showed that the cost ratio successfully predicted variations in shift-work across France, Japan, India, and Israel. The improvement in the predictions when the shift differentials were allowed to vary across countries provided indirect evidence that the shift differentials affected the probability of shift-work through the cost ratio in the manner predicted by the theory.

Our emphasis in the previous seven chapters has been on the causes or determinants of shift-work at the level of the individual factory. Although part of this emphasis has been retained in this chapter, some of the results presented have begun to shift the focus of our concern to other aspects of the subject. To illustrate, the evidence on the variety of country experiences suggests that the level of capital utilization could be substantially increased in many countries. It is of interest, therefore, to ascertain the effects of increases in shift-work on critical economic variables (e.g., capital requirements and employment levels).

Our interest in the effects of shift-work stems from two types of considerations. On the one hand, shift-work may change of its own accord, and indeed there has apparently been an upward trend in shift-work in several countries in the postwar period. Determining the effects of changes in shift-work is therefore of considerable interest. On the other hand, governments may wish to change the amount of shift-work in the economy by manipulating policy instruments. There are several reasons why society at large has an interest in the decisions that workers and managers make about shift-work. In the first place, the decisions of private parties may be affected by market failures; in particular, the shift differentials may respond very imperfectly to market forces. Second, society's concern about income distribution may motivate governmental intervention in private-sector decisions; this concern is prominent in developing countries with severe employment problems. Finally, many observers evidently believe that the decisions made by workers to accept onerous shift practices do not serve the long-run interests of these workers; these observers are mainly worried about the human costs of shift-work (i.e., its effect on health and family relations).

To put it very briefly, in Part IV (Chapters 9–11) we shall treat the effects of shift-work on production and income distribution. The other category of effects, the human costs of shift-work, will be discussed in the concluding chapter (Chapter 12), where we shall also summarize the implications of our findings for public policy.

Part IV is organized in the following manner: In Chapter 9 we concentrate on evaluating the potential contribution of shift-work to amelioration of the employment problem; our efforts include an analysis of the probable effects of changes in certain governmental policies on shift-work, employment, and capital requirements at the level of the individual factory. These policies, which would affect other variables as well as the level of shift-work, are a change of a certain percentage in the shift differential and a change of a certain percentage in the prices of labor and capital. Chapter 10 puts utilization into some models of economic growth. The emphasis here is on output effects. In particular, we investigate whether an increase in utilization (brought about, for example, by a change in the shift differential) will have a more powerful effect on output in a growth setting than in a static setting. Chapter 11 considers the same issues in a dual economy. Whereas in the preceding chapter we assumed that factor markets function perfectly, in Chapter 11 we assume that there is an industrial sector with a wage rate fixed at a level higher than in the rest of the economy.

PART IV

Implications

CHAPTER 9

Analysis of policy changes

As mentioned in the Introduction, much of the recent interest in shift-work among those concerned with developing countries derives from the hope that increased use of multiple shifts will contribute to solution of the employment problem. In Chapter 0 we explained why the phenomenon of substitution qualifies the favorable effects of shift-work on employment. To recapitulate, if the capital stock of the factory is taken as given, or if substitution possibilities are deemed to be absent, then increasing the number of shifts from one to two will double total employment per unit of capital stock. However, when the capital stock is regarded as endogenous and substitution possibilities are present, the choice of the double-shift system increases total employment per unit of capital stock by less than 100%, perhaps much less. One of the purposes of the present chapter is to present a theoretical treatment of this question.

The analysis of policy changes in a decentralized economy depends critically on whether or not the capital stock of factories is regarded as fixed. If it is, then a "big-push" policy package of increasing aggregate demand becomes quite appealing, because it seems that firms can increase output quite substantially by adopting multiple shifts. But if the capital stock of each factory can change, then the increase in aggregate demand may lead to an investment boom and to increased inflation instead of to the desired increase in multiple-shift operation. To get firms to change their shift-work decisions requires some change in the economic circumstances facing the firms.

Regardless of whether or not a big-push strategy is deemed desirable,[1] an analysis of the firm's long-run decision with respect to shift-work remains essential. One of our goals in this chapter is to

---

[1] A leading proponent of this strategy is Daniel Schydlowsky, who is directing a project at Boston University to research the implications of such a program (Schydlowsky 1972, 1979). For our comments on this strategy, see the work of Betancourt and Clague (1976) and especially Betancourt (1977, pp. 76–90).

determine the responses of firms to the changes in economic circumstances that governmental policy might bring about.

Many of the obvious policy measures designed to promote shift-work can be viewed as changes in two of the determinants of the cost ratio: the shift differential α and the capital share θ. Tax credits proportional to the amount of labor employed on shift-work are equivalent, from the firm's point of view, to reductions in α. In addition, removal of governmentally mandated shift premia (where these exist) can reduce the actual shift differentials. With respect to the capital share θ, it is widely believed that in the majority of less-developed countries the cost of labor in the modern sector is well above its opportunity cost, whereas real interest rates and the prices of imported durable equipment for established manufacturing enterprises are typically below the opportunity costs of the resources. Policies to bring the factor prices into line with opportunity costs (reducing the price of labor, raising that of capital) will normally affect the capital share θ.

Policies to "get the factor prices right" are also of interest in the present context because they directly encourage the substitution of labor for capital. We shall want to compare these "direct effects" of changes in factor prices with the "indirect effects" of changes in factor prices, which operate through changes in shift-work via the capital share.

The effects of changes in the shift differential and factor prices on the extent of shift-work can be calculated, on a probabilistic basis, with the aid of the logit regressions presented in Chapter 7. We can also calculate the effects of the policy changes on total employment per unit of capital. In this way we can get some idea of the contribution that these policy measures might make toward the solution of the problem of insufficient modern-sector employment.

The organization of this chapter is as follows: Section 9.1 presents a theoretical analysis of the effects of shift-work on the factory's level of total employment per unit of capital. Section 9.2 describes the procedures employed to estimate the effects of policy changes in our four countries; the estimates themselves are presented in Section 9.3. Some general equilibrium considerations are discussed in Section 9.4, and Section 9.5 adds some concluding observations.

9.1   The effects of shift-work: a theoretical formulation

In this section we formalize the relationship between substitution possibilities and the employment effects of shift-work by making use of the CES production function. The basic analysis has been presented in the literature (Winston 1974a; Betancourt and Clague 1975, 1976b). What is new in the present account is the incorporation of wear-and-tear depreciation into the theory. Some readers, however, may wish to concentrate on the case in which wear-and-tear depreciation is absent. We shall guide these readers through the section.

We allow for the possibility of wear-and-tear depreciation by permitting the price of owning a unit of capital stock for a day (r) to be different for the single-shift system and the double-shift system; that is, we distinguish r^2 from r^1, and r^2/r^1 exceeds 1.0. Following the discussion in Chapter 2, we shall think of r^2/r^1 as lying between 1.0 and 1.25. Thus, shift-work still reduces the price of capital *services;* this price is $r^2/2$ for system 2 and r^1 for system 1.

The equations needed for the analysis are presented in (2.2). From these we obtain[2]

$$\frac{L^2/K^2}{L^1/K^1} = \frac{2}{[(2 + \alpha)(r^1/r^2)]^\sigma} \qquad (9.1)$$

Equation (9.1) shows the ratio of total employment (first shift plus second shift) per unit of capital stock under shift-work to employment per unit of capital stock under single-shift operation. If $\sigma = 0$, the ratio is 2.0; that is, in the absence of substitution possibilities, shift-work doubles employment per unit of capital stock. As σ increases, the ratio declines. [Readers wishing to concentrate on the case in which wear-and-tear depreciation is absent may simply set r^1/r^2 equal to 1.0 in (9.1).]

But when there is wear-and-tear depreciation, employment per unit of capital stock is not a fully satisfactory measure of the employment effects of shift-work. Because capital wears out faster under double-shift operation, we need a measure of the resource cost of capital that takes this phenomenon into consideration.

The price of capital is $r^1 = P_K (i + d^1 + m^1)$ for system 1 and $r^2 = P_K (i + d^2 + m^2)$ for system 2, where P_K is the price of capital goods, i is the rate of interest, d is the annual depreciation, and m is the machine-related operating costs. These operating costs include maintenance and repair expenditures and the other costs of machine breakdown.

The price of capital r is what the decision maker considers when he makes his decision about the size of the capital stock and its rate of utilization. But the maintenance and repair component of r represents

---

[2] We must use r^1 in the equation for k^1 and r^2 in the equation for k_1^2, and we also use the fact that $L^2 = 2L_1^2$.

Table 9.1. *Effects of shift-work on employment per unit of capital-resource cost*

	$\sigma = 0$	$\sigma = 0.5$	$\sigma = 1.0$	$\sigma = 1.5$
A. Employment per unit of capital-resource cost, $\alpha = 0.20^a$				
$r^2/r^1 = 1.0$	2.0	1.348	0.909	0.613
$r^2/r^1 = 1.25$	1.661	1.252	0.944	0.711
B. Employment per unit of capital-resource cost, including maintenance labor in employment, $\alpha = 0.20^b$				
$r^2/r^1 = 1.25$	1.575	1.227	0.963	0.765
C. Employment per unit of capital-resource cost, $\alpha = 0^a$				
$r^2/r^1 = 1.25$	1.661	1.333	1.038	0.821

[a]Value of $[2(i + d^1)/(i + d^2)]/[(2 + \alpha)\,(r^1/r^2)]^\sigma$, where $(i + d^2)/(i + d^1)$ is set equal to 1.204 when $r^2/r^1 = 1.25$ and 1.0 when $r^2/r^1 = 1.0$.
[b]Maintenance labor adjustment factor taken from Table 9.3 for the case where $\theta = 0.30$.

mainly expenses for labor. For policy purposes, we are interested in separating capital resources from labor resources, primarily because one is thought to be overpriced and the other underpriced. Thus we shall define capital resource costs as $P_K K(i + d)$; this measure takes account of wear-and-tear depreciation through the term d. The only modification needed in our previous analysis is to divide both sides of (9.1) by $(i + d^2)/(i + d^1)$. The equation then shows the effect of shift-work on employment per unit of capital-resource cost. We shall refer to this expression as the "shift-work employment ratio." [Again, readers not interested in wear-and-tear depreciation may set $(i + d^2)/(i + d^1)$ equal to 1.0.]

We shall now illustrate the shift-work employment ratio with some numerical values of the parameters. We shall let r^2/r^1 take on values of 1.00 and 1.25. The latter value is a high one. When it obtains, we shall also assume that $(i + d^2)/(i + d^1) = 1.204$. This value is consistent with $r^2/r^1 = 1.25$ in a model of optimal machine life presented by Clague (1975, Section III). We set α at 0.20 initially and then let it fall to zero.

Table 9.1 shows the values of the shift-work employment ratio under the various assumptions. To repeat, a value of 2.0 means that shift-work doubles employment per unit of capital-resource cost. A value less than 1.0 means that shift-work actually reduces employment per unit of capital-resource cost.

Let us consider first the case in which wear-and-tear depreciation is absent ($r^2/r^1 = 1.0$). The dramatic effects of variations in the elasticity of substitution (σ) are shown in the first row of panel A of the table. The shift-work employment ratio falls from 2.0 when $\sigma = 0$ to less than unity when $\sigma = 1.0$. This row illustrates the important substitution phenomenon that was explained in Chapter 0 and in Part I.

The introduction of wear-and-tear depreciation (raising r^2/r^1 to 1.25) reduces the shift-work employment ratio when σ is low and raises it when σ is high. The reason for this result is easy to see when one looks at the algebraic expression for the shift-work employment ratio (see footnote a to Table 9.1). The term $(i + d^2)/(i + d^1)$ has the same effect on the expression regardless of the value of σ, but r^2/r^1 has an effect that depends on σ.

The labor required for maintenance and repair might be added to the operative labor in calculating the shift-work employment ratio. Shift-work normally involves more maintenance per unit of capital. Moreover, if σ is high, shift-work increases fixed capital per unit of operative labor. Hence, adding the maintenance workers would raise total employment by a larger proportion under shift-work than under single-shift operation. On the other hand, when σ is low, shift-work reduces fixed capital per unit of operative labor, and if σ is very low we might expect the addition of maintenance labor to add proportionally more to employment under system 1 than under system 2. A formal analysis of the employment generated by maintenance and repair is contained in Appendix 9.1. Panel B of Table 9.1 incorporates an illustrative figure taken from the appendix. The numbers in the table confirm the anticipated results.

Panel C shows the effects of setting α equal to zero. The reduction in α from 0.20 to zero increases the shift-work employment ratio. This result makes good sense intuitively. The cheapening of labor under system 2 encourages the substitution of labor for capital in that system; nothing is altered for system 1. Note that the increase in the shift-work employment ratio is not dramatic, particularly at low values of the elasticity of substitution.

The present section may be summarized by drawing the appropriate conclusions from Table 9.1. The contribution of multiple-shift operation to the resolution of the employment problem in developing countries depends on the typical value of the shift-work employment ratio. Those who argue the case for shift-work as a contribution to an employment policy package must contend that this ratio is typically substantially greater than unity. In light of Table 9.1, they must contend that the elasticity of substitution is typically less than unity. The lower the elasticity, the more favorable the shift-work employment ratio. But even the elasticity pessimists would concede that σ is normally greater than zero. Suppose we set σ at 0.5, a figure well below the consensus of the econometric estimates. With no wear-and-tear depreciation, the shift-work employment ratio is 1.35. The adjustments stemming from the introduction of wear-and-tear depreciation reduce the ratio still further to 1.25. Incorporating maintenance labor into employment only reinforces the conclusion that the employment-generating effects of shift-work are modest.

9.2   Estimating the effects of policy changes on shift-work, employment, and capital requirements

The purpose of this section is to describe the procedures by which the effects of policy changes in our four countries are calculated. The estimates themselves will be given in the next section.

We shall be concerned primarily with the effects of the policy changes on employment per unit of capital-resource cost. This variable is the most appropriate one for assessing the contribution of the policy changes to the solution of the employment problem.

Let us spell out the assumptions underlying the calculations. The output of each industry is assumed to be constant; one might say we assume industry demand curves to be vertical. Some general equilibrium aspects of shift-work will be discussed briefly in Section 9.4. With respect to factory outputs we made two alternative assumptions: that output of each factory was held constant, and that output per shift for each factory was held constant. Because the results of interest are practically identical for the two assumptions, the calculations presented here are based only on the first assumption.

The policy changes that we shall analyze can be categorized into those designed to reduce the shift-work premiums (α and α^1) and those designed to reduce the factor-price ratio (w_1/r). Because we are ignoring changes in industry output, we need not distinguish the ones that reduce w_1 from the ones that raise r. The specific policy changes we shall contemplate are reductions in the shift premiums (α and α^1) by 20 percentage points (making them negative in some of our countries) and a reduction in w_1/r by 20%.

We shall first describe how to calculate the effects of these changes on the expected number of shifts in each country. The logit equation for each country permits the calculation of the probability (P_m) of working more than one shift for each factory in the sample. The probability of working one shift is obviously $1 - P_m$. Because our logit regressions did not explain the choice between two shifts and three shifts in any of the four countries, we have used the sample frequencies to estimate the conditional probabilities of working two shifts and three shifts, given that some type of shift-work is undertaken. In other words, we calculated the probabilities of working two shifts (P_2) and three shifts (P_3) from the following formulas:

$$P_2 = P_m f_2 \quad \text{and} \quad P_3 = P_m f_3$$

where f_2 and f_3 are the fractions of shift-working firms in each country that work two shifts and three shifts, respectively ($f_2 + f_3 = 1$).

The expected number of shifts for each factory is then

$$P_1(1) + P_2(2) + P_3(3)$$

This expression was then averaged over the factories in each country to obtain the expected number of shifts in the country sample.

The change in the expected number of shifts resulting from the policy changes can easily be calculated. The new cost ratio for each factory is inserted into the logit equation, and a new P_m is obtained. The procedure yields new values for P_1, P_2, and P_3 and for the expected number of shifts for each factory. The expected number of shifts is again averaged over the country sample.

Why do we go through this procedure instead of merely looking at the regression coefficients? If the empirical relationship were a linear regression of the shift-work dummy variable on the shift differential and the (w_1/r) ratio, we could simply multiply the regression coefficient by the assumed magnitude of the policy change to obtain the change in the probability of working shifts. But we have a nonlinearity in the relationship of the shift premiums and w_1/r to the cost ratio, as well as a nonlinear (logit) relationship between the cost ratio and the probability of working shifts. These nonlinearities require us to calculate the effects on each factory and then to average over factories.[3]

We turn next to the calculation of the expected level of employment per unit of capital-resource cost. Our procedure was to calculate expected employment and expected capital-resource costs for each factory, before and after the policy changes. These changes were averaged over all factories in a country sample, and then the change in employment per unit of capital-resource cost was calculated for the country sample.

Expected employment ($\overline{L}$) for a factory can be written as

---

[3] This procedure is a much simpler alternative to the one suggested by Westin (1974).

$$\overline{L} = P_1(L^1) + P_2(L^2) + P_3(L^3)$$

Hence

$$\overline{L}/L^1 = P_1(1) + P_2(L^2/L^1) + P_3(L^3/L^1) \tag{9.2}$$

Expressions for L^2/L^1 and L^3/L^1 can be developed from the theoretical analysis of Chapter 2. These expressions are derived in Appendix 9.2. The point that needs to be made here is that they depend on the values of α, θ, and σ.

Expected capital-resource cost $(\overline{KRC})$ for a factory can be written

$$\overline{KRC} = P_1(KRC^1) + P_2(KRC^2) + P_3(KRC^3)$$

Hence

$$\frac{\overline{KRC}}{KRC^1} = P_1(1) + P_2\left(\frac{KRC^2}{KRC^1}\right) + P_3\left(\frac{KRC^3}{KRC^1}\right) \tag{9.3}$$

Expressions for KRC^2/KRC^1 and KRC^3/KRC^1 are derived in Appendix 9.2.

The policy changes affect (9.2) and (9.3) in two ways. They alter the probabilities and they change the expressions for L^2/L^1, KRC^2/KRC^1, etc. In addition, the policy change consisting of a fall in w_1/r by 20% has a direct effect on factor proportions. It can be shown that

$$K^1/K^0 = [\theta + (1 - \theta)(0.80)^{1-\sigma}]^{\sigma/(1-\sigma)}$$
$$L^1/L^0 = [\theta(1.25)^{1-\sigma} + (1 - \theta)]^{\sigma/(1-\sigma)}$$

where the superscript 0 refers to the initial situation and 1 refers to the new situation.

9.3   Results of policy changes

The results presented next are based mainly on the same assumptions as those employed in estimating the logit regressions. That is, we use our estimated values of the elasticities of substitution; we set $r^2/r^1 = 1.0$; and in calculating the cost ratios, we assume a constant-β technology for France and Japan and a semi-U technology for India and Israel. Nevertheless, we shall indicate briefly the sensitivity of the results to changes in the first two of these assumptions.

Table 9.2 shows the results of the policy changes. Looking at the first row for France, we find the mean values of the capital share (θ), the cost ratio (CR^1), and the expected number of shifts per factory in the original situation. As a result of the reductions in the second-shift and third-shift wage differentials, the mean cost ratio falls, and the

Table 9.2. *Effects of policy changes*

	$\bar{\theta}$	$\overline{CR^1}$	Expected shifts	Proportional change in L/KRC^a
France				
Original	0.304	0.942	1.540	
Reduce α, α^1	0.304	0.862	1.639	1.032 (1.043)
Reduce (w_1/r)	0.309	0.938	1.545	1.227 (1.114)
Japan				
Original	0.295	1.018	1.446	
Reduce α, α^1	0.295	0.941	1.559	1.018 (1.037)
Reduce (w_1/r)	0.295	1.018	1.445	1.248 (1.125)
India				
Original	0.385	0.818	2.085	
Reduce α, α^1	0.385	0.744	2.171	1.081 (1.069)
Reduce (w_1/r)	0.393	0.811	2.092	1.212 (1.107)
Israel				
Original	0.320	0.898	2.187	
Reduce α, α^1	0.320	0.817	2.376	1.099 (1.118)
Reduce (w_1/r)	0.323	0.895	2.197	1.235 (1.128)

[a]The figures in parentheses were calculated on the assumption that the elasticities of substitution were half their estimated values. Both sets of figures actually represent changes in $(I/L^1)/(\overline{KRC/KRC^1})$.

expected number of shifts increases (second row). The 20% reduction in w_1/r increases the mean value of θ slightly,[4] reduces the cost ratio, and increases the expected number of shifts.

The fourth column in the table shows the proportional change in employment per unit of capital-resource cost (L/KRC). The change in α and α^1 increases L/KRC by only 3.2%, whereas the reduction in w_1/r increases L/KRC by over 20%. Most of the impact of the change in w_1/r is the "direct effect" on capital–labor substitution, for as we can see, the effect of w_1/r on the expected number of shifts (column 3) is quite small.

The overall patterns of the results are rather similar for the other three countries. The main difference is that the proportional increases in L/KRC for the changes in α and α^1 are larger in the two countries (India and Israel) in which shift-work is more prevalent. This result

[4] A familiar proposition in the theory textbooks is that a fall in w_1/r will increase (decrease) the capital share if the elasticity of substitution is below (above) unity. If σ is close to unity, θ will not change very much.

occurs because part of the effect of the reductions in α and α^1 is to encourage firms already working shifts to become more labor-intensive.

The effects of the policy changes were also calculated under some alternative assumptions. First, wear-and-tear depreciation was introduced by letting r^2/r^1 be 1.25 and r^3/r^1 be 1.50. This change in assumptions reduced the effect of the α policy on L/KRC somewhat; in France, for example, the proportional change fell from 1.032 to 1.027. The impact of the w_1/r policy was practically unaffected.

Second, the elasticities of substitution were cut in half. The proportional increases in L/KRC for this set of assumptions are the figures in parentheses in the last column of Table 9.2. The impact of the w_1/r policy was cut approximately in half for each country. The impact of the α policy was increased somewhat in three of the four countries but decreased in the fourth (India). Note that with this set of assumptions for Israel the α policy is nearly as powerful as the w_1/r policy in its effect on L/KRC.

In brief summary, our logit regressions and our sample data suggest that a policy to reduce shift differentials will work in the right direction on L/KRC but will have a rather modest effect. The effect will be greater in those countries where shift-work is already more common. Our policy simulations also suggest that a change in factor prices of the same magnitude as the change in shift differentials[5] will have a greater impact on L/KRC. The impact of this policy, however, is quite sensitive to the assumed values of the elasticities of substitution.

9.4   General-equilibrium considerations

Up to this point this chapter has dealt with the effects of shift-work in a microeconomic setting. The wage rate and the price of capital stock were taken as given, and the effects of shift-work on the composition of output were ignored. However, policy makers are ultimately interested in the effects of shift-work on the whole economy. When the effects of shift-work decisions of individual firms are added up, what is the aggregate impact?

Let us envisage a model of an economy with two sectors; in one

---

[5] The two policies are probably not of the same magnitude in terms of political cost or other costs of implementation. The loss to the Treasury, for example, of subsidizing second- and third-shift work would be less than that of subsidizing all wages.

sector, shift-work is feasible, but in the other it is not. For ease of exposition, the first sector will be called manufacturing, and the second will be called agriculture. The production functions of each sector exhibit constant returns to scale, and the factor markets function well, so that the prices of capital and daytime labor are the same in the two sectors. The manufacturing sector is also assumed to be more capital-intensive under single-shift operation than the agricultural sector.

In a general-equilibrium model the factor endowments are assumed to be fixed. Suppose that initially the shift-work wage premium is kept very high by government legislation and shift-work is not undertaken in either sector. Then the government legislation is repealed, the shift premium falls, and the manufacturing sector increases its number of shifts from one to two. What will be the effect of this change on real factor prices?

It can be shown that the elasticity of substitution in manufacturing plays a key role in this situation. More precisely, if the elasticity of substitution exceeds unity, the adoption of shift-work must raise the return to capital and depress the wage rate of daytime labor, where both factor prices are measured in terms of manufacturing goods.[6] If the elasticity of substitution is rather low, on the other hand (say below 0.5, to be on the safe side), the adoption of shift-work must raise the daytime wage rate and depress the return to capital. For elasticities of substitution between 0.5 and 1.0, the effects of the adoption of shift-work depend on the values of other parameters in the model (the capital share in manufacturing, the shift premium, and the elasticity of demand for manufacturing output).

These results from the general-equilibrium model are exactly what we would expect, in light of the results from the microeconomic model. In the micro model, in which factor prices are given, the individual firm will reduce total employment per unit of capital stock when it adopts shift-work, if the elasticity of substitution is greater than unity.[7] If a great many firms adopt shift-work and their elasticities of substitution are greater than unity, we should expect there to be excess demand for capital stock and excess supply of labor, which will cause the price of capital to rise and the price of daytime labor to fall. Conversely, if a great many firms adopt shift-work and their elasticities of substitution are substantially less than unity, we should expect there to be excess supply of capital and excess demand for labor, which

[6] These results are derived in our unpublished paper (Betancourt and Clague 1979).

[7] We assume here that there is no wear-and-tear depreciation.

will raise the price of daytime labor and depress that of capital. We shall, of course, expect the general-equilibrium model to incorporate additional parameters that will influence the outcome, but we should not be surprised to find that the elasticity of substitution plays a central role in determining the effects of shift-work on factor prices.

9.5   Concluding remarks

The present chapter has been primarily concerned with shift-work as a possible contribution to ameliorating the employment problem in developing countries. Whether increased shift-work would make a positive contribution depends critically on the typical values of the elasticity of substitution between labor and capital services. When we used our own estimated values of the elasticity of substitution (which averaged around 0.9) in our simulations, the policy of reducing the shift-wage premium made a rather modest contribution to solving the employment problem; more precisely, a reduction in the premium by 20 percentage points increased employment per unit of capital-resource cost by 1.8% to 9.9% in the four countries. When the elasticities were cut in half, the estimates tended to rise, and the range became 3.7% to 11.8%. Moreover, cutting the elasticities in half dramatically reduced the effectiveness of an obvious alternative policy, that of reducing the ratio of the wage rate to the price of capital.

The introduction of wear-and-tear depreciation tends to weaken the case for shift-work, especially when the elasticity of substitution is less than unity. A two-sector general-equilibrium model confirms the insights about the elasticity of substitution that were derived from the partial-equilibrium model.

Whereas this chapter has emphasized the effects of shift-work on the distribution of output, a complete analysis of the topic must also take into consideration the effects of shift-work on the level and rate of growth of output. Examination of this aspect of the matter permits a more favorable assessment of the effects of shift-work, as we shall demonstrate in the next chapter.

Appendix 9.1 Employment generated by maintenance and repair

In this appendix we modify (9.1) to incorporate the employment generated by maintenance and repair. We shall need some additional notation. Let λ be the fraction of machine operating costs that is due to labor expenses. Then let ML^1 be defined as

$$\mathrm{ML}^1 = \lambda m^1/(i + d^1)$$

ML^1 is thus the ratio of labor operating costs to $i + d^1$ under system 1. Analogously, we define ML^2 as

$$\mathrm{ML}^2 = \lambda m^2/(i + d^2)$$

The total employment (including labor for maintenance) for system 1 is

$$L^1 + g_1 P_K K^1 = L^1[1 + g_1(P_K K^1)/L^1]$$

where g_1 is the maintenance labor required under system 1 per unit of the value of capital stock. Letting w_1 be the wage rate of maintenance labor (as well as of operative labor) under system 1, we have

$$\frac{w_1 g_1}{i + d^1} = \mathrm{ML}^1$$

Since

$$\frac{\theta}{1 - \theta} = \frac{(i + d^1)P_K K^1}{w_1 L^1}$$

we have, by simple manipulation of these two equations,

$$g_1 = \mathrm{ML}^1 \frac{i + d^1}{w_1} = \mathrm{ML}^1 \frac{\theta}{1 - \theta} \frac{L^1}{P_K K^1}$$

Hence

$$g_1 P_K K^1/L^1 = \mathrm{ML}^1 \theta/(1 - \theta).$$

Total employment becomes

$$L^1[1 + \mathrm{ML}^1 \theta/(1 - \theta)] \tag{9.A1}$$

Total employment under system 2 is

$$2L_1^2 + g_2(P_K K^2) = 2L_1^2[1 + g_2(P_K K^2)/2L_1^2]$$

where g_2 is defined analogously to g_1. Letting w_1 be also the wage rate for maintenance labor under system 2, we have

$$\frac{w_1 g_2}{i + d^2} = \mathrm{ML}^2$$

Hence

$$g_2 = \mathrm{ML}^2 \frac{i + d^2}{w_1} = \mathrm{ML}^2 \frac{i + d^2}{i + d^1} \frac{\theta}{1 - \theta} \frac{L^1}{P_K K^1} \tag{9.A2}$$

From (9.1)

$$\frac{L^1}{K^1} = \frac{2L_1^2}{K^2}\frac{1}{2}\left[\frac{2 + \alpha}{1}\frac{r^1}{r^2}\right]^\sigma \tag{9.A3}$$

Substituting for L^1/K^1 into (9.A2) gives

$$g_2 = \text{ML}^2\frac{i + d^2}{i + d^1}\frac{\theta}{1 - \theta}\frac{2L_1^2}{P_K K^2}\frac{1}{2}\left[\frac{2 + \alpha}{1}\frac{r^1}{r^2}\right]^\sigma \tag{9.A4}$$

Now

$$\frac{\text{ML}_.^2(i + d^2)}{\text{ML}^1(i + d^1)} = \frac{m^2}{m^1} = 1 + B$$

where $1 + B$ is defined as the ratio of annual operating costs under the two systems. Then (9.A4) may be written

$$\frac{g_2 P_K K}{2L_1^2} = \frac{1}{2}\left[\frac{2 + \alpha}{1}\frac{r^1}{r^2}\right]^\sigma \text{ML}^1(1 + B)\frac{\theta}{1 - \theta}$$

Total employment under system 2 becomes

$$2L_1^2\left[1 + \frac{1}{2}\left[\frac{2 + \alpha}{1}\frac{r^1}{r^2}\right]^\sigma \text{ML}^1(1 + B)\frac{\theta}{1 - \theta}\right] \tag{9.A5}$$

The ratio of total employment under the two systems, obtained by dividing (9.A5) by (9.A1), is

$$\frac{2L_1^2}{L^1}\left[\frac{1 + \frac{1}{2}\left(\frac{2 + \alpha}{1}\frac{r^1}{r^2}\right)^\sigma \text{ML}^1(1 + B)\frac{\theta}{1 - \theta}}{1 + \text{ML}^1[\theta/(1 - \theta)]}\right] \tag{9.A6}$$

The term in brackets in (9.A6) will be referred to as the maintenance labor adjustment factor.

This factor is illustrated in Table 9.3, where (9.A6) is calculated for various values of σ and θ. Again, r^2/r^1 is set at 1.25, $1 + B$ is set at 1.287, and ML^1 is set at 0.40. Although different values could, of course, be selected for these parameters, they are consistent with one another in the model presented by Clague (1975, Section III). ML^1 is exogenous. In the example from which the other numbers are taken, $m^1/(i + d^1) = 0.80$; thus, choosing $\text{ML}^1 = 0.40$ implies that labor accounts for half of machine-related operating costs. Changing ML^1 would not alter the qualitative aspects of the results to be presented.

The first point to note about Table 9.3 is that when σ is zero, the adjustment factor is less than unity. That is, maintenance labor is a smaller fraction of operative labor under system 2 than under system 1. The reason for this result, of course, is that under system 2 the capital

Table 9.3. *Maintenance labor adjustment factor*[a]

	$\sigma = 0$	$\sigma = 0.5$	$\sigma = 1.0$	$\sigma = 1.5$
$\theta = 0.10$	0.985	0.994	1.006	1.021
$\theta = 0.20$	0.968	0.987	1.012	1.046
$\theta = 0.30$	0.948	0.979	1.019	1.074
$\theta = 0.40$	0.925	0.969	1.028	1.106

Note: $\alpha = 0.20$ throughout the table.
[a]Value of

$$\frac{1 + \dfrac{1}{2}\left(\dfrac{2 + \alpha}{1}\dfrac{r^1}{r^2}\right)^{\sigma}(1 + B)\mathrm{ML}^1\dfrac{\theta}{1 - \theta}}{1 + \mathrm{ML}^1\dfrac{\theta}{1 - \theta}}$$

where $r^2/r^1 = 1.25$; $B = 0.287$, $m^1 = 0.8$, and $\mathrm{ML}^1 = 0.40$.

stock is only half as large as under system 1. To be sure, the capital stock must be serviced and repaired more often per year under shift-work, but not twice as often, according to the optimal machine-life model presented by Clague (1975). This feature of the model also accords with our impression of the reality of maintenance and repair requirements.

As σ increases, the adjustment factor increases. This result occurs because as σ increases, $(K^2/L_1^2)/(K^1/L^1)$ increases. Thus, for high values of σ, the adjustment factor exceeds unity, implying that maintenance labor is a larger fraction of operative labor under system 2 than under system 1.

Appendix 9.2 Derivation of $(L^2/X^2)/(L^1/X^1)$, etc.

From equation (2.3) in Chapter 2 and the facts that $L^2 = 2L_1^2$ and $2\phi(\overline{X}) = 1 + e_{cx}^2$, we have

$$L^2/L^1 = (1 + e_{cx}^2)[\theta(2 + \alpha)^{\sigma-1} + (1 - \theta)]^{\sigma/(1-\sigma)} \qquad (9.\mathrm{A}7)$$

Because in Chapter 2 total outputs were assumed to be the same for the two systems $(X^1 = X^2)$, we may write the left-hand side of (9.A7) as $(L^2/X^2)/(L^1/X^1)$ without changing the right-hand side. If the expression is generalized to allow r^1 to differ from r^2, it becomes

$$\frac{L^2/X^2}{L^1/X^1} = (1 + e_{cx}^2)\left[\theta\left(\frac{2 + \alpha}{1}\frac{r^1}{r^2}\right)^{\sigma-1} + (1 - \theta)\right]^{\sigma/(1-\sigma)} \tag{9.A8}$$

The expression for three shifts corresponding to (9.A8) is

$$\frac{L^3/X^3}{L^1/X^1} = (1 + e_{cx}^3)\left[\theta\left(\frac{3 + \alpha + \alpha^1}{1}\frac{r^1}{r^3}\right)^{\sigma-1} + (1 - \theta)\right]^{\sigma/(1-\sigma)} \tag{9.A9}$$

From (2.2) and (2.3) in Chapter 2 we obtain

$$\frac{K^2/X^2}{K^1/X^1} = \left(\frac{2 + \alpha}{1}\frac{r^1}{r^2}\right)^{\sigma}\frac{1 + e_{cx}^2}{2}\left[\theta\left(\frac{2 + \alpha}{1}\frac{r^1}{r^2}\right)^{\sigma-1} + (1 - \theta)\right]^{\sigma/(1-\sigma)} \tag{9.A10}$$

The corresponding expression for three shifts is

$$\frac{K^3/X^3}{K^1/X^1} = \left(\frac{3 + \alpha + \alpha^1}{1}\frac{r^1}{r^3}\right)^{\sigma}\frac{1 + e_{cx}^3}{3}\left[\theta\left(\frac{3 + \alpha + \alpha^1}{1}\frac{r^1}{r^3}\right)^{\sigma-1} + (1 - \theta)\right]^{\sigma/(1-\sigma)} \tag{9.A11}$$

These expressions must be multiplied by $(i + d^2)/(i + d^1)$ and $(i + d^3)/(i + d^1)$ to obtain $(KRC^2/X^2)/(KRC^1/X^1)$ and $(KRC^3/X^3)/(KRC^1/X^1)$.

CHAPTER 10

Capital utilization and economic growth

One section of the preceding chapter described the effect of shift-work on factor prices in a general-equilibrium static model. The stock of capital and the total labor force were assumed to be given. The present chapter will analyze the effect of shift-work in a growth model, in which the stock of capital is the result of the accumulation of past savings.

To see more clearly the differences between the general-equilibrium model and the growth model, let us imagine a one-sector static macroeconomic model in which capital utilization is a variable. The stock of capital and the labor force are given. It is obvious that an increase in capital utilization will increase total output and the wage rate. These gains may be called the static effects of the utilization change. Now let us convert our static macroeconomic model into a growth model in which the labor force grows exogenously and the capital stock at any given time is the accumulation of past savings. In the growth model an increase in utilization at any given time will still have the static effects on output and the wage rate, but it may also change the rate of capital accumulation and hence the ratio of capital stock to labor. If an increase in utilization leads to a higher capital-stock-to-labor ratio than would have existed otherwise, then we may say that utilization is more powerful in a growth context than in a static context. Whether or not this is so is one of the key questions to be addressed in this chapter.

The change in utilization can be viewed as having been brought about by a change in the shift premium α. Thus α may be thought of as either as a policy parameter subject to collective control or as a parameter reflecting the preferences of the population with respect to shift-work. In the latter case, a change in α may represent a change in society's tastes, or the analysis may be viewed as the comparison of two economies, identical in all respects except for these tastes and the implications of these tastes for important economic variables. Alternatively, one can view the change in utilization as a factor that is given, in which case the analysis here is simply an examination of the consequences of the given change.

The theoretical literature on capital utilization and economic growth essentially began with Marris (1964). He pointed out that in a Harrod-Domar model an increase in utilization not only increases current output but also increases the rate of growth; in this respect the utilization rate is like the rate of saving, and Marris emphasized that increases in utilization and increases in savings are substitute ways of achieving a given rate of growth. Neoclassical growth models in the 1960s sometimes contained (e.g., Conlisk 1969) a capital-employment parameter, which measured the fraction of the capital stock actually employed in production, and the effects of changes in this parameter were derived. Because this capital-employment parameter enters the production function in the same manner as the rate of capital utilization, we may say that some of the mathematics of the effect of a change in utilization were worked out, but the economic interpretation of the parameter as a measure of capital utilization was missing. It is interesting that in surveys of economic growth and textbooks on economic growth (Hahn and Matthews 1964; Solow 1970; Burmeister and Dobell 1970; Hamberg 1971; Britto 1973; Jones 1975) we find no mention of Marris's contribution nor of capital utilization as a variable.

We shall introduce capital utilization into some fairly simple neoclassical growth models. Our work represents an advance over Marris's in that we consider a production function with substitution possibilities. (The microeconomic and general-equilibrium theories of shift-work should alert us to the fact that the effects of changes in capital utilization may depend in part on substitutability.) Our formal results are in some respects similar to those obtained with the capital-employment parameter by Conlisk (1969), but our interpretation of the parameter as a rate of capital utilization leads us to consider the impact of changes in utilization on the rate of savings and on the rate of depreciation. The incorporation of these variables leads to new results.[1]

---

[1] Quite recently, Calvo (1975) introduced capital utilization into a neoclassical growth model in order to ascertain the optimal rate of utilization. He claimed that his measure of utilization (m) could be interpreted either as a measure of the speed of machines or as a measure of the number of shifts worked. His assumption about depreciation, however, made more sense for the former than for the latter interpretation. He assumed, in effect, that wear-and-tear depreciation per day was proportional to m^2. This assumption is not very plausible if m is interpreted as the number of shifts worked or as the fraction of the day the machines are in operation. Moreover, there

Although it has received little attention in the growth-theory literature, capital utilization has been more prominently treated in studies of growth accounting. Denison devoted several pages (pp. 152–4, 171) to shift-work in *Why Growth Rates Differ* (1967), and Jorgenson and Griliches (1967), building on Foss's finding (1963) that the hours of operation of electric motors had increased during the postwar period, attempted a drastic reassessment of the role of capital services in accounting for U.S. growth.[2]

Although growth theorists have neglected capital utilization, several authors interested in utilization have emphasized Marris's conclusion that in a Harrod-Domar model, utilization has a powerful effect on growth. Winston (1971, 1974, 1977) has disseminated this result widely, and Schydlowsky (1979) has made some dramatic calculations of the effects on growth rates in Latin American countries of increases in shift-work. His calculations were explicitly based on Harrod-Domar assumptions. Generalization of these assumptions, therefore, is eminently desirable.

This chapter will be organized in the following way: Utilization is introduced into a static macroeconomic model of the economy in the next section. This model will serve as the point of reference for the growth models. Subsequently (Section 10.2) capital utilization will be introduced into a simple Solow-Swan growth model with an exogenous savings rate. In the following section (Section 10.3) we shall give a numerical illustration of the effects on growth over a fifteen-year period of an increase in capital utilization on the one hand and an increase in the savings rate on the other. In Section 10.4 the growth model is extended by incorporating a savings rate that depends on the rate of interest, as well as a rate of depreciation that depends on the rate of utilization. In the last section a summary and some conclusions of the analysis are presented.

were no welfare costs to working at night in his model. His results were also different from ours. He found that an increase in the capital stock per head always reduced the optimal level of m. In our model, the effect of an increase in capital stock per head on the optimal rate of utilization will depend on the elasticity of substitution.

[2] The full set of exchanges between Jorgenson-Griliches and Denison is collected in *Survey of Current Business*, Vol. 52, No. 5 (May 1972, part II), and Brookings Reprint No. 244. Treatments of this subject in the same spirit, but for other countries, are available in the studies cited in Chapter 8 by Heathfield (1972) for the United Kingdom and by Kim and Kwon (1977) for Korea.

10.1   Utilization in a static macroeconomic model

Assume an economy with labor force L, capital stock K, and production function $Q = F(uK,L)$, where u is the rate of utilization, defined so that $u = 1$ for single-shift operation. Because the production function exhibits constant returns to scale, we may write output per worker as $q = F(uK/L,1) = f(uk)$, where $q = Q/L$ and $k = K/L$.

Appendix 10.1 derives some expressions for E_{qu}, E_{wu}, and E_{iu}, the elasticities of output per worker (q), the wage rate (w), and the interest rate (i) with respect to u. We have

$$E_{qu} = \theta^* \tag{10.1}$$

$$E_{wu} = \theta^*/\sigma \tag{10.2}$$

$$E_{iu} = 1 - [1 - \theta^*]/\sigma \tag{10.3}$$

where θ^* is the share of capital in total output at the given level of u (when $u = 1$, $\theta^* = \theta$), and σ is the elasticity of substitution between labor and capital services.

Consider a society weighing the benefits and costs of an increase in utilization. Equation (10.1) provides the intuitively appealing result that the benefits of an increase in u will be positively related to the capital share, θ^*. Equations (10.2) and (10.3) show that the distribution of these benefits between labor and capital will depend on σ. Capitalists will lose if σ is less than $1 - \theta^*$. Workers will always earn higher wages, but because they are the ones who have to work the second shift, whether they gain or lose in welfare depends on their distaste for second-shift work, as measured by the shift differential α. If we assume that u initially equals unity, then the elasticity of the daytime wage (w_1) with respect to u (see Appendix 10.1) is

$$E_{w_1u} = -\alpha + \theta/\sigma \tag{10.4}$$

(The asterisk is dropped from θ^* because u is initially unity.) Workers will benefit from the increase in u if and only if the daytime wage increases, and by (10.4) the condition for the daytime wage to increase is that θ exceed $\alpha\sigma$.

10.2   A simple neoclassical growth model[3]

This section introduces utilization into the basic Solow-Swan model of growth. In that model, the labor force grows at an exogenously given

---

[3] Understanding the derivations in this section requires familiarity with elementary growth theory.

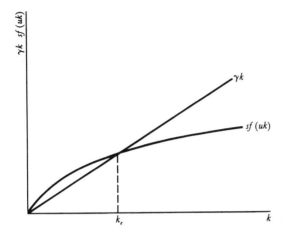

Figure 10.1. Capital utilization and the equilibrium capital–labor ratio.

constant rate and the savings rate (cf. p. 198, 10.4, line 2) is exogenous and constant. The equations of the basic model are

$$\dot{L}_t/L_t = \gamma \tag{10.5}$$

$$Q_t = F(uK_t,L_t) \tag{10.6}$$

$$\dot{K}_t = sQ_t \tag{10.7}$$

where γ is the rate of growth of the labor force, s is the rate of savings, and a dot indicates a time derivative (i.e., $\dot{L}_t = dL_t/dt$).

This model differs from the static model of Section 10.1 in making the capital stock endogenous. As explained in the chapter introduction, there is a key question: What is the effect of an increase in u on the ratio of capital stock to labor, k? To answer this question, let us describe first the solution of the model.

The growth rate of the capital–labor ratio k can be written as

$$\dot{k}_t/k_t = \dot{K}_t/K_t - \dot{L}_t/L_t$$

$$= sQ_t/K_t - \gamma$$

$$= sf(uk_t)/k_t - \gamma \tag{10.8}$$

Hence[4]

$$\dot{k}_t = sf(uk_t) - \gamma k_t \tag{10.9}$$

Equilibrium requires that $\dot{k}_t = 0$, which requires by (10.9) that

[4] In this chapter, parentheses are used to indicate functional relationships. Multiplication is indicated by square brackets or other symbols.

$sf(uk_e) = \gamma k_e$, where k_e is the equilibrium capital–labor ratio. This equilibrium is depicted graphically in Figure 10.1. For a "well-behaved production function," the $sf(uk)$ curve will intersect the γk line just once.

It is easy to see from Figure 10.1 that an increase in s and an increase in u will have the same effect: They will shift up the $sf(uk)$ line and thereby increase k_e. Under constant returns to scale, the equilibrium growth rate is affected in either case (since that growth rate is given by the growth rate of the labor force),[5] but the economy moves to a higher equilibrium path. Later we shall say more about the transition from one path to another. The important point at the moment is that the increase in u necessarily leads to a higher capital–labor ratio in the long run. The explanation is simple: An increase in u must increase output, and part of the additional output is saved. The accumulation of capital is speeded up temporarily, and hence k must rise.

Expressions for E_{ku} and E_{wu} are derived in Appendix 10.1. We have

$$E_{ku} = \theta^*/[1 - \theta^*] \tag{10.10}$$

$$E_{wu} = \theta^*/\sigma[1 - \theta^*] \tag{10.11}$$

Expression (10.10) confirms that E_{ku} must be positive. If we compare expression (10.11) with the corresponding one for the static model $[E_{wu} = \theta^*/\sigma$, from (10.2)], we see that an increase in u does indeed have a greater impact on w in a growth context than in a static context. Section 10.4 will examine whether or not this conclusion holds true when the simplicity of the model is eliminated through the introduction of endogenous rates of savings and depreciation.

Suppose now the economy is in an initial equilibrium at k_e. An increase in either s or u will start the economy moving toward a new and higher equilibrium growth path. During the transition period, the growth rate will be higher than the equilibrium rate. Considerable interest attaches to the transition period, which may be quite long. Moreover, the effects of changes in s and u turn out to be rather different during the transition period. Therefore the nature of the

---

[5] The introduction of technical change can alter this conclusion. For instance, with some kinds of endogenous technical change, an increase in either s or u raises the equilibrium capital–labor ratio (Atkinson and Betancourt 1971) and the equilibrium growth rate (Conlisk 1969). Note, however, that the direction of the impact of s and u on the equilibrium values of the capital–labor ratio and the rate of growth remains the same even in these models.

transition to the new growth path will be illustrated with some numerical calculations in the next section. These calculations will be based on a Cobb-Douglas model with the simplest kind of technological change.

10.3   The effects of utilization on growth: a numerical illustration

The production function is now written in Cobb-Douglas form:

$$Q_t = e^{gt}[uK_t]^{\delta}[L_t]^{1-\delta} \qquad (10.12)$$

where g is the rate of technological change and δ is the output elasticity of capital services. Let us assume that the economy is on its equilibrium growth path initially. We shall contemplate an increase in u on the one hand and an increase in the savings rate on the other.

For this numerical example, let us assume that the savings rate is initially 0.12, the labor force grows at 1.5% per year, the output elasticity of capital services is 0.30, and the rate of technological change is 1.75% per year. These figures imply (see Appendix 10.1) that output grows at 4% per year.

The changes in u and s that we contemplate are as follows: First, the utilization rate will be allowed to rise from 1 to 1.333 over a period of ten years, thereafter remaining at 1.333. The implied annual growth rate of u is 2.9% for the ten years. Second, the savings rate will be allowed to rise from 0.12 to 0.20 in one year and to remain at this higher level forever.

As a result of these changes in utilization or savings, the economy will move to a new and higher growth path, and the growth rate of Q will asymptotically return to the original rate of 0.04. Table 10.1 shows the calculated effects on output after ten years and fifteen years. The entries in the table are the ratios of output on the new growth path to output on the original growth path. (The equations used to calculate the paths are given in Appendix 10.1.) The interesting point to emerge from the calculations is that the change in utilization delivers its gains more quickly than the change in savings. Although the asymptotic gain in output from the savings change is 24%, the gain after ten years is only 6.6%. The change in utilization yields an asymptotic gain of only 13%,[6] but after ten years it is already 9.2%. Although the increase in

---

[6] Of the 13% asymptotic gain in output, 8% may be attributed to the static effect (that is, the rise in u with K remaining on its previous path) and the rest to the growth process.

Table 10.1. *Effect on level of output of increases in utilization and rate of savings*

	Change in	
	Utilization	Savings
After 10 years	1.092	1.066
After 15 years	1.096	1.091
Asymptotic ratio	1.131	1.245

This table shows the ratio of output on the new growth path to output on the original growth path.

savings in the long run is more powerful, the increase in utilization produces greater gains over the first ten years (and even the first fifteen years).

Let us add a few words of qualification to these calculations. In the first place, depreciation has not been explicitly considered. Second, the analysis is, of course, confined to the Cobb-Douglas case. Third, the model and the calculations neglect the problem that capital goods installed during the period when u equals unity are not in general in the form most suitable for maximizing production when u is higher than unity. This problem is perhaps not too serious for our calculation, since we are assuming a gradual increase in u at an annual rate of 2.9%.

*10.4   Extensions: endogenous savings rate and endogenous depreciation

In this section we return to the neoclassical model of Section 10.2 and extend that model in two directions. First we let the savings rate be a function of the rate of interest. Then we let depreciation be a function of the rate of utilization. Our treatment of depreciation will be extremely brief.

When the rate of interest changes as a result of a change in utilization, there is both an income effect and a substitution effect on the savings rate, since the change in the rate of interest is accompanied by a change in the productivity of capital (Bailey 1957). The substitution effect of an increase in the rate of interest works to increase the savings rate, whereas the income effect normally decreases it. Empirical studies have often found the interest rate to have a weak or insignificant effect on savings, but a recent study has found evidence of a significant positive interest elasticity of savings (Boskin 1978). We shall assume this elasticity to be positive for simplicity of exposition; however, we shall note the implications of a negative elasticity at the relevant points in the discussion.

The approach to the savings rate in this section is fundamentally different from that of Sections 10.2 and 10.3. There the savings rate was regarded either as a constant or as a policy variable that could be used to influence the growth of capital and output. Here the savings rate changes in response to changes in the rate of utilization. As in Section 10.2, the crucial question is whether or not an increase in utilization increases the capital–labor ratio.

To keep matters simple, we shall leave the rest of the Solow-Swan model intact while savings is made a function of the rate of interest. [For a treatment of savings in a growth model in which individuals maximize lifetime utility and different generations are treated explicitly, see the work of Diamond (1965).] The rate of interest, which equals the marginal productivity of the capital stock, is given by $i = f'(uk)u$. The following expression can be developed[7] for E_{ku}:

$$E_{ku} = \frac{\theta^* + E_{si}\left[1 - \dfrac{1 - \theta^*}{\sigma}\right]}{1 - \theta^* + E_{si}\left[\dfrac{1 - \theta^*}{\sigma}\right]} \tag{10.16}$$

where E_{si} is the elasticity of the savings rate with respect to the rate of interest. If E_{ku} is positive, then we say that utilization is more powerful in a growth context than in a static context. If it is negative, then the growth effects of an increase in u are unfavorable.

We first note that (10.16) collapses to (10.10) if E_{si} is set equal to zero. In that case, E_{ku} must be positive, as we saw in Section 10.2.

---

[7] The equilibrium condition (10.9) becomes

$$s(i)f(uk) = \gamma k \tag{10.13}$$

Differentiating (10.13) with respect to u,

$$sf'\left[u\frac{dk}{du} + k\right] + f\frac{ds}{di}\frac{di}{du} = \gamma\frac{dk}{du} \tag{10.14}$$

Now

$$\frac{di}{du} = f' + uf''\left[u\frac{dk}{du} + k\right] \tag{10.15}$$

We substitute (10.15) into (10.14) and collect terms containing dk/du on the left. After some manipulation and use of (10.A2) and (10.13), we obtain the expression in the text.

Suppose now that E_{si} is positive. Because the denominator of (10.16) is necessarily positive, the sign of E_{ku} depends on the numerator. The term in brackets in the numerator determines whether the increase in utilization raises or lowers the rate of interest when k is held constant [see (10.3)]. If σ exceeds $1 - \theta^*$, this expression is positive, and E_{ku} must be positive. If σ is less than $1 - \theta^*$, the bracketed term is negative, and if E_{si} were large enough, E_{ku} would be negative. The requirement is that E_{si} must exceed $\theta^*/\{[1 - \theta^*]/\sigma - 1\}$, where the denominator must be positive. Given our uncertainty about σ and E_{si}, we cannot be confident that E_{ku} is positive. For example, if $\theta^* = 0.2$ and $\sigma = 0.4$, the bracketed term in the numerator of (10.16) would be negative, and if E_{si} exceeds 0.2, E_{ku} would be negative.

If E_{si} is negative, there is the possibility that the growth model is not stable.[8] Stability requires, in this case, that $|E_{si}| < \sigma$; if this condition is met, the denominator in (10.16) must be positive. The sign of E_{ku} still depends on the numerator. It can be shown that for E_{ku} to be negative, $|E_{si}|$ must exceed θ^* and σ must exceed unity.[9] We shall not pursue this case further here, except to note that if E_{si} is negative, presumably it is

---

[8] Stability is assured in our model if E_{si} is positive. To demonstrate this result, we note first that stability requires that $d\dot{k}/k$ be negative at the point where $\dot{k} = 0$. Differentiating (10.9) with respect to k [letting s be a function of $f'(uk)u$] gives

$$\frac{d\dot{k}}{dk} = \left[\frac{ds}{di}f''u^2\right]f + sf'u - \gamma$$

Now $\dot{k} = 0$ implies $\gamma = sf/k$. Hence

$$\frac{k}{f}\frac{d\dot{k}}{dk} = \left[\frac{ds}{di}ukf''\right]u + s\left[\frac{ukf' - f}{f}\right]$$

$$= -E_{si}s[1 - \theta^*]/\sigma - s[1 - \theta^*]$$

Thus if E_{si} is positive, this expression must be negative, as required for stability. If E_{si} is negative, stability requires $|E_{si}| < \sigma$.

[9] For the numerator of (10.16) to be negative when E_{si} is negative, we must have

$$|E_{si}|\frac{1 - \theta^*}{\sigma} < -\theta^* + |E_{si}|$$

This inequality shows that $|E_{si}|$ must exceed θ^*. Manipulating this condition further yields

$$\sigma > \frac{1 - \theta^*}{1 - \theta^*/|E_{si}|} > 1$$

That is, σ must exceed unity.

small in absolute value; it seems reasonable to suppose that $|E_{si}|$ would be less than θ^*.

The effect of u on w can be found by substituting (10.16) into (10.9). We obtain, after simplification,

$$E_{wu} = \frac{\theta^*}{1 - \theta^*} \frac{1 + E_{si}}{\sigma + E_{si}} \qquad (10.17)$$

If E_{si} equals zero, this equation collapses to (10.10). E_{wu} must be positive in any case, but, of course, that condition does not mean that the increase in average wages is enough to compensate workers for the disutility of shift-work. One interesting question is whether E_{wu} is higher in (10.17) than in (10.10), that is, whether or not wages go up by more when the savings rate is a positive function of the rate of interest. The answer is that an increase in E_{si} raises E_{wu} if σ exceeds unity but lowers E_{wu} if σ is less than unity.

Another interesting question is whether or not the growth effects on w of the increase in u are favorable, that is, whether E_{wu} in (10.17) is higher than $E_{wu} = \theta^*/\sigma$ in the static model [see (10.2)]. Manipulation of the two expressions shows that (10.17) may be less than θ^*/σ; the conditions are that σ be less than $1 - \theta^*$ and that E_{si} exceed $\theta^*/\{[1 - \theta^*]/\sigma - 1\}$. This condition is exactly the same as the condition for E_{ku} in (10.16) to be negative. The fact that the two conditions are identical makes good intuitive sense and justifies our earlier emphasis on E_{ku}.

In summary, under the savings function with a positive interest elasticity, the growth effects of an increase in utilization may be unfavorable. To be sure, an increase in utilization must increase the equilibrium levels of output per worker and the wage rate, but that is also true of a static model. Favorable growth effects come about when the increase in u raises k. Although this result necessarily follows in the simple growth model, it is not necessary in the model considered in this section. A necessary but not sufficient condition for k to fall is that σ be less than $1 - \theta^*$. A sufficient condition for k to fall is that in addition to σ being less than $1 - \theta^*$, E_{si} must exceed $\theta^*/\{[1 - \theta^*]/\sigma - 1\}$.

The model can also be extended to incorporate wear-and-tear depreciation. We shall not take the time here to present the mathematics, but we shall mention some of the conclusions that can be derived. We assume that the annual rate of wear-and-tear depreciation is a positive function of the rate of utilization. Obviously the introduction of this kind of wear-and-tear depreciation detracts from the favorable effects of shift-work. In a static model, such depreciation reduces the desirable effects of shift-work simply by using up more resources. In a growth model with a constant savings rate, it introduces the possibility that increased utilization will have unfavorable output effects. Wear-and-tear depreciation also increases the chance that increased utilization will lower the rate of interest. Consequently, in a growth model with a positive interest elasticity of savings, the introduction of such depreciation increases the chance that the growth effects will be unfavorable. This outcome does require, however, a rather special set of circumstances: the elasticity of substitution must be low, the interest elasticity of saving must be high, and depreciation must be quite sensitive to utilization. We may still regard as normal the case in which increased utilization has favorable growth effects.

10.5   Concluding remarks

One issue addressed in this chapter is whether, under a neoclassical production function, an increase in utilization has a greater effect on output and the wage rate in a growth context than in a static context. This question boils down to whether the increase in utilization increases the ratio of capital stock to labor, k. It must do so in the simple model, in which the savings rate is constant and there is no wear-and-tear depreciation. It need not do so in models in which either the savings rate depends on the rate of interest or the depreciation rate depends on the rate of utilization.

Prior literature has introduced into the neoclassical growth model a capital-employment parameter e, defined as the fraction of the capital stock actually employed; e enters the production function in the same manner as our capital-utilization parameter u. Because in the basic model the roles of e and u are formally the same, our result that an increase in u must raise k can be said to have been available, at least formally, in the literature. Our finding that an increase in u can under certain circumstances lower k is, to our knowledge, novel; this new result stems from making the depreciation rate and the savings rate functions (directly or indirectly) of u. Inasmuch as previous authors did not think of e in the same way that we think of u, it is not surprising that they did not see the connection between this parameter and the rates of savings and depreciation.[10]

---

[10] Because the prior literature has analyzed more complex models with this capital-employment parameter included, this literature permits a straightforward extension of certain results to the issue of interest. For instance, in modified Solow-Swan models with endogenous technical-change frontiers, both savings rates and capital-employment or utilization rates are positively related to the capital–labor ratio and to the equilibrium growth rate. It immediately follows that the positive growth effects of increased utilization will be stronger in those models than in the ones discussed here.

The wage effects of increased utilization are more favorable as the elasticity of substitution decreases. This conclusion holds where the savings rate is constant and where the savings rate is a positive function of the interest rate. The conclusion also holds in the presence or absence of wear-and-tear depreciation.

Although in certain circumstances the growth effects of increased utilization may be unfavorable, these circumstances are rather unusual. One set of such circumstances involves a low elasticity of substitution and a high interest elasticity of savings. Another set involves these two elements together with a rate of wear-and-tear depreciation that is quite sensitive to the rate of utilization. The normal situation, however, is that in which an increase in utilization has favorable growth effects. This conclusion is the most important one in the present chapter, for it adds a new dimension to the case in favor of shift-work-promoting policies.

It is interesting to note that a high elasticity of substitution, which tends to make shift-work have unfavorable distributional effects, tends to ensure that shift-work will have favorable growth effects in the presence of a positive interest elasticity of savings. Moreover, an increase in the elasticity of substitution (in the presence of a positive interest elasticity of savings) always increases the favorable growth effects of shift-work. Thus, if future research reveals that typical values of the elasticity of substitution are quite high and confirms that the savings rate is a positive function of the rate of interest, a strong case in favor of shift-work might be made on the basis of its growth-inducing effects. It would have to be assumed that the negative distributional effects could be ameliorated by other policies. Shift-work would be proposed and defended, under these conditions, *in spite of* rather than *because of* its distributional implications.

Appendix 10.1 Derivation of equations

Since $q = f(uk)$, we have

$$E_{qu} = \frac{u}{q}\frac{\partial q}{\partial u} = \frac{ukf'}{f} = \theta^* \tag{10.1}$$

The wage rate is

$$w(u) = f(uk) - ukf'(uk) \tag{10.A1}$$

Hence

$$\frac{\partial w}{\partial u} = f'k - k[uf''k + f'] = -uk^2f''$$

(Here and throughout this chapter, parentheses are used to indicate functional relationships. Multiplication is indicated by square brackets or other symbols.) Now the elasticity of substitution (σ) can be written[11]

$$\sigma = - \frac{f'[f - ukf']}{ukff''}$$

Hence

$$ukf'' = - \frac{f'[f - ukf']}{\sigma f} = - \frac{f'}{\sigma}[1 - \theta^*] \qquad (10.\text{A}2)$$

where $1 - \theta^*$ is the labor share in total output. In view of (10.A2), the elasticity of w with respect to u is

$$E_{wu} = \frac{u}{w}\frac{\partial w}{\partial u} = \frac{uk}{[1 - \theta^*]f}\frac{f'}{\sigma}[1 - \theta^*] = \frac{\theta^*}{\sigma} \qquad (10.2)$$

The rate of return to capital is $i = f'u$. Hence

$$\frac{\partial i}{\partial u} = f' + ukf'' = f'\left[1 - \frac{1 - \theta^*}{\sigma}\right]$$

The elasticity of i with respect to u is

$$E_{iu} = \frac{i}{u}\frac{\partial i}{\partial u} = 1 - \frac{1 - \theta^*}{\sigma} \qquad (10.3)$$

Because the proportions of day and night man-hours are $1/u$ and $[u - 1]/u$, the relationship between the day wage (w_1) and the average wage (w) is

$$w_1\frac{1}{u} + w_1[1 + \alpha]\frac{u - 1}{u} = w$$

Hence $w_1 = hw$, where

$$h = \left\{\frac{1}{u} + [1 + \alpha]\frac{u - 1}{u}\right\}^{-1}$$

Now

$$\frac{\partial w_1}{\partial u} = w\frac{dh}{du} + h\frac{\partial w}{\partial u}$$

If we assume that initially $u = 1$, then $h = 1$ and $dh/du = -\alpha$. In view of (10.2), we have

[1] See the work of Allen (1967, p. 48); uk is substituted for k in his formula.

$$E_{w_1 u} = \frac{u}{w_1} \frac{\partial w_1}{\partial u} = -\alpha + \frac{\theta}{\sigma} \tag{10.4}$$

We turn now to the growth model. To derive (10.10) we set k_t equal to zero in (10.9) and differentiate the resulting equation with respect to u.

$$sf' \left[u \frac{dk}{du} + k \right] = \gamma \frac{dk}{du}$$

$$\frac{dk}{du} = \frac{-sf'k}{sf'u - \gamma}$$

$$E_{ku} = \frac{u}{k} \frac{dk}{du} = \frac{-sf'u}{sf'u - \gamma} = \frac{-sf'u}{sf'u - sf/k}$$

$$= \frac{-ukf'}{ukf' - f} = \frac{\theta^*}{1 - \theta^*} \tag{10.10}$$

To derive (10.11) we differentiate (10.A1) to obtain

$$\frac{dw}{du} = -ukf'' \left[u \frac{dk}{du} + k \right] = \frac{kf'}{\sigma} [1 - \theta^*][E_{ku} + 1]$$

$$E_{wu} = \frac{u}{w} \frac{dw}{du} = \frac{ukf'}{w} \frac{1 - \theta^*}{\sigma} [E_{ku} + 1] = \frac{\theta^*}{\sigma} [E_{ku} + 1] \tag{10.A3}$$

Substituting (10.10) into (10.A3) yields

$$E_{wu} = \frac{\theta^*}{\sigma} \left[\frac{\theta^*}{1 - \theta^*} + 1 \right] = \frac{\theta^*}{\sigma[1 - \theta^*]} \tag{10.11}$$

Next we turn to the numerical illustration with the Cobb-Douglas production function. Differentiating (10.12) logarithmically (with u held constant) yields

$$\dot{Q}/Q = g + \delta[\dot{K}/K] + [1 - \delta]\gamma$$

In equilibrium, $\dot{Q}/Q$ and $\dot{K}/K$ must be equal. Call this common growth rate λ. Then

$$\lambda = g + \delta[\lambda] + [1 - \delta]\gamma$$

Hence $\lambda = \gamma + g/[1 - \delta]$. The ratio of Q to K is implied by the equality of savings and investment, or $sQ = \lambda K$, which may be written

$$Q/K = \lambda/s = \{\gamma + g/[1 - \delta]\}/s$$

The year-to-year changes in the model's variables can be calculated sequentially from (10.A4), (10.A5), and (10.A6):

$$[Q/K]_t = [Q/K]_{t-1} \frac{1 + [\dot{Q}/Q]_{t-1}}{1 + [\dot{K}/K]_{t-1}} \tag{10.A4}$$

$$[\dot{K}/K]_t = [Q/K]_t s \tag{10.A5}$$

$$[\dot{Q}/Q]_t = g + [1 - \delta]\gamma + \delta[\dot{u}/u]_t + \delta[\dot{K}/K]_t \tag{10.A6}$$

If the new level of income is denoted Q_t^* and the original is Q_t, then the ratio Q_t^*/Q_t will approach an asymptote. This asymptotic ratio will now be calculated for each of the changes.

For the change in utilization, we have

$$Q_t^* = e^{gt}[u^* K_t^*]^\delta [L_t]^{1-\delta}$$
$$Q_t = e^{gt}[u K_t]^\delta [L_t]^{1-\delta}$$

Hence

$$Q_t^*/Q_t = [u^*/u]^\delta [K_t^*/K_t]^\delta \tag{10.A7}$$

Now $K_t = sQ_t/\lambda$ [from (10.A5)], and asymptotically $K_t^* = sQ_t^*/\lambda$. Hence

$$K_t^*/K_t = Q_t^*/Q_t$$

Substituting this equation into (10.A7) and manipulating the result yields

$$Q_t^*/Q_t = [u^*/u]^{\delta/[1-\delta]}$$

For the change in savings, (10.A7) continues to hold, but $u^*/u = 1$. We also have the asymptotic result that $K_t^* = s^* Q_t^*/\lambda$, from which it follows that

$$K_t^*/K_t = [s^*/s][Q_t^*/Q_t]$$

Substituting this equation into (10.A7) yields

$$Q_t^*/Q_t = [s^*/s]^{\delta/[1-\delta]}$$

CHAPTER 11

Shift-work and the dual economy

In the growth models of the preceding chapter, we assumed that factor markets function perfectly. Although such an assumption may be reasonable in developed economies, it is rather questionable in developing countries. Dualistic models have been a prominent feature of the development literature for some time (Lewis 1954; Fei and Ranis 1964). Although the concept of unlimited supplies of labor is no longer as popular as it was fifteen to twenty-five years ago (e.g., Kelley et al. 1972), the notion of an industrial wage set by institutional forces at a level above the agricultural wage is still widely accepted (e.g., Little et al. 1970, pp. 80–99, 335–6; Healey 1972; International Labour Office 1973; Morawetz 1974). The present chapter will use this assumption to construct a model of economic growth and capital utilization.

The model to be presented in this chapter is a model of the industrial sector. Formally, it differs from that of Chapter 10 only in that the wage rate is fixed, but the present model should be viewed as a component of a larger model containing at least two sectors, rather than as a model of the entire economy. The implications of the fact that there are other sectors in the economy will be mentioned at various points in the discussion.

Just as in Chapter 10, we shall distinguish between the static effects and the growth effects of an increase in utilization. For this reason it is convenient to begin (in Section 11.1) by constructing a static aggregate model in which the capital stock is given. The static effects of an increase in utilization are then described. In Section 11.2 the static model is converted to a growth model by specifying the mechanism of capital accumulation, and the effects of utilization in this context are examined. Finally, in Section 11.3 we compare the dualistic model developed here with the standard model described in Chapter 10.

11.1 The static model

When we say that the wage rate is fixed in this model, we are referring to the wage rate of the day workers. If w_1 is this daytime wage, the second-shift wage is $w_1[1 + \alpha]$. With the capital stock given in the static model, employment is determined by the condition that the marginal product of labor equals the average wage, or[1]

$$f(uk) - ukf'(uk) = w_1 \left[1 + \frac{u-1}{u} \alpha\right] \qquad (11.1)$$

where the notation is the same as that of Chapter 10. That is, u refers to the rate of utilization, defined so that $u = 1$ for single-shift operation, k refers to the ratio of capital stock (K) to labor (L), α is the shift differential, and $f(uk)$ is output per worker. Equation (11.1) determines k, given u and the other parameters. Because K is given, L can be found from K and k.

In Appendix 11.1 we derive expressions for E_{Lu}, E_{iu}, and E_{Qu}, which are the elasticities of employment (L), the interest rate (i), and output (Q) with respect to utilization (u). To simplify the formulas, we assume that $u = 1$ initially. We have

$$E_{Lu} = 1 - \alpha\sigma \frac{1}{\theta} \qquad (11.2)$$

$$E_{iu} = 1 - \alpha \frac{1-\theta}{\theta} \qquad (11.3)$$

$$E_{Qu} = 1 - \alpha\sigma \frac{1-\theta}{\theta} \qquad (11.4)$$

where θ is the capital share under single-shift operation and σ is the elasticity of substitution.

Let us note in passing that the condition for E_{iu} to be positive is the same as the condition that the cost ratio be less than unity under a Leontief production function [see Chapter 2, equation (2.5)]. It is intuitively reasonable that the condition for shift-work to cut costs at given factor prices be the same as the condition for the owners of capital to benefit from shift-work when the prices of daytime and second-shift labor are fixed. The relevant cost ratio is the Leontief ratio, because we are using only a first-order approximation to the output increase (the change in u being assumed to be small).

When the industrial wage is fixed, the "favorable" effects of an increase in u from the point of view of workers must be measured in terms of industrial employment rather than the wage rate. The

---

[1] We follow the convention of the preceding chapter that parentheses indicate functional dependence; multiplication is indicated by square brackets or other symbols.

condition for employment to increase with u is that θ exceed $\alpha\sigma$. If σ is greater than unity, the condition can easily be violated, in which case the static effects on employment will be unfavorable. The effects on employment will be more favorable (or less unfavorable) the lower is σ, the lower is α, and the higher is θ.

11.2   The growth model

To convert the static model into a growth model, we need only add to (11.1) the equation $\dot{K} = sQ$, or

$$\dot{K}/K = sQ/K = sq/k = sf(uk)/k \qquad (11.5)$$

This equation determines the rates of growth of capital, labor, and output. The condition for the growth rates to increase with u is that $sf(uk)/k$ increases.

If this condition is met, an increase in utilization will increase the rate of growth of each of the three variables. In that case, we may say that utilization is more powerful in a growth context than in a static context. If, on the other hand, $sf(uk)/k$ falls, the growth rates of the three variables will fall, and the growth effects of utilization will be less favorable than the static effects.

Let us consider first the case in which s is constant. Then the condition for favorable growth effects is that $f(uk)/k$ increases with u. A moment's reflection reveals that the condition on the parameters for this increase to occur is the same as the condition that output increase when the capital stock is held constant, and that condition is that E_{Qu} be positive in (11.4). The same condition is formally derived in Appendix 11.1.

Unfavorable growth effects, on the other hand, will occur when E_{Qu} is negative. Is it possible for shift-work to be profitable for entrepreneurs and still generate unfavorable growth effects? The answer is yes. Shift-work is profitable if the cost of ratio is less than unity, a condition that implies that E_{iu} in (11.3) is positive. E_{iu} can be positive while E_{Qu} is negative, if σ exceeds unity. Although this situation is unusual,[2] when it does arise an increase in utilization reduces $f(uk)k$ and (with s constant) reduces the rate of growth.

Suppose now that the savings rate has a positive interest elasticity. This circumstance can only be favorable to utilization, since all that is

---

[2] An example will illustrate how unusual this situation is. Suppose that $\theta = 0.3$ and $\alpha = 0.3$. The cost ratio is 0.955. The expression $\alpha[1 - \theta]/\theta$ is 0.7, and σ would have to exceed $1/0.7 = 1.43$.

required for the interest rate to rise with u is that the cost ratio be less than unity [by (11.3)]. It can be shown that the condition for $sf(uk)/k$ to rise with u when s is a function of $f'u$ is

$$1 - \alpha\sigma\frac{1-\theta}{\theta} + E_{si}\left[1 - \alpha\frac{1-\theta}{\theta}\right] > 0 \tag{11.6}$$

where E_{si} is the interest elasticity of the saving rate. This condition is a generalization of the condition that E_{Qu} in (11.4) be positive, since if we set E_{si} equal to zero, we obtain that condition. The term in brackets in (11.6) must be positive if the cost ratio is less than unity. Thus a positive interest elasticity makes it even more unlikely that an increase in u will reduce the rate of growth.

The long-run effects of an increase in u on industrial employment will be favorable if the growth rate of the industrial sector increases. Thus, even if the static effects of u on employment are negative, employment will be higher in the long run when u is higher, provided condition (11.6) is met.[3]

11.3   Comparison of standard and dualistic models

This section will compare the effects of shift-work in the dualistic model with the effects of shift-work in the standard model, which was discussed in Chapter 10. We shall begin by considering the effects on workers' welfare, and then we shall discuss the effects on total output.

In the standard model the interests of workers are best served by an increase in the daytime wage rate, whereas in the dualistic model, since the daytime wage for industrial workers is fixed, the workers are interested in an expansion of industrial employment. If we confine ourselves for the moment to the static components of the growth models, the relevant expressions are E_{Lu} in the dualistic model and E_{w_1u} in the standard model. Table 11.1 lists the two expressions for the case in which $u = 1$ initially, and we find that the condition for workers to benefit is exactly the same, namely, that the product of the shift differential and the elasticity of substitution must be less than the capital share.

In the growth context there is one fundamental difference between

---

[3] It should be noted again here that the other sectors have been left out of our growth model. The increased output of the industrial sector would lead to a deterioration of the terms of trade of that sector (compared with what would have happened if u had remained constant), which would limit the expansion of industry.

Table 11.1. *Conditions for favorable effects on labor in dualistic and standard growth models*

	Dualistic	Standard
Static	$E_{Lu} = 1 - \alpha\sigma\dfrac{1}{\theta}$	$E_{w_1 u} = \theta/\sigma - \alpha$
Growth with constant s	Growth rate depends on $1 - \alpha\sigma\dfrac{1 - \theta}{\theta}$	$E_{w_1 u} = \dfrac{\theta}{1 - \theta}\dfrac{1}{\sigma} - \alpha$
Growth with positive E_{si}	Growth rate depends on $1 - \alpha\sigma\dfrac{1 - \theta}{\theta} + $ $E_{si}\left[1 - \alpha\dfrac{1 - \theta}{\theta}\right]$	$E_{w_1 u} = \dfrac{\theta}{1 - \theta}\dfrac{1 + E_{si}}{\sigma + E_{si}} - \alpha$

Note: All the expressions in the table were derived on the assumption that $u = 1$ initially.

the two models. The growth rate itself depends on u in the dualistic model, but not in our version of the standard model. Therefore, in the dualistic model the growth-rate effects of a change in u must eventually overwhelm the static effects. In the standard model, on the other hand, we speak of static effects and growth effects, but the growth effects are changes in the equilibrium capital–labor ratio, not in the growth rate. Thus in the standard model the static effects can be added to the growth effects to give the overall effects. Consequently, we shall compare the growth-rate effects in the dualistic model with the overall effects in the standard model.

Consider first the case in which the savings rate is constant. Table 11.1 indicates the condition under which the growth rates (of employment, output, and capital stock) will rise with an increase in u in the dualistic model and the condition under which the daytime wage will rise in the standard model. The two conditions are the same! Thus the parallelism of the two models is quite striking.

We can push this parallelism one step further. The condition for shift-work to be profitable to entrepreneurs is the same for both models, namely, that $1 - \alpha[1 - \theta]/\theta$ must exceed zero. It is impossible for shift-work to be both profitable to entrepreneurs and detrimental to labor's interest if the elasticity of substitution is less than unity. (This statement may be confirmed by examining the expressions in Table 11.1 for the case in which the savings rate is constant.)

Let us note that whereas the conditions for favorable effects on workers are the same, the magnitudes of the favorable effects are quite different in the two models. In the standard model, the daytime wage moves toward a new and higher equilibrium value. In the dualistic model, on the other hand, the favorable effects consist in a higher growth rate of employment, and the cumulative effects of such a change over a long period of time will be enormous. This statement must be qualified by reference to the fact that we have modeled only one sector of what must be viewed as a model with at least two sectors. The expansion of the industrial sector may be limited by market restraints. Nevertheless, the favorable effects of shift-work (when they are favorable) would seem to be larger in the dualistic model than in the standard model.

The parallelism breaks down when we introduce a positive interest elasticity of savings. As shown in Table 11.1, the conditions for favorable effects on labor are now somewhat different in the two models. It remains true for both models, however, that if the elasticity of substitution is less than unity, shift-work cannot be profitable to entrepreneurs and harmful to workers' interests.

We turn finally to the effects of increased utilization on output in the two growth models. In the standard model, in which the labor force is exogenous, it can be shown that the flow of capital services (uk) always increases, and consequently total output is always larger when u is increased. The output effects will be more favorable, of course, if E_{ku} is positive;[4] we have listed in Table 11.2 the condition for E_{ku} to be positive in the different versions of the standard model. For the dualistic model, since the growth rate of output will normally change when utilization increases, we have listed again in Table 11.2 the conditions for the growth rate of output to rise in the different versions of the model.

Table 11.2 shows that when the savings rate is constant, the growth effects on output are always favorable in the standard model, but the growth effects may be negative in the dualistic model. The introduction of a positive interest elasticity of savings creates the possibility of negative growth effects in the standard model; these effects are possible if the increase in utilization makes the interest rate fall. In the dualistic model, the introduction of a positive interest elasticity of savings is always favorable to growth, provided the cost ratio is less than unity.

An interesting point to emerge from Tables 11.1 and 11.2 is that the elasticity of substitution plays contrasting roles in the two models. In the standard model, a high elasticity of substitution always makes increased utilization have unfavorable distributional implications, but

[4] It can be shown that $E_{qu} = \theta^*(1 + E_{ku})$.

Table 11.2. *Conditions for output effects to be favorable in dualistic models and for E_{ku} to be positive in standard models*

	Dualistic	Standard[a]
Growth with constant s	Growth rate depends on $1 - \alpha\sigma\dfrac{1 - \theta}{\theta}$	E_{ku} always positive
Growth with positive E_{si}	Growth rate depends on $1 - \alpha\sigma\dfrac{1 - \theta}{\theta} +$ $E_{si}\left[1 - \alpha\dfrac{1 - \theta}{\theta}\right]$	E_{ku} positive if $\sigma > 1 - \theta$; in the event that $\sigma < 1 - \theta$, E_{ku} positive if $E_{si} < \theta/\{[1 - \theta]/\sigma - 1\}$

Note: All the expressions in the table were derived on the assumption that $u = 1$ initially.

[a] Because the output effects are always positive in the standard model, we have listed the conditions for E_{ku} to be positive. The larger is E_{ku}, the greater the output effects.

a high elasticity of substitution is never harmful to output. In the dualistic model, on the other hand, a high elasticity of substitution is unfavorable for both employment and output.

In conclusion, let us add emphasis to a point already mentioned. Suppose the elasticity of substitition is less than unity, as many observers believe. Then if shift-work is profitable to entrepreneurs, it must benefit workers, in both models. But the magnitude of the workers' gains, as well as the magnitude of the increases in output, will be greater in the dualistic model than in the standard model. Therefore, to the extent that important features of an economy are captured by the dualistic model, the case for shift-work-promoting policies is much stronger than it would be if factor markets functioned perfectly as in the standard model.

Appendix 11.1 Derivation of equations

We start by deriving the elasticity of k with respect to u, or E_{ku}. Differentiating (11.1) totally,

$$f'd(uk) - ukf''d(uk) - f'd(uk) = w_1[1/u^2]du$$

$$d(uk)/du = -w_1\alpha/[u^2ukf'']$$

For simplicity, we set $u = 1$ initially. With $u = 1$, $w_1 = w = [1 - \theta]f$. Since $ukf'' = -f'[1 - \theta]/\sigma$, by (10.A2), we have

$$u\frac{dk}{du} + k = -\frac{\alpha\sigma f}{f'}$$

$$E_{ku} = \frac{u}{k}\frac{dk}{du} = -1 + \frac{\alpha\sigma f}{kf'} = -1 + \frac{\alpha\sigma}{\theta} \qquad (11.A1)$$

Since $k = K/L$, we have

$$\frac{u}{k}\frac{dk}{du} = -\frac{u}{L}\frac{dL}{du} = -E_{Lu}$$

where E_{Lu} is the elasticity of employment with respect to u. Hence

$$E_{Lu} = 1 - \alpha\sigma/\theta \qquad (11.1)$$

Next we find the elasticity of i with respect to u. Since $i = f'(uk)u$, we have

$$\frac{di}{du} = f' + uf''\left[u\frac{dk}{du} + k\right]$$

$$= f' + ukf''\left[\frac{u}{k}\frac{dk}{du} + 1\right]$$

$$= f' - \frac{f'}{\sigma}[1 - \theta]\left[\frac{\alpha\sigma}{\theta}\right]$$

Using the fact that $f' = i/u$,

$$E_{iu} = \frac{u}{i}\frac{di}{du} = 1 - \frac{1-\theta}{\theta}\alpha \qquad (11.2)$$

To obtain the elasticity of total output Q with respect to u, note first that $Q = Lf(uk)$. Hence

$$\frac{dQ}{du} = f\frac{dL}{du} + Lf'\left[u\frac{dk}{du} + k\right]$$

$$\frac{u}{Q}\frac{dQ}{du} = \frac{f}{Q}\frac{dL}{du}u + \frac{L}{Q}ukf'\left[\frac{u}{k}\frac{dk}{du} + 1\right]$$

Note that $f/Q = 1/L$ and $L/Q = 1/f$.

$$\frac{u}{Q}\frac{dQ}{du} = \frac{dL}{du}\frac{u}{L} + \frac{ukf'}{f}\left[\frac{u}{k}\frac{dk}{du} + 1\right]$$

$$= 1 - \alpha\sigma/\theta + \theta[\alpha\sigma/\theta]$$

$$E_{Qu} = 1 + \alpha\sigma\left[1 - \frac{1}{\theta}\right] = 1 - \alpha\sigma\frac{1-\theta}{\theta} \qquad (11.3)$$

Finally, we derive the condition for $f(uk)/k$ to increase with u:

$$\frac{d[f(uk)/k]}{du} = \frac{k^2 f' \left[\dfrac{u}{k}\dfrac{dk}{du} + 1\right] - f\dfrac{dk}{du}}{k^2}$$

The numerator will be positive if

$$E_{ku} + 1 - \left[\frac{f}{ukf'}\right]\frac{u}{k}\frac{dk}{du} > 0$$

$$\alpha\sigma/\theta - [1/\theta][-1 + \alpha\sigma/\theta] > 0$$

$$1 - \alpha\sigma[1 - \theta]/\theta > 0$$

This is the same as the condition that E_{Qu} be positive [see (11.3)].

CHAPTER 12

Conclusions and speculations

Our first task in this final chapter is to summarize the main conclusions of Chapters 1 through 11. This task will occupy us in Section 12.1. Then in Sections 12.2 and 12.3 we shall discuss, in a tone more subjective and speculative than in the rest of the book, the human costs of shift-work and the public-policy issues raised by our general subject.

12.1   Summary of findings and conclusions

The conclusions will be listed under the headings of methodological issues, substantive findings on the determinants of shift-work, and the productive and distributive effects of shift-work. With the exception of statements 3, 4, 10, and 17, which apply to shift-work exclusively, all of the following conclusions are applicable to both shift-work and capital utilization.

12.1.1   Methodological issues

1. According to economic theory, shift-work is both cause and consequence of capital intensity. On the consequence side, this statement has been part of conventional wisdom for a long time; the causal aspect was pointed out first by Marris (1964). The following implication of the statement, however, has not been widely appreciated: Observed correlations between capital intensity and shift-work do not provide empirical confirmation that capital intensity is a cause of shift-work.

2. Shift-work may be both cause and consequence of scale. Shift-work is always a cause of large scale in the sense that the undertaking of shift-work causes total factory output to be larger than it would otherwise be. Shift-work may be a consequence of large scale in that a larger optimal single-shift output may increase the profitability of shift-work; it will do so if the firm faces output restraint and its technology is of the semi-U type. The implication of our initial statement is that observed correlations between total output (or total employment) and shift-work provide singularly unconvincing evidence

shift-work are less favorable to workers the higher the elasticity of substitution. With a positive interest elasticity of savings, however, the output effects of shift-work will always be more favorable the higher the elasticity of substitution.

25. In the growth model with a fixed wage rate, an increase in utilization may increase or decrease the growth rate of output and employment. An increase in the growth rate is more likely the smaller the shift differential, the larger the capital share, and the smaller the elasticity of substitution.

We have completed our summary of the major conclusions from Chapters 1 through 11. Before discussing the implications of our findings for public policy, we shall describe in some detail the human costs of shift-work.

12.2 The human costs of shift-work

Shift-work requires people to work at abnormal hours, and it frequently involves changing one's hours of work at weekly or fortnightly intervals. The parties primarily affected by these working hours are the workers themselves and their employers. There are, however, some external effects of the decisions made by employers and workers. For example, an increase in shift-work may reduce the peak-load electricity requirements of the community, or it may reduce traffic congestion at morning and evening rush hours. Shift-work may also weaken the sense of community by preventing workers from participating in social and civic activities. We shall return to the theme of external costs and benefits in Section 12.3. The present section is concerned with the disutility that workers experience from shift-work.

This section is organized in the following manner: Subsection 12.2.1 describes the physiological problems engendered by shift-work. Because the majority of shift-workers seem to rotate, the physiological difficulties of rotating shift-work will be emphasized. Subsection 12.2.2 addresses the question of rotation itself by asking whether or not a system of permanent shifts would substantially reduce the human costs of shift-work. Subsection 12.2.3 attempts to quantify the human costs by presenting some data on explicit shift differentials. We find, however, that the explicit shift differentials frequently do not fully reflect the human costs of shift-work. Finally, Subsection 12.2.4 discusses the advantages and disadvantages of instituting arrangements by which the explicit shift differentials would reflect more closely the human costs of shift-work.

12.2.1 Physiological effects of shift-work[1]

The human body exhibits pronounced circadian (i.e., twenty-four-hour) rhythms in a number of biological variables: temperature, pulse, blood pressure, breathing rate, chemical composition of blood and urine, and of course brain activity. Under normal conditions the various rhythms exhibit a fairly high degree of synchronization. Although it is possible under highly controlled conditions (such as submarine life) to bring about a substantial inversion of the circadian rhythms, studies of industrial workers on permanent night shifts[2] have generally found that the circadian rhythms of such workers were reduced in amplitude and somewhat desynchronized. For instance, Carpentier and Cazamian (1977, p. 17) reported that the worker permanently on the night shift usually changes his sleeping and waking hours on the weekend to conform to those of other people. Moreover, the rotation of shifts produces a marked disruption in bodily rhythms for several days in most people. Walker (1971, p. 80) stated that "the body temperature rhythms usually change relatively easily but other rhythms such as the secretion of potassium in the urine are resistant to change. . . . The time required for body temperature to adjust is in the order of four days to a week." Individual variations in the time required for adjustment, however, are quite large. There is a presumption that those who make more rapid adjustments in their circadian rhythms find permanent shift-work and the rotation of shifts to be less burdensome.

Studies have quite consistently found a higher incidence of sleep problems among night-shift workers. The problems are more serious for those who rotate, but even permanent night workers tend to have more frequent difficulties involving the duration and quality of sleep than do permanent day workers. Once again, individual variations are important, as Winston (1970) emphasized. Farooq and Winston (1978, p. 229) stated that "studies of U.S. shift workers have concluded that 'the central problem of working shifts is getting adequate sleep' [reference to Mott et al. (1965, p. 235)], yet the most striking result of

---

[1] The literature on physiological effects of shift-work has been summarized by Mott et al. (1965), Winston (1970), Walker (1971), Maurice (1975), and Carpentier and Cazamian (1977).

[2] The physiological problems of shift-work arise primarily in connection with shift systems that involve night work (Mott et al. 1965, pp. 9–17; Walker 1971, p. 78). The inconvenience of two-shift systems not involving night work will be discussed in the next subsection.

the empirical studies in general is the large proportion of workers (30 to 80 percent) who profess to *no* problems of repeated sleep adjustment."

Shift-work also aggravates problems of digestion and elimination in some people, but the magnitude of the effect is difficult to detect because the shift-working population is a selected one. Studies have found that workers subjected to many years of shift-work are on the average as healthy as or more healthy than other workers. Because a selection factor is operating here, one cannot be sure that shift-work has been harmless, even for these workers; they might have been even healthier in the absence of shift-work. This point may seem to be rather picky, but it is mentioned here to indicate that the available evidence does not disprove the prevailing opinion among physiologists that disruption of circadian rhythms is bad for one's health.[3]

12.2.2 Shift-work without rotation

A system of permanent night work would seem to involve less violence to the circadian bodily rhythms than would three-shift rotation at weekly or biweekly intervals. In addition, surveys of workers have sometimes found that those on permanent night work are more satisfied with their working hours than those on rotating shifts that involve night work [Mott et al. 1965, p. 306; National Board for Prices and Incomes (NBPI) 1970, p. 89; Walker 1971, p. 88]. These findings have led Mott et al. (1965) and Winston (1970) to recommend permanent shifts rather than rotating shifts.

The fact is, however, that rotation is an extremely common practice.[4] Why do shifts typically rotate, if permanent shifts would be better for workers? It is hard to believe that management would object to permanent shifts if the workers preferred such a system. There may be several answers to this question,[5] but one of them centers on the implications of permanent shifts for family and social life. In the study of Mott et al. the permanent afternoon workers expressed considerable

---

[3] In a study of adult mice it was found that inverting the twelve-hour light–dark cycle once a week reduced the life span of the experimental group by 6% (National Institute of Mental Health 1970, p. 134).

[4] Permanent afternoon and night shifts are quite rare in Europe (NBPI 1970, p. 59; Maurice 1975, pp. 27–32). Permanent shifts are more widely used in the United States than in other countries (Northrup 1951; Maurice 1975, p. 85).

[5] We shall consider another answer in Subsection 12.2.4.

dissatisfaction because of being cut off from family (especially children) and from organized social activities.

It seems psychologically reasonable that the dissatisfaction because of being cut off from family and friends will increase with the length of time that one is so isolated.[6] This phenomenon could help to explain why shift systems typically rotate.[7] One certainly cannot infer from the relative satisfaction among samples of permanent night workers that permanent night shifts would be widely acceptable. Moreover, the evidence seems to indicate that recruiting permanent night workers requires a substantial monetary compensation when workers are free to choose day work as an alternative.[8] We turn to this evidence in the next section.

12.2.3 Magnitude of human costs of shift-work

An obvious way of attempting to quantify the human costs of shift-work is to look at pay differentials for different shifts. Data on these differentials are notorious for their scarcity, and we have reason to believe that they do not measure the human costs accurately. Nevertheless, they do provide useful information.

Where shifts rotate, workers sometimes receive the same pay regardless of the shift worked. This practice is understandable, since the system of rotation ensures that the burden of unpopular shifts is

---

[6] For a summary of relevant psychological evidence, see the work of Scitovsky (1976, Chapter 3).

[7] Perhaps the higher incidence of permanent shifts in the United States and the longer intervals of rotation in this country (Maurice 1975, p. 27) as compared with Europe reflect a higher value placed on physical comfort and a lower value on family and social contacts. This hypothesis would be consistent with Scitovsky's interpretation (1976) of the differences between American society and European society.

[8] There may well be variations in shift patterns that would be preferable to existing arrangements. Whereas the permanent afternoon shift was unpopular in the study of Mott et al. and is apparently rarely observed in Europe, the system of alternating double days received warm support from its workers in the NBPI study. It would seem that a discontinuous three-shift operation could be manned with lower human costs by combining alternating double days with one permanent night shift than by the currently widespread practice of rotation through all three shifts. Another new system that has been surprisingly acceptable is a three-shift continuous rotation at intervals of two or three days (Walker 1971, p. 89; Carpentier and Cazamian 1977, p. 59).

equitably shared. The more common arrangement under rotating shifts is that extra pay is awarded to those working afternoon and evening shifts, but there is little reason to think that such pay differentials fully compensate the workers for the disutility of being obligated to rotate through all three shifts. Under rotation, the appropriate measure of the human costs of shift-work would be derived by comparing the average wage rates of shift workers with those of comparable workers on permanent day work. Such a comparison would yield an implicit shift differential, and if the labor market were functioning smoothly, this differential would reflect the workers' perception of the human costs of shift-work.

Under a system of permanent afternoon and evening shifts, the explicit pay differentials (vis-à-vis the day shift) in the collective bargaining agreement would seem more likely to reflect the human costs of shift-work than would the shift differentials under rotation. In fact, Northrup (1951) reported that for his sample of fifty U.S. firms there was a tendency for shift differentials to be larger where shifts were fixed than where they were rotating. Nevertheless, there is evidence that even these fixed shift differentials fail to compensate workers fully for the unpopular shifts. Collective bargaining agreements in the United States typically specify that the choice of shift is governed by the seniority of the worker (Maurice 1975, p. 85, citing a 1950 U.S. Department of Labor compendium of collective bargaining provisions; Zalusky 1978, p. 6).

Data from collective bargaining agreements in the United States yield an average shift differential of approximately 4% for the second shift and 5% for the third shift.[9] These figures represent a combination of the premiums for fixed shifts and the premiums for second and third shifts within systems of rotation. We would not expect the premiums in either case to reflect fully the human costs of shift-work, and indeed the percentages strike us as very low.

Maurice (1975, p. 81) cited several examples of shift differentials of 10% to 15% in selected industries in France, Italy, and Germany.

---

[9] The source is O'Connor (1970). The average cents-per-hour differentials in 1967-8 were 10.0 cents for the second shift and 12.8 cents for the third shift. With an average hourly wage of $3.00 (Statistical Abstract 1973, p. 241), these differentials work out to 3.3% and 4.3%. Some collective bargaining agreements provide for uniform percentage differentials; the averages of these differentials are 7.6% for the second shift and 9.9% for the third shift. The weighted averages of the cents-per-hour and the uniform percentage differentials are the figures given in the text.

These figures appear to be explicit shift differentials within systems of rotation.

The National Board for Prices and Incomes (NBPI) made an attempt to deal with the difficulties of calculating shift premiums, and their data for the United Kingdom seem to be the most relevant for estimating the human costs of shift-work as perceived by the workers. An anaylsis of 130 collective bargaining agreements in 1969 showed that "the average shift payments . . . represented an addition to minimum hourly rates of 24.7 percent for permanent nights, 14.9 percent for discontinuous 3-shift and 12.2 percent for double days" (NBPI, 1970, p. 61). Another study of about 100 agreements in 1970 showed the "modal range" of the shift premiums to be 17% to 20% for double days, 19% to 21.5% for three-shift systems, and 25% for night work only (NBPI, 1970, p. 101). The NBPI also looked at earnings data for shift-workers and day-workers and after appropriate qualifications noted that "it would be safe, however, to infer that given equality in other respects manual shift-workers might expect to earn about 20 percent more than dayworkers although this will vary with different shift systems" (NBPI, 1970, p. 62).[10]

Note that a 12% premium for alternating double days has the same impact on costs as a 24% premium for a permanent afternoon shift, and a 15% premium for three-shift rotation is equivalent to 22.5% for the second and third shifts. Therefore, the figures reported here indicate a substantial preference for daytime work.

For less-developed countries there is also evidence that workers prefer daytime work to rotating shifts or night work. Thoumi (1978, p. 121) reported that the World Bank surveys found average night-shift differentials of 25% in Israel, 15% in Malaysia, and 10% in the Philippines. These figures are *not* legislated night premiums, which exist in several Latin American countries (Millan 1975, p. 223; Thoumi 1978, p. 121). Millan estimated the implicit second-shift premium in manufacturing in Peru (which does not have a legislated premium) by regressing average factory wage on several independent variables, including a dummy for second-shift operation. He estimated the second-shift premium for production workers at around 20% (Millan 1975, p. 159). Millan also reported on a survey of some fifty plants in Peru by a team headed by Roberto Abusada; wide variety was observed among shift premiums.

[10] Marris (1964, p. 139) estimated the percentage increase in unit hourly labor costs on double days to be between 20% and 30% for the United Kingdom in 1951.

Farooq and Winston (1978) surveyed day-workers and shift-workers in Pakistan and documented the considerable human costs of shift-work in that country. The shift-workers, most of whom were rotating, reported much higher incidences of sleeping problems, eating problems, and general health problems than did the day-workers.

Several authors have commented on the absence of shift differentials in particular less-developed countries: Farooq and Winston (1978, p. 238) in Pakistan, Baily (1974, pp. 77–9) in Kenya, Betancourt (1977, pp. 43–4) in Sri Lanka, and Wangwe (1977, pp. 67–8) in Tanzania. The evidence cited by these authors by no means implies that the human costs of shift-work are negligible in these countries. In the first place, most of these authors were referring to the absence of an *explicit* shift differential; moreover, their observations were consistent with the emergence of an implicit shift differential in the form of higher wages for factories requiring shift-work. Second, even if we assume that the poor functioning of the labor market in these countries prevents an implicit shift differential from emerging, most workers would still prefer day-work to shift-work if given a choice.

Farooq and Winston emphasized that the unemployed in Pakistan would be quite willing to accept shift-work even with no pay differential. Given the wage differentials between modern manufacturing and other sectors in most less-developed countries, it is quite believable that the unemployed would respond in a similar way in other poor countries. The difficulty with deriving policy implications from this finding is that the policies designed to provide shift-work jobs to the unemployed may turn out to provide shift-work jobs for those who would otherwise have been employed on day-work. Because the question of shift-work policy will be taken up in Section 12.3, we shall not pursue the topic further here. The point to be emphasized at present is that from the point of view of workers, day-work is not equivalent to shift-work; in this sense there are human costs to shift-work in less-developed countries as well as in developed countries. It may be plausible that the wage premium that makes the two types of work equally desirable is lower in poor countries than in rich countries, but there does not seem to be any solid evidence on which to base such a statement.

12.2.4 *Monetizing the human costs of shift-work*

It is apparent from the previous subsection that the disutility of shift-work is frequently not reflected in explicit shift premiums. An interesting question is whether or not it would be desirable to make the shift premiums more responsive to the balance of demands for shift-work on the part of employers and supplies of shift-work on the part of workers.

Consider a factory in which there are permanent day-workers and either rotating shift-workers or permanent afternoon-workers and night-workers. Suppose further that the jobs performed by the different groups are sufficiently comparable to permit transfer from one system to another. Finally, suppose the union and the management have agreed to set the shift differentials for the various systems and to let the individual workers choose the systems they prefer. If there were excess supply or excess demand for workers on a particular system, the shift premium would be adjusted. We are not supposing a finely tuned mechanism, but merely one in which shift differentials would adjust to gross discrepancies in supply and demand. Presumably management would have to retain the right to assign workers temporarily to an undesired shift system to meet temporary staffing needs.

Such a system would have the advantages normally claimed for the price system. Those who choose to work shifts would be those who find shift-work less disagreeable than others. The shift premiums that emerge would give the correct signals to management as to whether to expand or contract shift-work.[11]

Explicit shift premiums of the type just described might also alter the mix of permanent and rotating shift-work. In Subsection 12.2.2 we suggested that one reason for rotation might be that this system responds to the workers' desires not to be cut off from family and friends for extended periods. But another reason for the widespread practice of rotation may be that the premiums for permanent afternoon and night shifts are not permitted to rise to a level at which the human costs of these shifts are fully compensated.

We must reemphasize the importance of individual variations in physiological adaptability and family situation. The permanent afternoon shift, for example, is usually not physiologically demanding, and although it may be extremely undesirable for unmarried workers interested in evening social life and for married workers with children, it may be quite tolerable for other categories of workers. Similarly, there are some workers who can adapt to the physiological demands of night-work and some who cannot, and an arrangement of equilibrating shift differentials combined with freedom of choice would sort the workers into appropriate systems.

---

[11] This statement must be qualified by reference to possible external costs and benefits of shift-work, as mentioned at the beginning of Section 12.2.

Existing arrangements in the labor markets of developed countries undoubtedly do permit some sorting of workers into shift systems that are appropriate for them. Workers do move from one factory to another and in the process probably generate an implicit shift differential.[12] It is obvious, however, that the proposed system of explicit shift premiums within the factory would render the sorting process more efficient. Such a system would also make the labor costs of shift-work more visible to management and would probably sharpen their calculations of the private profitability of shift-work.

The use of the price system to allocate resources occurs very naturally to the economist. It does not occur so readily to workers, to managers, or even to other social scientists. Moreover, proposals to use the price mechanism in new areas often encounter resistance. The fact of this resistance, whether well-founded or not, must be recognized in order to understand why a system of equilibrating shift differentials is not more extensively practiced. What good arguments can be advanced against the use of the price mechanism in the present context?

In principle, a valid objection to the use of the price mechanism is that decision makers do not recognize or follow their own true self-interests. In the present context, the argument might be that shift-workers are undermining their long-term health either without realizing it or without giving it sufficient consideration. Although this phenomenon is possible and, as we pointed out earlier, is not ruled out by the available evidence, there is very little evidence to support the proposition that it is likely to be a serious problem. As long as workers are free to take other jobs in the same factory at lower pay, it seems to us unlikely that they would undermine their health by continuing on shift-work.

An extremely paternalistic attitude was adopted by Carpentier and Cazamian (1977), who seem to reflect a set of attitudes quite prevalent in France and other Continental countries. These authors apparently distrust the decisions that workers would make if they were permitted to choose among shift systems in the presence of shift differentials. Consequently, they recommended the banning of night-work "wherever its practice is motivated solely by the financial consideration of making costly equipment pay for itself more quickly" (p. 70), and they said that "the reduction of hours of work would seem to be a logically more satisfactory compensation than financial compensation, because

---

[12] Brown (1980) recently surveyed the evidence on the theory of compensating wage differentials and found the empirical support for the theory to be uncomfortably weak.

only an improvement in opportunities for rest can remedy the fatigue of night work" (p. 63). The government of France has recently placed restrictions on the extension of shift-work to new situations (Sloane 1978, p. 129; Bosworth and Dawkins 1978, pp. 4–5); the new French law was preceded by an official report that emphasized the medical and sociological problems of shift-work.

The idea of letting shift premiums within the factory be set by the forces of supply and demand is extremely foreign to the thinking of trade union leaders and members. In spite of the best efforts of economists to explain the merits of such a scheme, we predict that it is unlikely to come into widespread use in the United States or any other country. Such arrangements may also have subtle disadvantages that usually escape the attention of economists. In any case, the absence of an efficient sorting mechanism implies that the human costs of shift-work (as we have defined them) will not be minimized, and in our judgment they will remain substantial. These human costs, therefore, should be given some weight in the evaluation of public policies toward shift-work.

12.3   Reflections on public policy regarding shift-work

It will become apparent in the course of our discussion that economic analysis does not generally provide clear-cut policy recommendations on this topic. We have seen that shift-work generates a variety of beneficial productive effects, but whether or not the distributional implications of increased shift-work are favorable depends importantly on the relevant values of the elasticity of substitution, a matter on which there is much uncertainty. Although it is reasonable to hope that future research will shed light on this important question, certain other key questions concerning the desirability of shift-work will probably remain unanswerable for the foreseeable future. We shall begin our discussion with the situation in developed countries and then take up the rather different situation in developing countries.

12.3.1   Developed countries

If we rely primarily on the market to allocate resources, we should be careful to identify external benefits and costs, and if these are of sufficient importance we should try to devise a set of policies that will internalize the externalities. We have already mentioned (Subsection 12.2.3) externalities in connection with the electricity peak load and traffic congestion. Another category of external effects concerns the fact that if shift-work is more common in a community, it is a less lonesome and presumably less burdensome experience (Marris 1964, pp. 20–3). These considerations suggest that when a worker accepts shift-work he is generating an external benefit to the rest of society. But this conclusion is not certain, for we have failed to consider possible personal losses imposed on the diurnal majority of society by the decision on the part of one worker to accept nocturnal working patterns.

On the plausible assumption that shift-work has favorable growth effects, there may be an external benefit from shift-work to the extent that the private rate of discount exceeds the social rate of discount. If there is pure time preference for the present, however, one could less plausibly argue that shift-workers themselves may undervalue the long-term undermining of their health that shift-work may cause and that this loss outweighs the benefits.

We see that there is ample room for the construction of arguments that the free market leads to either excessive or insufficient levels of shift-work in developed countries. We do not find any of these arguments to be sufficiently compelling to justify our advocating a national policy of intervention either in favor of or against the adoption of shift-work. Incidentally, our personal preferences would be to favor removal of the still widespread prohibitions on night-work for women. Those who place a high value on economic growth, however, could use our long-run analysis to justify governmental intervention in favor of shift-work.

12.3.2 Developing countries

In many developing countries governmental interventions seem to have unintentionally but substantially reduced the extent of shift-work.[13] In particular, policies to insulate the industrial sector from international competition have aggravated scale barriers to shift-work and have provided firms with sufficient profits for managers to indulge their preferences for avoiding the bother of multiple shifts (Lecraw 1978). The underpricing of capital and the overpricing of labor can lead to reductions in the capital share and thereby reduce the extent of shift-work, although our policy simulations in Chapter 9 suggested that this effect has not been substantial in magnitude. More important in some countries have been governmental restrictions on the firing of

---

[13] For more extended discussions of this topic that stress short-run considerations, see the work of Schydlowsky (1979) and Betancourt (1977).

workers; such restrictions might easily have discouraged experimentation with multiple shifts. In addition, some Latin American countries have legislated rather high wage premiums for night-work (Millan 1975, p. 223).

Our recommendations of trade liberalization, removal of capital subsidies, reduced restrictions on the discharge of labor, and elimination of legislated night-wage premiums are quite familiar to development economists. For this reason we shall not dwell on these recommendations here, but we must emphasize that they are our most important policy prescriptions for developing countries.

We turn instead to a more difficult question. Suppose that for political reasons it is impossible to "get the factor prices right." In particular, let us assume that labor in the modern industrial sector is priced above its opportunity cost. As a result, we find unemployed workers willing to engage in shift-work with no wage premium. Our question is this: Should the government subsidize shift-work in this situation?

In this context, Farooq and Winston (1978, p. 242) stated that "the relevant comparison for workers' welfare in a country with high levels of unemployment is not the relative costs of day work and shift work, but the relative costs of shift work and no work at all, and the evidence is clear that the workers put the satisfactions of a shift job above those of unemployment. So a policy of increased employment through increased capital utilization, hence increased shift working, appears justified despite the clear present social costs of shift working revealed by our survey."

Schydlowsky (1979) made a similar point (p. 14) and was even more explicit on the policy implications (p. 63): "To what extent these direct measures [i.e., subsidies linked to second and third shifts] are desirable depends in part on what can be done on wage policy and to what extent tax tools must be used to offset the differential between market and shadow wage and between the day and night shift."

The recommendation to subsidize shift-work to offset the overpricing of industrial labor would make good sense if the capital stock were exogenous or if the elasticity of substitution were zero. In our model, however, shift-work subsidization, which may be thought of as a decline in the shift differential, may actually reduce employment per unit of capital stock if the elasticity of substitution is near unity. Even if this elasticity is well below unity, subsidizing shift-work involves substituting some nighttime employment for some daytime employment, and the question becomes whether or not the employment gains outweigh the human costs of shift-work.

The resolution of our question thus depends on the typical values of the elasticity of substitution and on the magnitude of the human costs of shift-work. In conclusion, our feeling is that there is a strong case for increasing the extent of shift-work by allowing the market to function more freely. The case for intervention on behalf of shift-work in market-oriented economies is less strong. In societies where there is substantial dissatisfaction with both the level of output and the rate of growth of output, however, our presumption is that a case for market intervention in favor of shift-work can be made on the basis of the long-run analysis.

References

Abusada-Salah, R. 1975. "A statistical shift-choice model of capital utilization." Unpublished mimeograph, Boston University.

Acharya, S. 1974. "Fiscal/financial intervention, factor prices and factor proportions: a review of issues." World Bank staff working paper No. 183.

Acheson, K., and Willmore, L. 1974. "Capital utilization in economic development: a comment." *Economic Journal* 84:159–66.

Allen, R. G. D. 1967. *Macro-economic theory.* London: Macmillan.

Amemiya, T. 1975. "Qualitative response models." *Annals of Economic and Social Measurement* 4:363–72.

Arrow, K., Chenery, H., Minhas, B., and Solow, R. 1961. "Capital labor substitution and economic efficiency." *Review of Economics and Statistics* 43:225–50.

Atkinson, L., and Betancourt, R. 1971. "A neo-classical growth model with endogenously positioned technical change frontier: a comment." *Economic Journal* 81:616–19.

Bailey, M. J. 1957. "Saving and the rate of interest." *Journal of Political Economy* 65:279–305.

Baily, M. A. 1974. "Capital utilization in Kenya manufacturing industry." Unpublished Ph.D. dissertation, Massachusetts Institute of Technology.

——— 1976. "The effect of differential shift costs on capital utilization." *Journal of Development Economics* 3:27–48.

Bain, J. 1956. *Barriers to new competition.* Cambridge: Harvard University Press.

Batra, R., and Ullah, A. 1974. "Competitive firm and the theory of input demand under price uncertainty." *Journal of Political Economy* 82:537–48.

Baumol, W. 1959. *Business behavior, value and growth.* New York: Macmillan.

Bautista, R., Hughes, H., Lim, D., Morawetz, D., and Thoumi, F. 1979. "Capital utilization in developing countries: a case study of Colombia, Israel, Malaysia and the Philippines." (Oxford University Press, forthcoming.)

Betancourt, R. 1977. "The utilization of industrial capital and employment promotion in developing countries: multiple shifting as an emergency employment scheme in Sri Lanka." World Employment Programme working paper No. 2-24/W.P.6, International Labour Office.

Betancourt, R., and Clague, C. 1975. "An economic analysis of capital utilization." *Southern Economic Journal* 42:69–78.

——— 1976a. "Working capital and shift-work in imperfect capital markets." Unpublished mimeograph, University of Maryland.

——— 1976b. "Multiple shifts and the employment problem in developing countries." *International Labour Review* 114:187–96.

——— 1977. "The theory of capital utilization in labor-managed enterprises." *Quarterly Journal of Economics* 91:453–67.

——— 1978. "An econometric analysis of capital utilization." *International Economic Review* 19:211–27.

1979. "Shift-work and general equilibrium." Mimeograph, University of Maryland.

Bhalla, A. (ed) 1975. *Technology and employment in industry.* Geneva: International Labour Office.

Boon, G. 1964. *Economic choice of human and physical factors of production.* Amsterdam: North Holland.

Boskin, M. J. 1978. "Taxation, saving, and the rate of interest." *Journal of Political Economy* 86:S3–S28.

Bosworth, D., and Dawkins, P. 1978. "Proposed changes in the extent and nature of shiftworking: some important policy issues." Occasional research paper No. 21, Department of Economics, University of Loughborough.

Britto, R. 1973. "Some recent developments in the theory of economic growth: an interpretation." *Journal of Economic Literature* 11:1343–66.

Brown, C. 1980. "Equalizing differences in the labor market." *Quarterly Journal of Economics* 94:113–34.

Burmeister, E., and Dobell, A. 1970. *Mathematical theories of economic growth.* New York: Macmillan.

Calvo, G. A. 1975. "Efficient and optimal utilization of capital services." *American Economic Review* 65:181–6.

Carpentier, J., and Cazamian, P. 1977. *Night work.* Geneva: International Labour Office.

Clague, C. 1969. "Capital-labor substitution in manufacturing in underdeveloped countries." *Econometrica* 37:528–37.

1975. "The theory of capital utilization: some extensions." Unpublished mimeograph, University of Maryland.

1976. "The theory of capital utilization and the putty rubber production function." *Journal of Development Economics* 3:277–88.

Collins, N., and Preston, L. 1968. *Concentration and price-cost margins in manufacturing industries.* Berkeley: University of California Press.

Conlisk, J. 1969. "A neo-classical growth model with endogenously positioned technical change frontier." *Economic Journal* 79:348–62.

Corden, M. 1971. "The substitution problem in the theory of effective protection." *Journal of International Economics* 1:37–57.

Debreu, G. 1960. Review of R. D. Luce: *Individual choice behavior: a theoretical analysis. American Economic Review* 50:186–8.

Denison, E., assisted by Poullier, J. P. 1967. *Why growth rates differ.* Washington, D.C.: The Brookings Institution.

1972. "The measurement of productivity." *Survey of Current Business* 52:3–111.

1974. *Accounting for United States economic growth: 1929–1969.* Washington, D.C.: The Brookings Institution.

Desai, M. 1977. *Applied econometrics.* New York: McGraw-Hill.

Diamond, P. A. 1965. "National debt in a neoclassical growth model." *American Economic Review* 55:1126–50.

Domencich, T., and McFadden, D. 1975. *Urban travel demand: a behavioral analysis.* Amsterdam: North Holland.

Farooq, G., and Winston, G. 1978. "Shift working, employment, and economic development: a study of industrial workers in Pakistan." *Economic Development and Cultural Change* 26:227–44.

Fei, J. C. H., and Ranis, G. 1964. *Development of the labor surplus economy.* Homewood, Ill.: Richard D. Irwin.

Feldstein, M., and Rothschild, M. 1974. "Towards an economic theory of replacement investment." *Econometrica* 42:393–424.

Forsythe, D., McBain, N., and Solomon, R. 1977. "Technical rigidity and appropriate technology in less developed countries." Mimeograph, Department of Economics, University of Strathclyde.

Foss, M. 1963. "The utilization of capital equipment: postwar compared with prewar." *Survey of Current Business* 43:8–16.

Gaude, J. 1975. "Possibilities for substitution between capital and labor: lessons from experience." In Bhalla, A. (ed.) 1975. *Technology and employment in industry.* Geneva: International Labour Office.

Georgescu-Roegen, N. 1935. "Fixed coefficients of production and marginal productivity theory." *Review of Economic Studies* 3:40–9.

  1969. "Process in farming versus process in manufacturing: a problem of balanced development." In Papi, U., and Nunn, G. (eds.) 1969. *Economic problems of agriculture in industrial societies.* New York: Macmillan.

  1970. "The economics of production." *American Economic Review* 60:1–9.

  1972. "Process analysis and the neo-classical theory of production." *American Journal of Agricultural Economics* 54:279–94.

Goldberger, A. 1964. *Econometric theory.* New York: Wiley.

  1968. *Topics in regression analysis.* New York: Macmillan.

  1973. "Correlation between binary outcomes and probabilistic predictions." *Journal of the American Statistical Association* 68:84.

  1974. "Unobservable variables in econometrics." In Zarembka, P. (ed.) 1974. *Frontiers of econometrics.* New York: Academic Press.

Goldfeld, S., and Quandt, R. 1972. *Nonlinear methods in econometrics.* Amsterdam: North Holland.

Goodman, L. 1960. "On the exact variance of products." *Journal of the American Statistical Association* 58:708–13.

Grieves, R. 1973. "An empirical estimate of the elasticity of substitution." Mimeograph, Department of Economics, University of Maryland.

Hahn, F. H., and Matthews, R. C. O. 1964. "The theory of economic growth: a survey." *Economic Journal* 74:779–902.

Haldi, J., and Whitcomb, D. 1967. "Economies of scale in industrial plants." *Journal of Political Economy* 75:373–85.

Hamberg, D. 1971. *Models of economic growth.* New York: Harper & Row.

Hausman, J., and Wise, D. 1978. "A conditional probit model for qualitative choice: discrete decisions recognizing interdependence and heterogeneous preferences." *Econometrica* 46:403–26.

Healey, D. 1972. "Development policy: new thinking about an interpretation." *Journal of Economic Literature* 10:757–97.

Heathfield, D. 1972. "The measurement of capital usage using electricity consumption data for the U.K." *Journal of the Royal Statistical Society* 135:208–20.

Henderson, J., and Quandt, R. 1971. *Microeconomic theory.* New York: McGraw-Hill.

Holthausen, D. 1976. "Input choices and uncertain demand." *American Economic Review* 66:94–103.

Hughes, H., Bautista, R., Lim, D., Morawetz, D., and Thoumi, F. 1976. "Capital utilization in manufacturing in developing countries." World Bank staff working paper No. 242.

International Labour Office 1973. *Fiscal measures for employment promotion in developing countries.* Geneva: International Labour Office.

1976. *World employment programme: research in retrospect and prospect.* Geneva: International Labour Office.

International Monetary Fund 1964. *International financial statistics.* Washington, D.C.: International Monetary Fund.

Jones, H. G. 1975. *An introduction to modern theories of economic growth.* New York: McGraw-Hill.

Jorgenson, D. W., and Griliches, Z. 1967. "The explanation of productivity change." *Review of Economic Studies* 34:249–83.

1972. "The measurement of productivity." *Survey of Current Business* 52:3–111.

Kabaj, M. 1965. "Shift-work and employment expansion." *International Labour Review* 103:47–62.

1968. "Shift-work and employment experience: towards an optimum pattern." *International Labour Review* 106:245–74.

1978. "Utilization of industrial capacity: shiftwork and employment promotion in developing countries." World Employment Programme Research working paper No. 2-24/W.P.11, International Labour Office.

Kan, A., and Prais, S. J. 1978. "Capital utilization in Britain, the United States and Germany: a re-examination of statistics on shiftworking." Mimeograph, National Institute of Economic and Social Research, London.

Kelley, A., Williamson, J., and Cheetham, R. J. 1972. *Dualistic economic development.* Chicago: University of Chicago Press.

Kim, Y., and Kwon, J. 1977. "The utilization of capital and the growth of output in a developing economy: the case of South Korean manufacturing." *Journal of Development Economics* 4:265–78.

Kim, Y., and Winston, G. 1974. "The optimal utilization of the capital stock and the level of economic development." *Economica* 41:377–86.

Kindleberger, C., and Herrick, B. 1977. *Economic Development.* New York: McGraw-Hill.

Lago, J. 1979. "A quantal choice model of the household's energy conservation decisions." M.A. thesis, University of Maryland.

Lecraw, D. 1978. "Determinants of capacity utilization by firms in less developed countries." *Journal of Development Economics* 5:139–53.

Lewis, W. A. 1954. "Economic development with unlimited supplies of labour." *Manchester School of Economics and Social Studies* 20:139–92.

Lim, D. 1976. "Capital utilization of local and foreign establishments in Malaysian manufacturing." *Review of Economics and Statistics* 58:209–17.

Little, I., Scitovsky, T., and Scott, M. 1970. *Industry and trade in some developing countries.* London: Oxford University Press.

Luce, R. 1959. *Individual choice behavior: a theoretical analysis.* New York: Wiley.

Maddala, G., and Nelson, F. 1974. "Analysis of qualitative variables." National Bureau of Economic Research working paper No. 70.

Mann, F. 1965. "Shift work and the shorter work week." In Dankwert, C. E., and Northrup, H. R. (eds.) 1965. *Hours of work.* New York: Harper & Row.

Marris, R. 1964. *The economics of capital utilization.* Cambridge: Cambridge University Press.

Maurice, M. 1975. *Shift-work: economic advantages and social costs.* Geneva: International Labour Office.

McFadden, D. 1974. "Conditional logit analysis of qualitative choice behavior." In Zarembka, P. (ed.) 1974. *Frontiers of econometrics.* New York: Academic Press.

Millan, P. 1975. "The intensive use of capital in industrial plants: multiple shifts as an economic option." Ph.D. thesis, Harvard University.

Moore, F. 1959. "Economies of scale: some statistical evidence." *Quarterly Journal of Economics* 73:232–45.

Morawetz, D. 1974. "Employment implications of industrialization in developing countries: a survey." *Economic Journal* 84:491–542.

   1975. "Capital utilization in Israeli industry." Discussion paper No. 753, Falk Institute for Economic Research in Israel.

   1976. "The electricity measure of capital utilization." *World Development* 8:643–53.

Morley, S., and Smith, G. 1977a. "The choice of technology: multinational firms in Brazil." *Economic Development and Cultural Change* 25:239–64.

   1977b. "Limited search and the technology choices of multinational firms in Brazil." *Quarterly Journal of Economics* 91:263–88.

Moroney, J. 1970. "Identification and specification analysis of alternative equations for estimating the elasticity of substitution." *Southern Economic Journal* 36:289–99.

Morrison, D. 1972. "Upper bounds for correlations between binary outcomes and probabilistic predictions." *Journal of the American Statistical Association* 67:68–70.

Mott, P., Mann, F., McLoughlin, Q., and Warwick, D. 1965. *Shift work: the social, psychological and physical consequences.* Ann Arbor: University of Michigan Press.

National Board for Prices and Incomes 1970. *Hours of work, overtime and shiftworking.* London: H. M. Stationery Office.

National Institute of Mental Health 1970. "Biological rhythms in psychiatry and medicine." Public Health Service publication No. 2088, U.S. Department of Health, Education, and Welfare.

Northrup, H. 1951. "Shift problems and practices." Studies in personnel policy No. 118, National Industrial Conference Board. New York: The Conference Board.

Norway, Central Bureau of Statistics. 1960. *Lonnsstatistikk 1960 (Wage statistics 1960).*

O'Connor, C. M. 1970. "Late-shift employment in manufacturing industries." *Monthly Labor Review* 93:37–42.

O'Herlihy, C. 1972. "Capital labor substitution and the developing countries." *Bulletin of the Oxford Institute of Economics and Statistics* 34:269–80.

Pack, H. 1975. "The choice of technique and employment in the textile industry." In Bhalla, A. (ed.) 1975. *Technology and employment in industry.* Geneva: International Labour Office.

Phan-Thuy, N. 1979. "Promotion de l'emploi du Maroc par la pleine utilisation de la capacité industrielle." World Employment Programme working paper No. 2-24/W.P.13, International Labour Office.

Pindyck, R., and Rubinfeld, D. 1976. *Econometric models and economic forecasts.* New York: McGraw-Hill.

Pratten, C. 1971. *Economies of scale in manufacturing industry.* Cambridge: Cambridge University Press.

Pryor, F. 1973. *Property and industrial organization in communist and capitalist nations.* Bloomington: Indiana University Press.

Ramos, J. 1975. "La ampliacion de turnos en la industria Chilena: la factibilidad de una politica de empleo productivo." Discussion paper No. 12, Boston University Center for Latin American Development Studies.

Reimboldt, T., and Almon, C. 1972. "Investment equations and comparisons of forecast with actual spending." Maryland Interindustry Forecasting Project No. 31.

Roemer, M. 1975. "The neoclassical employment model applied to Ghanaian manufacturing." *Journal of Development Studies* 11:75–92.

Rothenberg, T. 1973. *Efficient estimation with a priori information.* New Haven: Yale University Press.

Sandmo, A. 1971. "Investment and the rate of interest." *Journal of Political Economy* 79:1335–45.

——— 1974. "Investment incentives and the corporate income tax." *Journal of Political Economy* 82:287–302.

Sattah, S., and Tversky, A. 1976. "Unite and conquer: a multiplicative inequality for choice probabilities." *Econometrica* 44:79–90.

Scherer, F. M. 1973. "The determinants of industrial plant sizes in six nations." *Review of Economics and Statistics* 55:135–45.

Scherer, F., Beckenstein, A., Kaufer, E., and Murphy, R. D. 1975. *The economics of multiplant operation: an international comparisons study.* Cambridge: Harvard University Press.

Schydlowsky, D. 1972. "Latin American trade policies in the 1970's: a prospective appraisal." *Quarterly Journal of Economics* 86:263–89.

——— 1974. "Influencia del mercado financiero sobre la utilización de capacidad instalada." *Desarrollo Economico* 14:269–88.

——— 1975. "Price and scale obstacles to export expansion in LDC's." Discussion paper No. 11, Center for Latin American Development Studies, Boston University.

——— 1979. "Capital utilization, growth, employment, balance of payments, and price stabilization." pp. 315–55 in Behrman, Jere, and Hanson, James, eds. *Planning and short-term macro-economic policy in Latin America.* Boston: Ballinger.

Scitovsky, T. 1976. *The joyless economy.* New York: Oxford University Press.

Shri Ram Center for Industrial Relations 1970. *Human problems of shift work.* New Delhi: Shri Ram Center for Industrial Relations.

Sloane, P. J. 1978. "Economic aspects of shift and night work in industrialized market economies." *International Labour Review* 117:129–42.

Solow, R. M. 1970. *Growth theory: an exposition.* New York: Oxford University Press.

Statistical Abstract of the United States 1973. Department of Commerce, Bureau of the Census. Washington, D.C.: U.S. Government Printing Office.

Taubman, P., and Gottschalk, P. 1971. "The average workweek of capital in manufacturing." *Journal of the American Statistical Association* 66:448–55.

Theil, H. 1971. *Principles of econometrics.* New York: Wiley.

Thoumi, F. 1975 (revised 1978). "Fixed capital utilization in Colombian manufacture." Unpublished mimeograph, World Bank.

United Nations Industrial Development Organization 1967–8. *Profiles of manufacturing establishments, Vols. I and II (ID, Series 4 and 5).* New York: United Nations.

U.S. Department of Commerce. Various years. "Surveys of plant capacity." Current Industrial Reports, MQ-C1, Department of Commerce, Bureau of the Census.

U.S. Department of Labor 1975. "Area wage surveys: metropolitan areas, United States and regional summaries, 1973–74." Bulletin 1795–29, Bureau of Labor Statistics.

——— 1978. "6.9 million workers on late shifts." News, U.S. Department of Labor 78-188.

Various years. "Industry wage surveys." Bureau of Labor Statistics.

Visco, I. 1978. "On obtaining the right sign of a coefficient estimate by omitting a variable from the regression." *Journal of Econometrics* 7:115–17.

Walker, J. 1971. "A review of the literature on the human problems of shift-work." National Board for Prices and Incomes Paper I (Supplement).

Wangwe, S. M. 1977. "Factors influencing capacity utilization in Tanzanian manufacturing." *International Labour Review* 115:65–77.

Warner, S. 1962. *Stochastic choice of mode in urban travel: a study in binary choice.* Evanston: Northwestern University Press.

Westin, R. 1974. "Predictions from binary choice models." *Journal of Econometrics* 2:1–16.

White, L. 1978. "Appropriate factor proportions for manufacturing in less-developed countries: a survey of the evidence." *Economic Development and Cultural Change* 27:27–59.

Winston, G. C. 1970. "Capital utilization: physiological costs and preferences for shift work." Research memorandum No. 42, Center for Development Economics, Williams College.

1971. "Capital utilization in economic development." *Economic Journal* 81:36–60.

1974a. "Capital utilization and optimal shift-work." *Bangladesh Economic Review* 2:515–58.

1974b. "The theory of capital utilization and idleness." *Journal of Economic Literature* 12:1301–20.

1974c. "Factor substitution, ex-ante and ex-post." *Journal of Development Economics* 1:145–63.

1977a. "The concept of capacity: an integrated micro and macro analysis." *American Economic Review* 63:418–22.

1977b. "Increasing manufacturing employment through fuller utilization of capacity in Nigeria." World Employment Programme working paper No. 7, International Labour Office.

Winston, G. C., and McCoy, T. 1974. "Investment and the optimal idleness of capital." *Review of Economic Studies* 41:419–28.

Wonnacott, P. 1974. *Macroeconomics.* Homewood, Ill.: Richard D. Irwin.

Yugoslavia, Savezni Zavod za Statistiku (Federal Statistical Institute). Various years. *Statisticki godisnjak Jugoslavije (Statistical yearbook of Yugoslavia).* Belgrade.

Zalusky, J. 1978. "Shiftwork – a complex of problems." *The AFL-CIO Federationist* 85:1–6.

Index

241

DATE DUE